ONCE UPON A TIME IN
GOGINAN

To our dear friend Jim, with every good wish
Gwynne + Cecilie

ONCE UPON A TIME IN
GOGINAN

CEIRIOG GWYNNE EVANS

KAY +eeog

y Lolfa

I bobl Goginan, o'r gorffennol a'r presennol

Dedicated to the people of Goginan, past and present

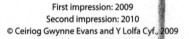

First impression: 2009
Second impression: 2010
© Ceiriog Gwynne Evans and Y Lolfa Cyf., 2009

*This book is subject to copyright
and may not be reproduced by any means
except for review purposes
without the prior written consent of the publishers*

Cover design: Alan Thomas

ISBN: 9781847710932

Printed on acid-free and partly recycled paper
and published and bound in Wales by
Y Lolfa Cyf., Talybont, Ceredigion SY24 5HE
e-mail ylolfa@ylolfa.com
website www.ylolfa.com
tel 01970 832 304
fax 832 782

Contents

Acknowledgements

The idea of writing a book of this sort has been gnawing at me for years. Eventually someone told me to get on with it or shut up about it! So I made myself sit down, and after getting a few chapters on paper, I plucked up the courage to ask my friends Daphne and John Payne to give their opinion on my efforts. John very politely switched off his favourite television programme to accommodate me, and instead of resuming his viewing when I departed, he took up my script and was still reading well into the early hours of the next morning! The following week, I was astounded when Daphne informed me that they had booked a week's holiday in mid Wales so that they could see the scene of the action for themselves! So my first thanks must go to them for inspiring me to write more.

So many other good friends, mentioned below, have subsequently contributed in several ways to make the book a reality; if I have omitted to mention any contributor, please accept my sincere apologies and put it down to advancing years, when senior moments often merge into minutes!

During the course of the text I have mentioned the valuable advice and consent given by Messrs. Tegwyn Jones, Simon Hughes and Gwyn Jenkins to peruse their various books, and for this I thank them most sincerely. My grateful thanks to Miss Nia Richards of the Research Department, Ceredigion Library, Aberystwyth for her work in finding so much useful information on the village and its environs.

To Mr Aled Bebb, the Reverend and Mrs Evan Mason Davies, Mr Cyril Evans, Mrs Morfudd Hamer, Mr Erwyd Howells, Mr

Gareth Jones, Mrs Tegwen Jones, Mrs Yvonne Rhys-John, Mr Graham Levins, Mrs Myfanwy Maclean, Mrs Iris Richards, Mrs Mair Selway and Mrs Bethan Williams, my grateful thanks for so many contributions, be they old photographs, historical (and hysterical) information or anecdotes.

I should also like to thank Mr Neil Castle for proof-reading and to Mr Kevin Hands for his skilled work with the computer. Also my very special thanks to Mrs Menna Bassett and Mr John Edwards for some valuable assistance and advice on content and presentation.

Dr Brian Evans and Mrs Eluned Mai Porter have constantly been at my side with their advice and suggestions, and I am deeply grateful to them for facilitating my efforts in the right direction towards publication. I am also very grateful to Mr Lefi Gruffudd and his staff at Y Lolfa for their professional skills and advice during publication.

Lastly my thanks to my dear wife, Cecele, for her patience and encouragement in the fulfilment of my dream.

Ceiriog Gwynne Evans

CHAPTER ONE

Coming Back Home

THE DRIVE FROM MY home in Trowbridge to Goginan, the village near Aberystwyth where I was born, is usually a very pleasant one. However, on this particular day it bode to be anything but pleasant. The wind blew in powerful gusts and heavy, squally showers swept down from a leaden sky. The weatherman on television told us that the old Severn Bridge was closed due to strong winds. My wife, Cecele, and I considered whether being buffeted while crossing the new M4 bridge was worth the risk – or the £5.10 toll at the other end. However, my ancient aunts, Mary (then aged a hundred and one) and her sister Betty (a mere hundred) were anxious to see us, and so the fates dictated that we should go. As it happened, the bridge crossing provided no major problems and the traffic on the M4 was relatively light.

The first major landmarks on the journey were the tollgates – they reminded us of those on the freeway between Houston and the International Airport, even down to the coin bins into which you could throw the correct amount of money instead of queuing to pay the attendant. All very modern and 'Big Brotherish.' I've always had a silly fear of using these bins lest I throw the wrong weight of money into the machine and endure dire consequences from the authorities. So we patiently queued, thankful that our journey so far was uneventful. Once we got off the motorway, we felt that we were at last in 'real Wales', with lovely green hills and fields which, despite the wind and gusty rain, looked peaceful and inviting.

Eventually we reached Abergavenny. Our journey usually takes us around the outskirts of the town itself, as it did on this day, but on the one or two occasions when we have stopped and ventured into the town centre, we found it very congenial. It seems to be a busy, bustling place, probably feeling more so because the main street is narrow with shops of all sorts crowding on to the pavements. It has a mediaeval castle – well, a few remains of one. The view overlooking the Vale of Usk is very pleasant and peaceful, which belies its horrible history. A Norman lord, William de Braose, invited a group of Welsh noblemen to a Christmas banquet here in 1176 – only to slaughter the lot of them. During World War II, Adolf Hitler's deputy, Rudolf Hess, was detained in the town's mental asylum for a time. On being given leave to wander in the surrounding hills, he apparently developed a real affection for Wales.

Abergavenny has quite a few good eateries and a famous food festival every September. I once stopped at a local café for a quick meal and to my delight found my favourite meal on the menu – chicken curry. I ordered and waited in eager anticipation for the culinary delight, noting that the clientele was made up of local people, which I thought bode well for the quality of the food to come. Then it arrived. It consisted of a plate of bilious-looking curry sauce (obviously from a packet), some of the most enormous chips I'd ever seen (four of them joined together would constitute a respectably-sized baking potato), and to cap it all, a whole chicken leg sticking upright – rather reminiscent of the stance a cat takes when licking its nether regions, or a volcanic island in a yellow sea. I shall remember that meal.

However, notwithstanding that experience, I find Abergavenny a very attractive town. I must mention the Sugarloaf Vineyard, situated just off the A40 on the southern slopes of the cone-shaped Sugarloaf Mountain. I was surprised to learn that they grew seven types of grapes here, and I must say, to my untrained palate the wine is of a wonderful quality.

We then passed through Glangrwyney. I love that name, which I assume to mean that the village is situated on the banks of the Grwyney river, though I have as yet failed to locate it. There does not seem to be much going on there, but I love the little terrace of houses situated on the left of the road with their lovely pastel colours.

Then on to Crug Hywel (Crickhowell) – *crug* means a hillock or a cairn. This is another pleasant place, with an ancient Celtic fort situated on a flat summit overlooking the town. It is very quaint, with Georgian streets leading down to the 400-year-old bridge over the River Usk. The Bear Hotel with its cobbled courtyard is an old coaching inn which, along with the historic streets, takes one back a few hundred years to the old-fashioned days of yore.

But what do we behold in passing? The Powys Balti? Raju's General Stores? Surely not in the heart of the Brecon Beacons! Yes, there they are; obviously the inhabitants of Crickhowell have succumbed to the exotic cuisine of the East. There is also a Chinese restaurant in a grand building on the main street with one concession to its location: a huge Welsh flag dominating the façade.

To the west of Crickhowell we left the A40 and turned north on the A479 to drive through the village of Tretŵr (Towertown) – so named, yes you've guessed it, because a huge round tower dominates the village. Incidentally, a visit to the castle ruins which date from Norman times and the later fourteenth-century manor house are well worth the short detour from the road. Then on through Cwm Du (black valley), a village owned by the National Trust, and aptly named on that day as the towering Black Mountains on our right and Bannau Brycheiniog (Brecon Beacons) on our left presented a majestic but forbidding vista under the grey, scudding clouds.

We were greeted in Llanfair ym Muallt (Builth Wells) by a huge mural. I think it depicts scenes of Llywelyn ein Llyw Olaf (Llywelyn our last prince); anyway, it is quite impressive and adds something to the scene by the town bridge on the River Wye. I always find the environment of Builth rather akin to that of Abergavenny, but on a smaller scale. The main street is narrow and rather congested, with most of the shops designed to cater for the needs of the local clientele – though as with nearly everywhere these days I overheard the strains of the Polish language on more than one occasion. The one-way main street takes one down to the riverside, which seemed very pleasant even on this cloudy day. After crossing the bridge and passing the mobile fish and chip stand, we went by the Royal Welsh Showground at Llanelwedd. Once I pass this, I always seem to feel that I am really on my way home, even though there are another sixty or so miles to go.

The town of Rhaeadr Gwy (falls on the Wye) had its usual sprinkling of shoppers and a few tourists, but its tranquillity belies its place in history as one of the centres of the Rebecca Riots in the mid nineteenth century, when farmers disguising themselves as women tore down the hated toll-gates that ruined the livelihood of many local travellers.

So we made our way upstream along the Wye Valley to the little village of Llangurig (Curig's Church), reputed to be the highest village in Wales. Many a time we have taken advantage of my cousin Myfanwy's hospitality here on our way west to Goginan and Aberystwyth, and spent many a pleasant evening enjoying wonderful cuisine and warm hospitality at the Black Lion Hotel in the centre of the village. For many years the hotel has been managed by Les, Doug, and John – three Londoners who settled in the village and became very popular members of the community. This time, however, there was no time to stop as it was already well after noon.

By this time the wind had eased considerably and the rain had petered out to the occasional isolated shower. Turning west as we climbed out of the village, our spirits rose as we encountered blue sky ahead. Scattered shafts of sunlight brought some brightness to the olive-green slopes rising from the upper Wye Valley. The road climbed steadily along flanks which were almost treeless – except for the occasional cluster of conifers clothing parts on both sides – culminating at the top of the pass in the little hamlet of Eisteddfa Gurig (Saint Curig's seat). Tradition has it that while Saint Curig rested here during his travels through Wales, he decided he would throw his staff and build a church wherever it landed. If this tale is true, I can only say that he would have been a tremendous asset to an Olympic javelin team, as his church at Llangurig is about five miles away!

From here the road meanders gently down towards the shores of Cardigan Bay in the west, and we were delighted to see a shimmering blue sea in the distance and the whole scene bathed in sunshine, making us feel that the journey was worthwhile after all. We passed through the village of Ponterwyd, where the road crosses the upper waters of the River Rheidol, and as we passed the Llywernog Silver-Lead Museum, my eye caught sight of several black dots circling high in the sky ahead. Eventually the dots grew bigger and we realised that we were seeing dozens of red kites. It was approaching three o'clock: feeding time for these magnificent birds and the highlight of the day at the Nantyrarian (Silver Stream) forestry centre. I've always puzzled as to how they knew it was feeding time.

On impulse, I turned right into the small car park at the centre. We climbed the small bank surrounding the park and there in front of us opened a sight which, though I had seen it several times before, never fails to set my spine tingling. This was the Melindŵr valley: my valley – where I was born, grew up and played all those years ago.

When I was a child in Goginan school, we used to recite a poem entitled 'Cwm Pennant' (Pennant Valley), composed by one of the foremost Welsh poets, Eifion Wyn – or to give him his real name, the Reverend Eliseus Williams:

Yng nghesail y moelydd unig,

Cwm tecaf y cymoedd yw.

(In the shelter of the lonely, bare mountains,

Lies the most beautiful of all valleys.)

They say that beauty lies in the eye of the beholder. To me, Cwm Pennant came a very poor second to what I could see before me here.

The Melindŵr (meaning water mill – there used to be a water mill here once to grind the corn of the local farmers) is a glaciated valley. The Pleistocene glacier was kind in not gouging too much of the surface rocks of the plateau, thus leaving gentle wooded slopes and a luscious green floor carefully looked after and nurtured over the centuries by countless generations of farmers. In my childhood these slopes were clothed by a variety of deciduous trees: oak, ash, sycamore and hazel. World War II necessitated the wholesale clearance of these slow-growing trees in favour of a uniform cover of quick-growing coniferous trees such as pine and spruce, to be made into pit props and for other purposes.

In the distance was the sea, and dominating the centre of the vista rose the hill fort of Pen Dinas with its vertical cannon-like stone structure erected to commemorate the victory of the Duke of Wellington at the Battle of Waterloo. However, the sight of that tower brought back memories of my days at the grammar school in Aberystwyth. Each spring term, one of the house competitions involved a cross-country race of six miles which took in the steep climb up the ploughed flanks of the hill – made more difficult by having to traverse the deep defensive ditches which still prevailed from the Iron Age. I remember one had to go round the monument at the top or one was disqualified. Oh, the pleasure of letting gravity take its course as one stumbled down the other side!

In the middle distance on the floor of the valley, I could see what I have long considered to be the spiritual foundation of my life, Jezreel Baptist Chapel – now sadly a crumbling ruin. Here, for many years I attended services three times on Sundays, accompanying my great-uncle John Hughes. Though he had suffered from hip disease as a young boy which necessitated using crutches, he would traverse the steep hill from his house in Goginan to attend all three services. My mother played the chapel's organ for seventy years, until her eyesight finally failed. It is so sad to realise that I shall never more hear the strains of that hymn singing, of the fervent sermons and prayers, or the dulcet tones my mother produced on the American organ. Even more sad is the ruinous condition of the building.

It is such a peaceful scene and yet, as the memories flooded back, I saw in my mind's eye a vibrant rural community which lived, laboured and died in this lovely valley. It is over fifty years since I left to seek work elsewhere and, though I have forgotten many of their names, I remember the inhabitants vividly: what they looked like, what they did and particular characteristics which made them stand out as individuals. I suppose one could say that their lives were of no consequence, being ordinary people who shone briefly, made their own little contribution then faded into oblivion – another pinpoint of light being extinguished. But to me they were more than that. In their own way they left their mark on me, and though they had no claim to fame in the world, their contribution to life in the valley was an important one. I therefore decided there and then that I would try to perpetuate the memory of these folk by gathering as much information as I could – anecdotal or otherwise – about the valley, the village of Goginan and some of the individuals who contributed to the fabric of society.

Reluctantly, we turned away from this idyllic scene and wended our way down the side of the valley towards the distant coast. Below us on our right was the small holding of Nantyrarian – the silver stream – an obvious reference to the fact that silver, along with lead, was produced at the local mine. Incidentally, the valley terminates here in an amphitheatre containing an air pocket, and during World War II, I remember the thrill of seeing aircraft such as Spitfires being caught in this pocket then flying almost at ground level along the valley floor towards the sea.

Across the valley on the opposite steep slope, now largely cleared of its covering of conifers, I spotted a mound of rubble which suddenly evoked memories of my uncle John Lloyd, my father's eldest brother. This pile of stones marks the entrance to Lefel yr Ych (the Ox's level); I gather that this name might be a misnomer for Lefel Uchaf (the uppermost level), to distinguish it from Lefel Newydd (new level) farther down the slope. Whatever the proper name, this was one of the last working areas in the valley. A level drainage tunnel (also known as an adit) had been dug into the hill to connect with a vertical shaft. John Lloyd worked here as a lad, and every morning he would run the three miles from his home at the Druid Inn in Goginan to his place of work at the mine, and repeat the exercise homewards in the evening.

We were now approaching the huge bend in the main road known as Y Goedwig (the forest) – with not a tree in sight! On negotiating the bend, we entered a minor tributary valley in which is situated the little hamlet of Cwmbrwyno. I am not sure where the name derived from. *Cwm* (valley) is easy to translate, but there are two conflicting interpretations of *brwyno*. It could indicate the presence of rushes growing in the valley, but there is another rather more dubious translation indicating sadness. I prefer to think of this as 'the valley of the rushes'.

Here the road follows the slope in a huge loop towards the little stream at the bottom of the valley. To our left we passed a small terrace of houses built to accommodate lead miners in the nineteenth century. Behind them, I spotted a little black and white bungalow nestling behind some bushes on the south-facing hillside. This cottage was quite familiar to me in my childhood, as I spent many fascinating hours listening to the experiences of the old gentleman who lived there on his own. His name was JE Jones and his bungalow was called Yr Hafan (the haven); what an apt name, for the little place was a haven of knowledge. He seemed very old to me as a lad, but he was so full of enthusiasm and gentle vigour. I remember his tall thin frame, his rather gaunt face surrounded by wisps of grey hair and his lively eyes which seemed to look right into one's being. He had been a brilliant statistician during his working life and had invented 'JEJ's Perpetual Calendar', by which he could work out the day upon which any date in history occurred. I was fascinated when he worked out that my birthday in October 1931 fell on a Tuesday (which explains a lot). He gave me a signed copy, and how I treasured that booklet for many years. He also compiled crossword puzzles for *The Times*. On reflection, I regret not paying more attention to the knowledge that emanated from his lips. It was such a privilege to know him.

In the small terrace of three houses by the side of the road lived Richard Richards with his wife and children. He was a frail little man, and his kind face bore the faint markings of hard work in his younger days – probably as a miner. He remains in my mind because he occasionally used to visit our chapel as a lay preacher when I was a child. There were quite a few Richards in the valley, so to distinguish him, we kids called him 'Double Dick' – not to his face, naturally!

As we moved down the huge curve in the road towards the bottom of the valley, I glanced up the north-facing wooded slope in front of us, and another remarkable character came to mind. He was another Richards – but we all knew him as Jonathan. He was a hill farmer, rearing a few cattle and sheep mainly, and lived in a small-holding called Pen Castell (castle head) – apparently there was an Iron Age fort near the site of the farm. Jonathan was very much a loner, his only close acquaintances being the local farmers. His appearance changed little with time: he always wore dark clothes and a red scarf or bandana around his neck. His cloth cap was pulled down over his left eye. As well as being a small farmer he was a butcher for a time and brought his meat in a basket to sell to the householders in Goginan.

What made Jonathan a remarkable man, however, was his gift for healing. One lunchtime when my aunt, Arwel, was six years old and living in another small hill farm called Nantbyr, not far from Jonathan's home, she accidentally tilted a saucepan on the kitchen fire. In trying to straighten it, she put her hand into the naked flame. She was in agony and her mother rushed her over to Jonathan's house. Arwel was terrified of Jonathan and would not go near him. However, he enticed her with the offer of a halfpenny, a considerable sum for a child in those days. The instant his hand came in contact with her burnt hand, the pain vanished and the hand was perfectly healed within three days.

When Arwel was sixteen and working in Aberystwyth, she had another mishap cooking ham and eggs in her lodgings, and once again badly burnt her hand. Despite having treatment at the local hospital, her condition worsened. Visiting home at the weekend, she rather reluctantly paid another visit to Jonathan who placed his hand over the wound. Once again the pain disappeared and the hand was healed in a few days.

My father related a similar story to me when I was a boy. The local policeman had been cleaning the engine of his motorcycle with petrol in a covered area at the Druid Inn, my father's home in Goginan. When he had finished, he reached over for a rag close to a lighted candle to dry his hands. Both his hands caught alight, leaving him in agony with heavy blisters. My father was instructed to use the motorcycle to travel the two miles to Jonathan's house. On being told the problem, Jonathan very calmly told him not to worry and that all was well with the policeman. My father returned, carrying some home-made ointment to rub into the policeman's hands, and to his amazement discovered him calmly drinking a cup of tea in no discomfort whatsoever. Apparently, the pain had gone about fifteen minutes earlier – roughly at the time when Jonathan was told of the mishap. What gift he had remains a mystery, but before he died he passed the secret on to a nephew who was the local coalman, and to another close friend who lived in a nearby farm called Ffynnon Wen (the white well). Incidentally, this farm reached the national newspapers when it was sold to the son of film stars Michael Wilding and Elizabeth Taylor for ten thousand pounds. It also created a bit of a stir when it was converted into a hippie colony – the first of its kind in the county of Cardiganshire.

On the sharp bend at the bottom of the hill lived Morris the Bridge. We kids were very wary of him. To us he was a giant of a man, at least eight feet tall. He always wore a dirty raincoat and a cloth cap pulled well down and seemed to glower at you through dark, piercing eyes under his shaggy eyebrows. He looked very furtive and always muttered, "They are after me, you know!" Who was after him we never dared ask. I remember on one occasion being terrified when I had to accompany my father into his house. All I recollect of that encounter was Morris, sitting in the twilight of the living room, glowering at us from his chair on one side of the fireplace, with an enormous heap of coal on the other. Obviously he liked to keep his creature comforts within easy reach!

A few yards down the road, we passed Tan-yr-allt (under the hillside), where the village shoemaker once lived. I think he was a deaf-mute, but this in no way impaired his skills at repairing shoes or anything else made of leather. In the days when footballs were made of leather and had a bladder inside them, we used to prolong their life by taking them to the cobbler for repair. Unfortunately, he did not have the appropriate equipment to do an internal repair of the hard leather, so the only solution was to stitch the panels together externally. You can imagine playing a game on a wet day with the ball heavy and greasy, and having to head it with your forehead in contact with the hard ridge created by the repair. Soccer in those days was a game fraught with serious dangers.

And so on past St Matthew, the little church on the right-hand side of the road, to Goginan, the village of my birth and childhood and of so many memories – of the school, the places of worship, the lead mine, the public houses and the many individuals who were so important in forming my character and influencing the shape of my life in later years.

CHAPTER TWO

The Village of Goginan

YOU WILL FIND GOGINAN on the A44, about seven miles to the east of Aberystwyth. Goginan is a hidden village – the type you drive through in a few seconds and, on seeing the exit sign, say, "Was that it?" Most of the village lies below the main road, clinging to the north-facing slope of the Melindŵr valley. There are a few clusters of cottages forming 'mini suburbs' here and there. The visible part of Goginan lies on the main road, which has right-angled bends at both ends of the village. As with many villages these days, the traveller will often not see a soul when passing through. It is rather reminiscent to me of driving along empty African roads knowing that the natives are somewhere close by in the bush.

Most people are intrigued by the name – how to pronounce it if one is foreign and, more intriguingly, what it means. Neighbouring villages seem to have more sensible and logical names, such as Cwmbrwyno (the valley of the rushes), Llangurig (Curig's Church) and Ponterwyd (Erwyd's bridge) – but Goginan?

When I was a child, the popular interpretation in the village was that Goginan referred to Cegin Ann (Ann's kitchen). Are we to assume that somewhere in the past a lady called Ann ran an embryo McDonald's-type diner here? Could be.

The most acceptable interpretation I have so far found is that the word derives from Go'r Ceunant. *Go* is an alternate word for 'beside', as in the name of the village in Anglesey that seems

to go on for ever: Llanfairpwllgwyngyll*go*gerychwyrndrobwll...
etc. (The church of Mary by the white hazel beside the fierce
whirlpool... etc.) *Ceunant* refers to a steep-sided valley. Thus,
Goginan can be interpreted as 'The village *beside* the steep-sided
valley.'

If one looks at an Ordnance Survey map of the area, one
will see that the village is divided into Goginan itself, near the
main road on the north-facing slope, and Old Goginan at the
bottom of the sunnier south-facing side. The site of Old Goginan
coincides with the confluence of a small, steep-sided tributary
valley and the Melindŵr valley. There are two very old farms
which possibly gave the village its name. A few hundred yards up
the side of the small tributary is Goginan Fach (beside the small
valley), while on the slope of the main Melindŵr valley is the
other farm, Goginan Fawr (beside the big valley). In my youth
we used to refer to Goginan Fawr as Bank Farm, as it was sited on
top of the south-facing slope, but eighteenth-century Ordinance
Survey maps place it at the foot of the slope.

A third interpretation which I heard recently postulates that
the name came from the word *cawginan*. *Cawg* is Welsh for a
basin, while the suffix *in* denotes small and *an* means a further
diminution. Thus *cawginan* means a very small basin. Whatever
the meaning, there is evidence that people have dwelt here for
many centuries and that the village has been recognised under
various names in the last few hundred years: Goginen, Coginan
and Kyginan.

The area has an interesting history. Ordinance Survey maps
show the presence of hill forts and tumuli (ancient burial sites).
The Castell was the site of one of these ancient hill forts and
was always a good viewing point and picnic spot when we were
children. One can imagine the ancient Celtic clans living in round
huts in enclosures on top of these hills, wearing home-spun,
woven and brightly coloured clothing, singing and telling stories

at their festivals. In the wooded slopes under the hill fort, they would have used their skills to hunt wild boar and other animals with bow and arrow, and to select and prepare wild roots, plants and berries for their cooking pots. They may have cultivated the gentler slopes on the summits with corn using light ploughs.

There are many intriguing questions regarding this period which remain unanswered. For instance: did the Druids who revered the oak and mistletoe visit the valley? There was a public house called the Royal Oak in Old Goginan; there is also the Druid Inn. Did these names have some remote connection through the mists of time to the ancient Celts and Druids?

One also wonders what the Celts made of the Roman incursion into their habitat. There is little evidence of any real conflict. Looking at the configuration of these iron-age settlements, there are no defensive ditches surrounding them, unlike Pen Dinas in Aberystwyth. Maybe there was co-operation and even social integration between the two races inland. Lead and silver were probably extracted from the area by the Romans around 70 AD but it is possible the Celts had appreciated the value of these ores even earlier. There is a legend that Caractacus, the great Celtic leader, tried to defend the workings in Goginan against intrusion by the Romans.

At this stage, I thought I should include a short account of the geology of the valley – with the help of my university notes – before giving a potted history of the area, from Roman times to the present.

The Melindŵr valley's location is almost in the middle of an area referred to as the Central Wales Orefield. Ore veins were formed during earth movements and the minerals were deposited from hot fluids that flowed from fractures in the rocks. These movements occurred in lower Palaeozoic sedimentary rocks – akin to shale – from the Devonian period, about 400 million years ago, through the Carboniferous period to the Permo-Triassic period about 230 million years ago, The veins contained ores of lead, zinc, silver and copper mixed with quartz (silica), magnesium and iron-bearing carbonate rocks. The rocks also contain small amounts of cobalt, nickel, antimony, arsenic, cadmium and very small traces of gold. The veins, except the gold, are associated with the presence of sulphur and are called sulphides. Of these, probably the most important in the Melindŵr valley was an ore called Galena which contains silver and lead. I remember as a child finding small lumps of this silver-grey ore in the spoil heaps left in the disused mine in Goginan, noting how heavy it was and how it sparkled in the light.

There is some evidence that the Romans' main interest in the area was the exploitation of lead and silver ores. Lead was a very useful and malleable material which could be used for making roofs, water pipes and guttering. When mixed with tin, it could be made into pewter. It is likely that the Romans extracted the ore by using opencast methods. The initial indication of its presence would probably be in outcrops exposed on the surface of the ground. A trench would be dug to follow the lead vein, which could be pursued to depths of up to seven or eight fathoms.

The Early Mines Research Group has recently suggested that 'fire setting' techniques could have been used even before Roman times, to break up the rocks. Fires were lit against a rock and kept burning for many hours, then cold water would be thrown over the hot rock to cause rapid cooling, contraction and cracking. This would have been an effective method to break up the well-jointed shales in the Cardiganshire area.

There doesn't seem to be any tangible evidence on the surface of the ground that any of these methods were used in Goginan mine, but many Roman relics have been found there including a key and a cache of coins. A Celtic urn has also been discovered. Near the confluence of the Rheidol and Melindŵr rivers, there are remains of a Roman fort built of earth and timber, surrounded by a defensive ditch. Since there is evidence of another Roman encampment near Llangurig, I believe it is reasonable to think that there could have been some communication between Celts and Romans throughout the valley. Furthermore, a few hundred yards to the west of the fort, near the Rheidol-Melindŵr confluence, ran Sarn Helen, one of the major Roman routes connecting North and South Wales. This can now be traced intermittently along certain contemporary minor roads.

Geological evidence suggests that agriculture of some form or other went on almost continuously here throughout the Mediaeval period. The soils weathered from the Pumlumon shales were yellow-brown and silty clay loams up to a height of 300 metres, ensuring good drainage. The ridge tops belong to the Hiraethog series which can be peaty and badly drained. However, rich soils on the valley bottom and good arable alluvial soil elsewhere made agriculture possible. There may have been a division of land utilisation involving cropping on the valley bottoms and rough pasture on the upper slopes.

During the Mediaeval period, the Roman Catholic Church was a very dominant influence and a monastery was built on the site of the present church at Llanbadarn Fawr, near Aberystwyth. For administrative purposes the land was divided into hundreds – the Melindŵr valley came under the control of the Llanbadarn hundred. The land was granted to gentry who lived in mansions such as Nant Eos (the nightingale's stream), Lovesgrove and Gogerddan. They in turn divided the land into smaller plots for the peasants, who swore allegiance to the lord of the manor in return. Such allegiance required them to work for a given period on the lord's land during the year, to fight for the lord should the need arise and hand over part of the crops (a tythe) to him each year. Thus there were freemen and bondsmen, or villeins as they were called.

These must have been tumultuous times for the people of

the valley, as there were several skirmishes with the English and
the Danes. The destruction of Aberystwyth's castle – only seven
miles away – would almost certainly have affected their lives.

It seems mixed farming remained as the economic base in
the Melindŵr valley during Mediaeval times. Due to the lack of
extensive flat land, I think it unlikely that any open field system of
agriculture – as used in the Welsh Marches and England – would
have been used here. It is possible that the lower valley would have
been divided into small fields, giving each peasant family a small
plot on which to grow subsistence crops such as potatoes, turnips,
beans, peas, onions, garlic, cabbage and possibly some medicinal
herbs. It is also possible that on another plot or on the hill slopes,
some cattle and sheep would be reared to provide meat, milk,
skins, bone and fat – the latter could be used as tallow for candles.
Pigs, ducks, chickens and geese would also have been important.
The land was under the control of the Gogerddan estate, and if
sheep were reared they would have provided a valuable source of
income for the lord of the manor.

It is not clear when all of the larger farms in the valley were
established, but there is evidence that many began during the
Tudor or Stuart period. Once this development took place, it is
likely that peasants would have concentrated on their own small
plot or garden, producing the basic subsistence crops and looking
after the animals to sustain the family.

With such basic foodstuffs and little attention to hygiene,
exogenetic diseases would have been a constant problem. Saint
Anthony's Fire, or gangrene, which emanated from disease in
cereals, was a common complaint. Tuberculosis was common,
due to the wet climate. Dysentery, diarrhoea, cramp and fever
were also endemic. Another common disease was leprosy, caused
by bacteria. Though leprosy was highly contagious, the Church in
Mediaeval times venerated sufferers due to the disease's association
with the ministry of Jesus Christ, and many of the older churches

in Cardiganshire had a special niche or window to one side of the altar where lepers could come to receive communion.

Whether the Black Death of the earlier Mediaeval period reached the valley is not certain, but it affected much of Wales and created such a shortage of labour that the difference between freemen and villeins was undermined. This in turn caused a change in the social makeup of society, because many former bondsmen became freemen.

There is not much evidence of the lead and silver ores in the valley being exploited before the reign of Henry VII. However, the Stuart period (1603-1714) saw much activity in the hills and underground, when entrepreneurs such as Sir Hugh Myddleton (a friend of Sir Walter Raleigh) and Thomas Bushell (a protege of Sir Francis Bacon – the pioneer scientist and politician in the reign of Elizabeth I and the early Stuart period) had a financial interest in the valley's minerals.

Other entrepreneurs at this time included Sir Carbery Pryse, the squire of the Gogerddan estate, Sir Humphrey Mackworth and William Waller, a mining engineer – all of whom took an interest in the development of the silver-lead mines, including that of Goginan. I will talk about their influence and economic impact on the mines of the Melindŵr valley at a later stage. Suffice to say here, this industrial development in late Tudor and Stuart times had a significant influence on the development of Goginan, as many houses were built to accommodate the miners and their managers. No trace of these dwellings has survived, but I think that this was the period when Goginan was given its name and became a village.

The Georgian era (1714-1837) was probably the busiest period in the county's mining history, with new technological developments and pioneers such as Lewis Morris, who for a time lived in Goginan. This era also saw changes in the agricultural system. Agriculture was becoming more entrepreneurial, with an

Goginan in the 1920s. The field in the foreground was later installed with sheep pens for the monthly mart. Note the two shops on the right of the picture.

Progress in Goginan of the 1950s. The nearer of the two shops in the picture above has been replaced by a smaller wooden structure. A new red brick house has been built and Emlyn Jones has installed a petrol station.

Goginan in the 1950s.

The 'Sunny Side' or Old Goginan taken in the 1920s showing the nineteenth-century houses built for the mine's agents, with Melindŵr House seen on the left.

economic focus to cope with the pressures of increasing population and the demand for food. The old system of subsistence farming was beneficial to peasants, but was inefficient and vulnerable to the spread of disease amongst crops and animals. The Enclosures Acts which were introduced in the eighteenth and early nineteenth centuries saw a great change in the utilisation of the land, by erecting hedgerows and fences to form the individual fields which can still be seen in the Melindŵr valley.

The practice of transhumance was also greatly expanded at this time – a practice which persisted right up to my childhood. In early summer it was a common sight to see flocks of sheep being driven eastwards along the main road through Goginan on their way up to the hilly areas on the slopes of Pumlumon, with a return journey in the autumn. The terms *hafod* for the upland summer shelter for the shepherds and *hendre* for their lowland winter quarters, are reflected in that there was a small holding above the village called Hafodau, and there is a Cefn Hendre in the locality.

Goginan developed on a larger scale with the expansion of mining activities in the 'Golden Period' of the mid to late nineteenth century. This was when the village as we knew it in the last generation – and to some extent the present one – took its form. In the early to mid nineteenth century, what we called 'Sunny Side' – mostly quite large houses catering for management – developed in close proximity to the mine workings. Until recently, there were quite a few ruins of terraced houses on or near the site of the mine which probably housed the workers. During the mid nineteenth century, there was an influx of miners from other parts of the United Kingdom, especially from Cornwall and Devon – and also from Ireland – which necessitated an increase in housing. There seemed to have been some segregation of the workers, possibly due to the language barrier, as terraces had names such as Cornish Row and English Row.

Aeial view of Goginan, taken in 1985.

The main turnpike road, now the A44, was built along the southern slope of the valley in the early nineteenth century, and there seemed to have been a sort of tug-of-war between the mine workings and the attraction of the main road for the siting of houses. One of the main developments along the road was the Druid Inn – a public house and a post for changing the horses of the stage coach which plied from Aberystwyth east to Llangurig and beyond. The first proprietor was a David Sayer; to some extent he was instrumental in getting more houses built to the east of the Druid. This little section – which contained one detached house and a terrace of four houses on one side of the road and a larger detached house, 'The Mount', on the other – was called 'Sayer's Village', or Pentre Sâr in Welsh. When I was young, the older villagers still called it by that name. These houses accommodated the managers and agents of the mine workings and formed another little ghetto of English speakers. Then, along the slope under the main road, a variety of small stone cottages and terraces was built to cater for the workers.

Religion was an important part of village life, and three non-conformist chapels were initially built at the bottom of the valley to cater for the mine workers. An English Wesleyan chapel was opened at the very edge of the mine workings at what is now the farm of Troedrhiwcastell (the foot of castle hill). At the turn of the twentieth century, when activities ceased in the Goginan mine, this chapel closed and the building was incorporated into the farm house. Then a piece of land was leased from the owner of Gogerddan estate, Pryse Pryse MP, and the miners raised money by public subscription to build Jezreel Baptist Chapel in 1849.

A small Methodist chapel was also erected early in the nineteenth century, which for a time served as a school; it was replaced by a much larger chapel, the Dyffryn (valley) Methodist Chapel, erected in 1862. In the late 1860s, St Matthew's Anglican Church was built on the main road about half a mile east of the village. Towards the end of the nineteenth century two shops were built on the main road to cater for the needs of the miners and villagers.

During the early years of the twentieth century, now that the last of the mines had closed, there was a period of relative stagnation in Goginan's development. One or two houses deteriorated slowly and were eventually abandoned and dismantled. The school remained open, though numbers dwindled; one shop burned down in the 1930s but was replaced by another. The two remaining chapels and the church received worshippers regularly, though their numbers also diminished. The three public houses were reduced to one, as patronage from the miners dwindled (Goginan mine closed in 1886), leading to the closure of the Miners' Arms and the Royal Oak.

The next changes had to wait until after the end of the Second World War in 1945. One of the disadvantages of living in the village before the war was that there was no source of electric power, gas or water. Though there was a rumour of expansion –

a small council estate was to be built next to the school – the plan was abandoned due to the 'lack of facilities.' Eventually, in the 1950s and 60s, a small estate of privately-owned bungalows was built on Penbryn farmland to the west of the village, on a minor road leading to the disused mine. Water and electricity finally arrived, but drainage facilities remained primitive and there was a lack of an effective sewerage system.

The latter years of the twentieth century saw a gradual decline. One by one, the chapels and the church closed. Sadly, they are now deteriorating into ruins. The two shops were eventually forced to close due to lack of trade, as mobility improved with the advent of private cars. Gone are the little lanes and tracks along which we as children used to run or cycle; they have been replaced by roads capable of accessing houses by car or even lorry. Eventually, government policy dictated that the school should close due to lack of numbers, and children were bussed to neighbouring villages. The post office still remains, but has moved several times from its original site on the main road in the centre of the village where it served the community for over a century. At present it is sited at the old school on the periphery.

Even the disused lead mine has changed. The ugly spoil heaps have been removed, the old stone ruins of the workers cottages, the huge waterwheel, and the various engine and ore dressing rooms have gone. The sand hills, which we as children used to slide down and see who could jump farthest, are no more. Instead, the area has been given a covering of grass and for a time was the scene of a nine-hole golf course for the new inhabitants of Old Goginan.

Still, not all is gloom and doom. Existing houses have been renovated and improved in appearance. New houses are being built on the site of former mine workers' cottages, with beautifully landscaped gardens. A new form of culture exists: there are many talented artistic people who have moved in, engaging in cottage industries such as painting, pottery, and photography – and the village has a web site.

The Druid Inn still thrives and has become the cultural and social centre of the village. Its high standard of cuisine has attracted the attention of national papers and it was awarded 'Pub of the Year' in 2004. I was delighted to learn that it won a similar award from CAMRA (the Campaign for Real Ale) in 2008. Credit must be given to Lewis Johnson and Lorraine Edwards who took over as managers in 2007. Long may the tradition of the Druid continue!

The village is now prettier and tidier in many ways: the houses are neater and the main road is possibly safer with a double white line running through it. In my day it was much more rough and untidy (especially the houses, despite valiant efforts using rough tools, hard graft and the use of the whitewash brush on the outer front walls) and the mine was an ugly white and grey scar on the landscape. But it had life; it had soul.

When as a child I spent my Saturdays at the Royal Oak, running up and down the nearby spoil heaps, gazing in fear and wonder down the old shafts left by the miners, wandering a few tentative yards down Francis' large sloping adit, or helping my grandfather unearth the huge pieces of wood which once formed the circular base for the 'buddling' process in the ore dressing days. I felt a strange connection with those brave people who worked here from dawn to dusk six days a week, attended chapel on Sundays and choir or brass band rehearsals once or twice a week.

Yes, in those days there were distinct echoes of the past. Sadly, I don't feel them anymore.

CHAPTER THREE

Early Days in Goginan

THE BARBRA STREISAND SONG mentions 'scattered pictures' and 'misty waters' to describe her memories; the same applies to my recollections on my early life in Goginan during the 1930s.

I was born at about two in the morning on Tuesday, 27 October 1931 in Irfon House, Goginan. The midwife was Nurse Griffiths. I remember her in later years as a very kind lady with a lovely face, who always wore a navy-blue hood – like the ones nuns wear.

My mother had decided that if I turned out to be a boy, I should be called Caradog. Now, whatever my aspirations, I don't think it would have suited me, as the historical character of the same name had a little steel beehive hat covering some wild flowing locks, a huge spear, a big round shield, large beard and bare knees (at least that's how my early history book depicted him). Eventually, with the aid of the midwife, the gentler name of Ceiriog – after the old bald-headed, bearded station master of Caersws, John Ceiriog Hughes – was decided upon.

I don't know whether I have been entirely happy with Ceiriog either; though I must say I did like the romantic poems which my nineteenth-century namesake produced. The name has been subjected to certain variations in the past, such as Ceiliog – the Welsh name for a cockerel – or even Kelloggs. The main problem with the name emerged several years later when I settled in England. Very few people could pronounce it, let alone spell it:

"What's your name?"

"Ceiriog."

"Pardon? Could you spell it or write it down, please?"

So my second name, Gwynne, had to be substituted for the ease of my friends. This is the 'posh' version of the name; most poor Welshmen have to be satisfied with the usual Gwyn, but not me. Apparently, the name derives from a steel family in South Wales who lived earlier in the twentieth century. I don't know whether their company was prosperous or not, but I experienced no financial gain from the derivation. When another Ceiriog appeared in Goginan, I was called Ceiliog Gwyn (white cockerel), while he, since he had ginger hair, was called Ceiliog Coch (red cockerel) to distinguish us. Luckily, he left after a very short period, so I was left to rule the roost once again.

In my formative years, I would describe the parameters of my life as being dominated by the home, certain pathways and a few adult faces. Some people have vivid recollections of what they did in their prams but I am not one of those. I can only recall one occasion: I was staring at a grassy hedge on the steep hill which runs down from the village to the chapels in the valley. I know we were at a standstill and that it was sunny, but I don't know why we had stopped. My mother (if she was the person in charge of the pram at the time) probably needed a rest; or she had stopped as women often do, to chat with someone. Whatever it was, I have often thought it strange that the only glimpse of early babyhood that remains with me was that particular occasion. Psychiatrists could probably have a field day relating that moment to later developments in my life.

I remember a little more clearly, my spoon and pusher for eating – or spilling – my 'Force' corn flakes saturated with milk, during my 'sitting up in the high chair' stage. The packet always fascinated me: it pictured Sunny Jim in an Uncle Sam outfit, complete with silver-topped walking cane, striding over a small fence. I think Sunny Jim should feel very honoured in that this food was one of the few things I deigned to eat at that stage.

Another picture that comes to mind is sitting on the potty beside the fire on cold nights, and having to scamper into the back room complete with potty when there was a knock on the front door. Here I would sit, still enthroned on the potty, peeping through the door at any visitors, impatiently wishing that they would leave so that I could resume my former, warmer location.

It is said that if you hear music while in the womb, it will form a very dominant part of your life. In my case this might be true, as on several nights a week my mother would be engaged in some musical activity or other; accompanying the village choirs or taking soloists through their paces in the living room at home. The occasional kicks she endured during this period might have indicated a wrong note or an opinion from within on some slightly dubious rendering of a song. Whatever the reason, I was apparently born with an innate sense of rhythm. Sitting up in my pram or cot, I would always sway to the rhythm of whatever piece of music that was on the go. I don't know if this extended to my great-uncle John Hughes' violin playing. More than likely I would doze off to sleep long before he would ever be satisfied that he had tuned the instrument correctly; this took a very long time, I can tell you!

In Irfon House where I was born, the living room was a narrow, oblong shape about fifteen feet long and ten feet wide, with one small window to emit daylight on the narrow side near the front door. There was a short passage from the front door which opened into the room. If this was to keep the draughts out, it did not succeed. A heavy curtain was hung over the opening in winter which swayed gently on a windy night, despite valiant efforts with mats to repel the icy blasts blowing in from the north-east.

On entering the room, one had to avoid the dining table (on which stood the paraffin oil lamp), its four chairs and my uncle John's rather low wooden-sided easy chair, on which he could lounge fairly successfully despite his locked hips. A 'U-turn' on negotiating the short passage would bring one to my uncle's high desk by the window, where he would stand for hours doing his accounts for the Odd Fellows or secretarial work for the many organisations of the village. A busy man was my uncle John. Then there was the redwood sideboard where my mother kept a whole horde of paraphernalia: blankets, sheets, tablecloths and other boring stuff; but the drawers above were full of all sorts of interesting objects which busy little fingers would have a field day rummaging through – once they could reach.

The big black grate in the fire-place was a great focus for the little room. On one side there was a big black kettle which never seemed to move and was never used; I thought that rather unfair as the little kettle on the other side seemed to do all the work. To the right of the grate hung the bellows (which, incidentally, I still have in my possession, though the leather has long since deteriorated). Even to my infant eyes they looked beautiful. They had a picture of a lake scene, with the lake itself being made of mother-of-pearl. They also had gold designs on the black, lacquered handles, while the spout was made of gleaming brass.

The mantelpiece had all sorts of bits and pieces on it. On either end were two King Charles dogs made of 'blue' china which were apparently very old. Inside these were two gleaming brass candlesticks, and in the middle was an upright German chiming clock. The mantelpiece also contained several of my uncle's pipes and a packet or two of Ringer's Shag: a strong, evil-smelling concoction which both my uncle and my maternal grandfather smoked with relish. On the steel fender, a variety of pokers and tongs accompanied a little pot full of paper spills. My uncle made these from strips of newspaper for lighting his pipe.

On the wall beside the fireplace, a portrait of my great-grandmother Sarah Jane Hughes took pride of place. In front of it stood my uncle's upright armchair where he could sit to read the *News Chronicle*, the Liberal newspaper of the day. Next to the portrait, recessed into the wall, was a glass-fronted cupboard where my mother kept all the 'Sunday' china, as well as two beautiful brass and copper kettles and various table condiments; relics of a better life when they were ensconced on the tables of Hafod mansion (some of my immediate ancestors worked there). The cupboard beneath was another 'grotto' of all manner of things: polishers, dusters and boot lasts – which my uncle used most efficiently to repair our boots, often with bits of rubber or leather which had to be cut to shape before being tacked on.

On the other side of the door which led to the tiny back kitchen, stood a leather chaise lounge. Above that was a huge black and white framed picture, entitled 'The Hope of His Side', which depicted a fat little boy dressed in a white sun hat, armed with a very broad wooden cricket bat, taking guard of a wicket. I used to study that picture a lot, as my pram was always parked in front of it.

On the wall next to the table stood the most precious piece of furniture in the house: the piano – gleaming black from the daily polish my mother lavished on it. The brass candlesticks (I never recall seeing any candles in them) also shone brightly; as did the black and white keys. It was in remarkably good condition, considering that when my mother was a teenager it had probably been subjected to buffeting and the occasional beer spill when it stood in the drinking room of the Royal Oak. It was always in perfect tune as my great-uncle John, who had a very good ear for music, had acquired a tuning key and a tuning fork. He would spend literally hours carefully tuning each string – a time when my mother thought it judicious to take me out for a very long jaunt in my pram. On the flagstone floor were numerous little mats which gave the room some measure of warmth and comfort, and the ceiling had exposed rafters, painted black.

Was it comfortable? I would say so. It was spotlessly clean, and on winter evenings the yellow glow of the paraffin lamp and the wind whistling in the chimney, encouraging the fire to roar, would emanate a warmth and semblance of great comfort as we all engaged in our own little activities. My uncle would read the newspaper if sitting in the high-backed chair, or peruse a religious commentary in the low easy chair if it was approaching Sunday. My mother would be doing one of a variety of tasks: sewing, darning or practising a piece on the piano; while I would busy myself on the table by drawing, painting or playing with the few toys I had – seconding my toy soldiers from their usual duties to become actors on the stage I built out of odds and ends. Yes, I would say that life in that little room was on the whole a very pleasant and rewarding one.

As time went on, my strengthening little legs would carry me farther afield, like a bird venturing forth from the nest. I felt it was my duty to go and visit my various 'aunties'. It was rather strange that I used to call my real aunts by their first names and reserved the term 'auntie' to my adopted 'family'. Anyway, on many mornings I would go off in my 'car' or my 'lorry' to deliver pretend goods to these noble people. You may wonder how I distinguished between my 'car' and my 'lorry'. Well, it was all in the mouth and the legs, you see. If I took the 'car', I would adopt rather a high-pitched hum and would sprint on my toes. A 'lorry' on the other hand would require a much deeper sort of growl; the knees had to be bent and the feet would stamp rather heavily on the ground – and of course the steering wheel was enormous.

My route took me straight down the lane from the front door, alongside the wall of Mr Duggan's garden to the difficult right-angled bend at the bottom – especially tricky if I had the 'lorry'.

After negotiating this hazard, the lane alongside the bottom of the garden was easy, as was the third wall once the second corner was negotiated. Then up the curved lane to Eagle House, a small cottage (no longer there) where Gwilym and Mary Howells lived. They were a contrasting pair: Mary was quite tall and wore round glasses, and was always very sociable when one passed. Gwilym, on the other hand, was small in stature and rather more reserved. He always wore a cloth cap and moved with a very measured tread. I remember him in later years as the proud possessor of a drop-handled bicycle which took him everywhere.

I recall one incident Gwilym used to relate of a journey he took from Goginan to the village of Cwmystwyth (Ystwyth valley). On the homeward journey he had to drop down a steep hill which ended in a sharp bend next to the hotel in Devil's Bridge. Unfortunately, the brakes on the bicycle ceased to work and Gwilym hurtled at a rate of knots towards the bend at the bottom. It was impossible for him to negotiate the bend at the rate he was going, and he had no choice but to go straight towards a low wall which protected the terrace in front of the hotel from the two-hundred-foot deep gorge beyond. Luckily, Gwilym had the presence of mind to hurl himself off the bike and wrap himself around an ornamental tree that decorated the terrace. The bicycle vaulted the wall and landed in the gorge below.

Many of his tales were very amusing, if a little exaggerated at times, like the one he used to relate of being caught in a downpour while cycling back from Aberystwyth. Since he had no raincoat he did the next best thing: pedalling madly uphill for the last two miles so that the front edge of the rainstorm only affected the back mudguard, while he and the rest of the bike remained perfectly dry. He was indeed a memorable character who enriched the life of the community.

My route would then pass the bungalow of Mr and Mrs Pearce, called Gorffwysfa (resting place) – what lovely names many of the houses in the village had. Now it was time to turn right into Queen Street, the only lane in the village to be called a street. It was named after Queen Victoria, the reigning monarch at the time it was built. Sally, my mother's sister, lived in No. 1 with her husband, Dick Leonard Davies, and their five children: Megan, William John, Myfanwy (Fanw), Leslie and Eurona (Rona). (I don't know why my parents stuck with one child; after all, I don't think I turned out so badly!) Apart from William John, the Davies family were very musical and were all members of the local choir. Dick Leonard was one of 'God's children': he had such a perfect baritone voice that never needed training (unlike most of ours), and it was such a pleasure to hear when he could be coaxed to sing at local concerts. Sally was a little lady with a mass of curly, dark hair and a lovely soprano voice. The parents' talents were passed on to their children.

Megan, the eldest, was a sophisticated young lady who worked in Lloyd's Bank in Aberystwyth. William John – or 'Will John' as he was called to distinguish him from all the other Wills and Johns in the locality – was in the Royal Army Medical Corps, which even then I thought strange because he couldn't stand the sight of blood. I still have the Christmas card he sent our family from France in 1940, about the time of the evacuation of the British forces from Dunkirk. It is very special to me. Fanw was spared military service, but Leslie served in the Royal Air Force, being stationed for most of the war in India. Rona served with the Women's Auxiliary Air Force and surprised us all with her athleticism, becoming WAAF champion in many athletic events.

After a short stop at No. 1, it was time to visit Marged (Margaret) and Mary Thomas, two sisters who lived in the little cottage next door. Marged was a large, rotund lady with a big bosom under her floral 'brat' (wrap-around pinafore), a broad, smiling face which exposed the two teeth she had held on to, and kind, twinkling eyes. She paid very little attention to her mottled hair, which was always trained into a roll at the base of the neck. She was such a lovely, warm person whom I enjoyed visiting.

It is strange that the thought of Marged's burial in Cwmsymlog cemetery still brings back memories of warmth and sadness, even though I was not actually present at the funeral. I do remember that it was a hot, sunny day and a few of us youngsters climbed the hill to the north of Goginan, past the Royal Oak and Goginan Fach farm up to the Bwlch, then onwards over the ridge until we could see the cemetery about a mile away on the other side of the valley. We lay down in the grass and watched the black-clad mourners filing up behind the coffin to the graveside. It was so peaceful, except for the occasional hum of an insect or the chatter of a grasshopper in the heather. Then came the poignant echoes of 'O fryniau Caersalem' ('From the Hills of Jerusalem') – the standard hymn sung unaccompanied in Wales at the graveside – from across the valley. I have been involved with music all my life, conducting choirs and orchestras, but I can still hear those faint echoes quite clearly. What a fantastic way to remember dear Marged.

Her sister, Mary, was also a lovely person, but quite different. She was rather stout, but not nearly as rotund as Marged, and I always envisaged her as being in the shadow of her sister. She worked in Aberystwyth, which seemed to give her a certain aloofness like all the ladies who worked there. She didn't wear a 'brat' and I am certain that she used henna on her hair, because it seemed to have an unnatural fairness about it. There was also evidence of hot hair tongs being used to turn up the ends.

I was fascinated by their little house – well, at least the living-room, which was as far as I went. It was a smallish room with a potted aspidistra in the window. What fascinated me most were the two enormous Welsh dressers, both complete with a full set of plates and jugs. One day a few years later, I was saddened to see that only one dresser remained; the other had been sold by Marged to a passing tinker for five pounds.

My next port of call was the double-fronted house at the end of this little terrace, No. 4, where 'aunty' Maggie lived: sister-in-law to Sally, Marged and Mary. She was slim and quite tall – she could have been taller except that she hunched her shoulders. I always thought she was much older than the other ladies because she had white hair and was therefore wiser. When I was shedding baby-teeth, I used to visit her quite regularly as her shedding method seemed to be quick and fairly painless. One end of a piece of cotton thread would be tied to the offending tooth and the other to the door knob. The door was slammed shut and the process was over – very nifty. The only snag was that the Tooth Fairy had not yet arrived in Goginan, so I lost a lot of potential cash.

If time permitted, I would travel down to the end of the street, stopping for about thirty seconds with John Hugh Griffiths who was usually chopping firewood with a billhook outside his shed. He was a fairly tall, slim man who always wore a cloth cap settled firmly on his head. His rather sallow face was adorned with round tortoise shell spectacles, and a very neatly-trimmed white moustache. He was always very pleasant, but spoke in a pedantic manner with rather a loud voice, so that he greeted you as if you were one hundred yards away. This was a little disconcerting to a five or six year old. However, he was a very kind man and I would often see him armed with his two-pronged hay fork on his way to help with the harvest on some farm or other, greeting everybody in his loud fashion. I think this manner of speaking was engendered amongst people who were brought up in sparsely populated upland areas where houses were about a half a mile apart, so that any conversation between neighbours had to be conducted in high decibels. However, John Hugh, as he was known locally, was a very able man of letters: his *englynion* (four line verses written in a typically Welsh form of alliteration called *cynghanedd* – where a sequence of consonants in the first part of a phrase or sentence are repeated in the second part) were excellent, and he won many prizes on a national and local level.

Then on down to the dead end at the bottom where Mrs Richards might be standing on the doorstep of Tŷ Sgwâr (square house), grinning broadly at me. The house was made up of two 'semis'; Tommy Lewis and his wife Gertie lived next door. He was called Tommy Bach (little Tommy), though he was not small at all. It was because his father, Tommy Mawr (big Tommy), also lived in the village and they had to be distinguished somehow. Tommy Bach and Gertie shared their house with Queenie, a white bull terrier which to me looked rather big and fierce. My eyes were almost level with his mouth and he had big teeth, but he was quite lovable really. Then there was Joey the budgie, which chose choice words to hurl insults at the Nazis during the Second World War.

Having completed my chores in Queen Street, it was time to take my 'lorry', 'bus' or 'car' (whichever was the flavour of the day) up to the main road to pay my respects to whoever I encountered. The first person I usually met was Hannah. I never knew her surname; everybody called her Hannah or Hannah Fawr (big Hannah). She was big – really big – with grey hair drawn back from her florid face into a bun. She was always accompanied by a brown greyhound called Lucky. I don't know whether this was her dog or if she 'borrowed' it from the post office next door, but they were obviously great friends. In the middle of the night, one would occasionally hear her rather monotonous voice bawling out: "Lucky!" as she walked through the village looking for him.

I would then visit the post office, where there was always plenty of activity. Mary Elizabeth lived there with her four children: John Moses, Dick, Defi (David) Hugh and Jennie. Her husband,

Hugh M Evans, had died in 1933 after an illustrious career in local music. Such was his contribution to the choral music of the valley that he was called 'Eos Melindwr' (Melindwr's nightingale). I vaguely remember him visiting our house to rehearse or discuss a performance with my mother. He was a tenor who won many prizes at competitive meetings against better vocalists, despite not having a great voice. He managed this by singing very correctly – a lesson I heeded very closely in later years. For years after his passing, his name would often be on my mother's lips.

To enter the living quarters of the post office, one had to go down a passage between the 'shanty' – a sort of workroom full of junk – and the house itself, guided by the hum of constant activity emanating through the open back door of the kitchen. There would be Meri (Mary) Elizabeth, busily doing something or other, but she would always have time to greet such an important visitor as myself. John Moses was a bus driver at that time I think, so he wouldn't be around, but Dick and Defi Hugh would often be found tinkering with the motor cycle or the car. That was a fascinating object in those almost carless days, and to sit in one was an exciting privilege. It was a black Morris Eight, registration number CGU610; I always felt a quiver of excitement when the little red light came on when the ignition key was turned.

When I was older, Dick often used to give me a ride on the back of his motor-cycle when he had to go and empty the 'Sunny Side' post box on the other side of the valley. The only mishap I remember was when the motor-cycle toppled sideways and trapped my leg under the exhaust pipe. I didn't cry but I had a lovely red mark for a few days to commemorate the experience.

Jennie had a beautiful voice. It is difficult to describe as it had a unique silvery quality which thrilled me when I heard it, even as a very small boy. Nobody could outclass her when it came to *penillion* (verses sung to music), which were very difficult to do properly. A poem was given to the singer, and while the harp or

Hugh M Evans with his daughter, Jennie, outside the Post Office in Goginan in the late 1920s.

piano played a tune (usually a folk song), the singer would have to compose a tune in their mind to fit the metre of the verses and then harmonise with the instrumental music. In proper competitions the singer would be given some time beforehand to study the music and the verses. The difficulties didn't end there. The singer could not start singing straight away but had to blend in a few bars down the line as it were. However, both the singer and the instrument had to finish at exactly the same time. Sometimes, to make one a little crazier, the rhythm of the verses would be different from that of the instrumental tune. For instance, the music might be in waltz (three/four) time while the verses dictated singing in four/four time. If one is not very musical, then this might sound like gobbledegook. But as I have tried it, take it from me: it isn't easy. But Jennie was good: so good that we regularly heard her on the wireless in the thirties.

John Moses could be called a rough diamond with an eye for the ladies, but he was also one of the kindest and most talented people I knew in my childhood. He had a great sense of humour and a good tenor voice like his father. My father used to relate a few amusing anecdotes about John and his father, Hugh. Apparently, both had a passion for the pickles which Meri

Elizabeth used to store in vinegar in old sweet bottles. There was one incident where both John and Hugh made a simultaneous grab for the bottle and both hands entered it at the same time so that neither could extract his hand without letting go of the pickle. The altercation as to who should withdraw went on for half an hour until Hugh, emphasising his seniority as the father, won the day.

Another story was told about the Baptist minister, dear old Dafydd ap Morgan (David son of Morgan), visiting Hugh, who was precentor (leader of hymn singing) at the chapel. While they were discussing some matters, Hugh felt a tug on his sleeve, and there was the four-year-old John Moses.

"What is it, John bach?" asked Hugh, in his Sunday best manner.

"I want to do number two," whispered John, in an equally polite manner.

"Look on the sideboard, John bach, there's a pencil and piece of paper there," was the polite reply.

"Damn you, I want to shit!"

It's funny how thin the veneer of respectability is at times.

Having seen that everything was normal – or as near normal as to be expected – at the post office, it was time for me to move on. Quite often, outside the lower of the two village shops across the road from the post office, I would come across Tommy Lewis (Tommy Mawr). He lived in 'Sayer's Village' with his wife Charlotte, a rather large dominating lady, and his daughter, Lally (Elizabeth).

As well as Tommy Bach, they also had another son, Teddy, who appeared from London on occasion during vacations. I wasn't quite sure of Teddy, as he wore a camel-hair coat and had red tinges in his hair. When I went to teach in London many years later, Teddy very kindly invited me to dinner one evening at a

Tommy (Mawr) Lewis, with Enid Herbert, wife of David Herbert, the village schoolmaster, outside Emlyn Jones' wooden shop in the late 1940s.

Lyons' Corner House restaurant. At the time, Teddy was in charge of cutlery at Quaglino's, a very posh restaurant in Piccadilly (I made a mental note that I obviously didn't qualify to be entertained in such posh surroundings.) The first thing that he did at Lyons' Corner House was to inspect all the cutlery we had been given and ordered the whole lot to be replaced – which was a little embarrassing for a country bumpkin like me. What also astonished me was the number of cigarettes he went through during the meal; every mouthful of food had to be accompanied by a mouthful of smoke. He must have gone through over twenty cigarettes while we were sitting there.

But I must come back to my encounter with Tommy Mawr. He was quite a tall, well-built man with a cheery, ruddy face, round spectacles and the inevitable pipe, all crowned with the ubiquitous cloth cap. I'm not sure what he did, except that he was responsible for the distribution of the daily newspapers in the village which Lally delivered daily with her usual "'ullo!"

During the war, Tommy and his ferret did their bit for the food shortage by catching rabbits and selling them to the populace. He used to conscript one of us boys to go with him to carry back the spoils. He would place wire snares just outside a warren on the rabbits' escape track – quite a meticulous operation. The noose had to be placed centrally on the track, usually between two thick clumps of grass like a little canyon, and the snare had to be firmly secured to a vertical stick driven into the ground. Then the ferret – a smelly creature – would be taken out of its sack and a muzzle would be placed over its mouth before it was sent down the hole. Now it was time for a rest and a pipe of 'Ringer's Shag' while the ferret did its work below ground. There'd be a sudden commotion: out would shoot the rabbit into the snare, and with a quick thump on its head it would all be over. On a good day, Tommy might bag up to fifteen rabbits which, rather like a poor man's golf caddy, we would have to hump back to the village. The last part of the day's proceedings would be the share-out. Tommy would sit on a stone with the rabbits lying in a row in front of him, ready for the distribution which would be our wages for the day:

"One for me, one for you, and one for the little ferret."

So we would part ways, he carrying his ten rabbits while I would return home with five. I never questioned the distribution at the time, though it made me think in later years.

A visit to Emlyn or Dilys Jones at the lower shop could sometimes result in the gain of a sweet or some other delicacy. Emlyn (Jones the Shop) came to Goginan in a motor-bike and side car in the 1930s along with his wife, Dilys. (I don't know whether their son, Huw Gwynfryn, had been born then, but eventually they had two children, Gwyn and Mair, both of whom had illustrious careers in later life.) He was a very enterprising man and established all sorts of businesses in the village such as a petrol station, a car sales establishment and a taxi service. When he arrived, he took over the proprietorship of the lower of the two shops in the village, but disaster soon overtook him when the shop caught fire and burned to the ground. I remember that incident very clearly as our house was immediately below the shop, and sparks and flying embers rained down onto the roof and into the back garden. However, a smaller wooden shop soon replaced the old establishment.

Dilys was also enterprising, and often looked after the shop while Emlyn was engaged in other activities. She was also very kind and always ready to help out any unfortunates who happened to come along. In those days hobos or tramps would visit the village quite frequently. One would hear their singing – if one could call it that – from one end of the village to the other. I always thought that they had an uncanny sense of knowing where they would be given something to eat or drink. My mother was one of those 'softies' who would spare them a sandwich or a piece of cake and hot tea to fill their pots. They all seemed to make a beeline for our house which I thought very strange even at that young age. This puzzled me for a long time until someone later pointed out a small pile of stones that had been built up just around the corner from the back door. Apparently, this was the signal erected by members of the nomadic fraternity that this house was 'a good 'un'.

Dilys would occasionally show the same compassion, regularly providing sustenance for one particular tramp. Apparently, this personage would appear quite often and hold conversations with Dilys as he munched his food. Then he disappeared as quickly as he had arrived and was never seen again. I don't think Dilys ever suspected the truth: the tramp was in fact Jenny from the post office across the road, who would regularly put on a disguise that would have done credit to Sherlock Holmes!

My next port of call would be the top shop: a veritable grotto of all sorts of items. The wooden panels which separated the shop itself from the rest of the building were painted a pale green (or had been once in the dim and distant past). To my little eyes, this shop looked huge compared with the little wooden one down the road. It had a counter which ran along three sides of the room. On the left was the serving counter where John Davies stood, usually dressed in a sleeveless leather jerkin with his *pinze-nez* on the tip of his nose, over which he either beamed or glared at you depending on his mood. He also had a rather droopy moustache and the inevitable cloth cap. My first memory of him was when he lifted me onto the big seat at Jezreel Chapel at the age of three or four to make my debut as a soloist, singing the chorus from one of my namesake's verses, 'Yr Arad' Goch' ('The Red Plough').

The 'top' shop as it appeared in 1900. At that time it performed roughly the same function as it did during the thirties and forties, except that it also included the Post Office at that time, as shown by the three postmen in the photograph. In 1900 the shop was owned by a gentleman called Moses Roderick.

We usually exchanged a few pleasant platitudes – or rather he talked while I smiled inanely at him. Then he would return to whatever chore he was engaged in, such as totting up the amount of money the villagers owed him, as most people bought things to be paid for later. In the meantime, I would look around to see if anything exciting had been added since my last visit, especially in the sweet department.

The shop was very orderly, with similar types of goods neatly compartmentalised for the convenience of customers. To the left of the serving area were large, square tin boxes of biscuits (in those days the shopkeeper would weigh handfuls of loose biscuits and place them in white paper bags); to the right were stacks of sweet boxes containing such delicacies as liquorice or chocolate, backed by tall jars of boiled sweets, lemon sherberts, etc. Behind these were shelves containing all sorts of tins of meats and vegetables.

Further along the counter and along the back counter all the measureable foodstuffs such as butter, lard, bacon and sugar were stacked in large bags or on marble slabs and covered with gauze to keep the flies at bay. They were interspersed by the machines for slicing bacon or wire-cutting the cheeses and butters. The sugar, bacon, butter and cheeses were weighed, then neatly packed in brown paper.

The right-hand side of the shop was devoted to hardware, clothes and boots which were neatly displayed on the shelves on the wall behind. From the exposed rafters hung a variety of goods: hatchet or axe handles, buckets, brooms and brushes, paraffin lanterns and Wellington boots, to name but a few. Two doors opened out to the back rooms where the coal, paraffin and various seeds were kept. Here, John would measure out pints or quarts of oil into bottles the customers were obliged to bring, or he would weight hundredweights of coal into bags on the magnificent weighing machine he had there. Then, a quick wipe of the hands on a convenient towel which hung by the door and he was ready to slice the butter. I wonder what the Health and Safety people would make of it today!

The focal point of the whole room was the paraffin stove (I can still smell its fumes) situated in the centre of the room below the huge paraffin lamp which gave a faint illumination during winter evenings. Then there were the benches where customers could sit while they waited their turn for the sole attention of the shopkeeper. This was a particularly favoured spot on Saturday nights, when probably half the housewives of the village would congregate to do their weekly shopping and have a good gossip. To be served on a Saturday night could take upwards of four hours, as Mr Davies would have to enter the items bought by many of the customers into a ledger to be paid for at a later date, or in some cases, a much later date. On that night, the shop would often have to remain open until ten o'clock. Even then, some late-comer arriving on the last bus from Aberystwyth might plead with John or my cousin Fanw for some item or other, well after half-past ten at night.

The atmosphere in the shop would be considerably lightened when John was absent and Fanw filled in for him. From a very early age, Fanw had been employed to take charge of the domestic running of John's house under the supervision of his wife. Mrs Davies was a sort of early-day cross between Claire Rainer and Anthea Turner, the television presenters. If anyone had a problem, Mrs Davies was the person to sort it out; she was supposed to know everything and be able to do anything. I remember once playing cricket on the field near the school amongst the cow pats and clumps of grass. I was doing well, hitting the ball to all corners of the field, until one delivery hit the edge of a dry cow pat and hit me in the eye. There was a great panic as the blood poured from my eyelid. I was rushed up to Mrs Davies who did an expert job patching up my wound. I remember being so proud as on that very same day, the same accident occurred to my hero Denis Compton, the Middlesex and England batsman.

Mrs Davies was a great organiser and Fanw worked hard for long hours keeping the house going under her supervision, attending to the laundry in the big boiler in the kitchen and taking the washing up the steep steps to the back garden to be hung on the lines to dry. She cooked and cleaned every day, and as Christmas approached, the cooking became very onerous as Mrs Davies would prepare cakes, mince pies and Christmas puddings for every family in her 'empire'. So Fanw would be faced with the prospect of preparing six or seven cakes or puddings which would cook slowly overnight in the big boiler used for washing clothes. This meant regular visits to the boiler several times during the night. Then she would spend many hours each day serving in the shop – a job which included selling oil and coal. In keeping with many of her contemporaries, Fanw worked hard and diligently and was one of those faceless people who maintained life over the years in the village.

My last call of the morning was usually to see if my grandmother and aunt Betty were all right at the Druid Inn. A few short minutes in the 'black hole' were sufficient to see that all was well; then it would be time to return down the hill at a trot, saying "'ullo," to anyone I passed.

CHAPTER FOUR

Spreading One's Wings

As TIME WENT ON, my travelling scope widened to include unaccompanied forays across the valley to the Royal Oak, my maternal grandparents' house, in my 'lorry'. This became a regular Saturday event, and on a sunny spring or summer's day it was pure joy trotting down the hill, saying a quick "'ullo" to John and Marged Evans. They were a retired couple living at the only house remaining in what used to be called Pleasant Row. In later years, John worked at a pig farm called the Black Horse. My friend, Hedd Jones, and I would carry the waste food bin from the school to feed the pigs on Friday afternoons. John always reminded me of Father Christmas without his beard: a kindly man with a broad smiling face under a mass of white hair – though I must say he did not smell very sweet in the course of his work. Marged was a diminutive lady with gold-rimmed oval glasses and the most guttural North Wales Welsh accent I have ever heard, but she was always very welcoming.

I negotiated the steepest part of the hill – luckily I knew every stone in the lane so accidents were unheard of – and came to BrynMelindŵr Terrace – a row of seven small miners' cottages, each with four rooms. In No. 1 lived Mrs James (who was often bedridden) with her two daughters, Maud and Irene. I remember Maud as a very slight, dark-haired young lady with round black-rimmed glasses. Irene, on the other hand, was well built with a round face, laughing eyes and a perpetual grin on her rosy face. She was a jolly young lady who was a great asset to the community, especially at concerts when she used to delight everyone with her comic recitations.

Next door lived my favourite, Marged Anne Llywelyn, a dear little lady with unusual purple-tinted oval glasses. I liked her because when she visited my uncle John every day on her way to get water from the village pump, she always gave me sweets (people had to buy my friendship in those days).

My friend Danny lived in No. 7, but he and his mother had to be satisfied with a wave from me during those Saturday morning missions. Farther down the hill, I would often meet Dorothy Baxter. She was a very pleasant girl a few years older than I; unfortunately she had inherited St Vitus' Dance which handicapped her throughout her life. We used to manage a few pleasant words in passing.

Then my journey took me across the little bridge over the River Melindŵr, where in later years Danny and I would spend hours splashing in the shallow water. There was a stretch of about one hundred yards where the lane was framed by tall hedges. I mention this as it was the scene of a very unfortunate accident which made me aware of the value of mothers.

One day when I was four or five years old, my mother had gone by bus to that distant, magical town of Aberystwyth, and I was left forlorn to wander around the village. I was dressed in my usual 'playing-in-the-dirt' gear: ragged boots, crumpled knee-length stockings and short trousers held up by big leather braces or suspenders – fitted over my shirt but under my pullover – all decorated with stains and holes to prove that I was not a cissy. The braces were the problem. At school, Miss Williams was always at hand to undo the buttons to release the braces and at home it was no problem. However, due to something I had eaten, my little stomach started playing up and a visit to the toilet became a prime consideration. But what could I do? Here I was, stranded in the middle of the village *sans* mother or Miss Williams. One couldn't really approach a stranger and say, "Please will you undo my trousers?" The only solution was to run pell mell over the valley, a distance of about a mile, to the Royal Oak where my aunt Lill or my grandmother would perform the deed. I negotiated the hill very well, but on reaching the bridge things got rather desperate. A hundred yards further on, events overwhelmed me. The remainder of the journey was conducted at a very slow pace in great discomfort and misery, with not a few tears. Oh, the shame of it all!

As a surprise wedding present, a good old friend of mine presented us with an oil painting of Jezreel Baptist Chapel by Aberystwyth's most famous artist, Hywel Harries. On the right hand edge of the beautiful work is the lane where the incident occurred, and whenever I look at it I am always reminded of that day.

Those Saturday mornings running along the paths and rubble mounds of Goginan lead mine were idyllic. Even at that young age I felt a great freedom – just me and my imaginary 'friends' who would agree with my every wish. There was much potential danger: the deep shafts had been abandoned in an apparent hurry, with only a cursory wire fence placed between the curious and certain death. But there was a sort of innate awareness of such dangers. Though we as children would all venture close enough to throw stones into the holes – to hear them clatter against the sides and to listen for the distant splash when they reached the water at the bottom – we always kept a safe distance from the edge. I never heard of any accidents in what had become a playground for the village children. We engaged in activities such as seeing who could jump the farthest down a mound of soft sand, or building dams so that we could swim in the river nearby.

For some reason I enjoyed being alone with my 'friends'. Sometimes my muses would inspire me to stage a performance in the little amphitheatre that constituted my grandmother's washing line area. Otherwise, I would operate my imaginary bus route along the narrow path that connected the Royal Oak's valley with the main village. This was heavy stuff, involving bent knees and further wear and tear on abused boots. My imaginary colleagues would be driving the other 'buses' and were invariably called Dick or Dai, the standard name for most bus drivers at the time, I thought. It was very important to salute Dick or Dai when our 'buses' passed each other. I would recognise every stone or boulder embedded in the path and regarded them as friends in my lonely little world. So the day would pass with a welcome lunch (or 'dinner' as it was called) at twelve noon: cawl (soup) in a basin, followed by a plate of meat and vegetables which I scoffed – much to my mother's surprise.

Afternoons would often incur visits with my aunt Lill to various people's houses in Old Goginan, or 'Sunny Side' as we used to call it. The Saycells had been living in the first house for ages; in fact it was the same Saycell family member who used to give my mother piano lessons in 1913. I have vague memories of old Tom Saycell, but even though I was only six or seven then, I can still envisage his wonderful acre of ground entirely covered with daffodils in the spring. I wondered how he had the time to plant all those thousands of flowers each year.

Farther down the row lived the Rowlands family – a favourite drop-in centre for Lill. Tom Rowlands was old, but his elder sister was absolutely ancient. I don't think I had ever seen anybody as old as Miss Rowlands – I never knew her first name. She was a wizened little lady, rather hunched, with greying hair pulled back in a tight bun and little oval spectacles at the end of her nose. She was what I would envisage as the typical old lady, complete with walking stick and a shawl. I don't think I ever spoke to her; in any case I don't think she would have been able to hear my squeaks if I tried. No, I would linger behind my aunt, shift my weight from one foot to another and wonder what it was like to be that old and to live independently. She was not always independent: her favourite nephew, John Davies, would sometimes visit her from London.

Before she sadly passed away, my good friend Mrs Nanno Davies recalled the relationship between her father, John, and Miss Rowlands. Apparently, whenever John came home from London, nobody was allowed to do anything for Miss Rowlands except him. He would take her for the morning visit to the toilet at the bottom of the garden. Then she had to be fed her porridge. One morning, she quietly passed away the moment she had swallowed the last mouthful. Then something very strange happened. At her very advanced age, all her teeth had gone except one, right in the front of her mouth. The moment she expired, that last tooth crumbled into dust and tumbled down her chest as if to say that its work was done at last.

A little further down the lane was a large white gate which barred entry to a wooded drive leading to Melindŵr House, where the Misses Saycell lived. If there was anything approaching a manor house in Goginan at that time, it was Melindŵr House. Not that it was very big or grand, but it had a certain mystique about it, so that if ever one approached the gate, let alone the house, it was almost like entering the unknown. One felt obliged to wipe one's feet before even setting foot on the drive.

The two Misses Saycell were middle-aged visions in pastel, with a special fondness for powder-blue. I don't think I ever ventured to say anything to them except a shy "'ullo," but they always gave me a gracious smile and a little wave, rather like the Queen Mother used to do. They drove around gracefully at about twenty miles per hour in a powder-blue Wolseley car, in which they used to do their weekly shopping in Aberystwyth. They were very seldom seen in the village itself and about the only time we children would see them was on New Year's Day, when we would go singly or in small groups to greet the New

Year by singing Welsh songs outside people's houses in return for *calennig* (New Year's gift). Usually the tariff was a halfpenny or a penny, which we placed in the little bags our mothers put around our necks with a drawstring to stop the spoils from falling out. However, we kept our best songs for Melindŵr House, where if we sang well we would be rewarded with sixpence. This money-making 'racket' would have to stop by midday, otherwise dire consequences might ensue.

Talking of money-making rackets, the other caper in those days was to catch people out when they got married. Most of the weddings at the village would be in either of the two chapels in the valley. Since most of the brides and bridegrooms approached from the main road, their cars would have to negotiate the steep hill. This provided an excellent spot for a sort of hold-up. A rope would be held across the lane and the bridal cars were obliged to stop and hand over a sum of money. The quality of the wedding was assessed according to the amount of money gleaned. Absolutely rotten weddings were those that avoided the hold-ups by taking the lower road to the chapel.

Afternoon trips with Lill would, on occasion, take us far from home. Lill was never a strong lady and bouts of coughing would often ensue – I guess due to her liaisons with tobacco. Visits to her doctor took the form of a pilgrimage, as they involved walking across the valley to catch the afternoon bus to Aberystwyth. This would have been OK, but we had to get off at Lovesgrove and walk another three or so miles to the village of Bow Street. Here, her particular doctor held surgeries every Wednesday afternoon in a little one-storey cottage. We would have to sit for a long time in the small front room amid all the coughs, sneezes and aspidistras until the doctor, who operated somewhere in the back of the cottage, would call my aunt. She would eventually emerge, carrying one of those medicine bottles with the individual dosages etched on the side. I assume it contained cough mixture, as it was a horrid dark colour, and for this the doctor would relieve her of one shilling. Then came the operation in reverse and the three-mile trek back would have to be completed in time to catch the bus back to Goginan.

Then there would be the occasional afternoon jaunt to fetch butter from a farm with the lovely name of Trawsnant (across the stream) in Cwmerfin, a little hamlet over the hill in the next valley. It was a bit of a trek over rough ground, but it was well worth the effort to partake of a farmhouse tea with those enormous thinly-sliced loaves which one doesn't see anymore – and wonderful home-made fruit cake. Then, if the weather was fine we would spend a lazy afternoon picking blueberries amongst the heather on top of the hill on the way home.

★ ★ ★

Whenever I looked west down the Melindŵr valley in those days, the sky always seemed lighter and bluer and I would experience a certain joy, for a few miles away was Aberystwyth – that distant 'Mecca' which one might visit on Bank Holiday Mondays. The Sundays beforehand would be delightful days of excitement and anticipation which even the ritual of three services in chapel could not dim. Everybody went to town on Bank Holiday Mondays, invariably demanding a duplicate Crosville at half-past one – lovely chocolate-coloured buses with a cream band along the side. This meant I could feast my eyes on not one but two of my heroes: the drivers seated high up in their separate cabs.

Once in town, my favourite port of call was the seaside. In those days the promenade was a hive of activity with hundreds of deckchairs, 'Uncle Tommy and his Pierrots' on the bandstand, a dozen or so donkeys plying their hundred-yard course along the road, and of course the ice cream stands. The beach was full of would-be swimmers or paddlers, intermingling with the dozen or so vociferous old sailors in their peaked caps and jerseys enticing punters to go for a trip in the bay or a more distant afternoon voyage to Aberdovey and back on the 'Pride of the Midlands' – that brave old motor-boat that risked life and limb to bring British troops back from Dunkirk in 1940. It was so exciting just to be a spectator. It must have been a similar scene when, as a child, my mother was taken to Aberystwyth on the old horse-drawn brake. In those days, however, the first chore which the family had to undertake was to visit the water's edge and line up for a few spoonfuls of sea-water, which was supposed to cure all sorts of ailments.

After the seaside, I would head to Woolworths. In those days the store was equipped with long solid counters, with an assistant behind each one. Oh, the joy of being given the privilege of choosing a toy. Books were a 'no-no' – I headed straight for the toy cars, lorries or tanks, and hoped for a few toy soldiers to replenish the little army already billeted at home that had been mostly decapitated by little teeth (what is all this about lead poisoning?).

Talking of books, which were not near the top of the list as far as presents were concerned, I recall one incident during the Second World War that regularly returns to haunt me. It gives one an insight as to how cruel and selfish young children can be. It was Christmas 1941 and presents were very hard to come by. I woke up early on Christmas morning and groped down the bed to where I knew my sock had been strategically placed the night before. Yes, it was there and seemed to be quite full. I fumbled inside, hunting frantically for the lorry or tank which I had been hinting at for weeks, casting aside the traditional orange and apple and a few stocking fillers. I reached the bottom of the sock: no tank, no lorry; in fact not a thing that I had hoped for. I sat back, staring broodily at the bottom of the bed. In the gloom, another shape suddenly began to emerge. This was it, Santa hadn't forgotten after all! I took a dive towards the bottom of the bed, grabbed what I made out to be a rectangular box and hastily ripped off the wrapping paper. It was *A Compendium of Fairy Tales* by Hans Christian Andersen! I glared in disbelief at the monstrosity. How could Father Christmas get it so wrong?

For days I moped and stormed around the house, feeling that I was the most unlucky, unfortunate boy in the village. What did I care that the book was beautifully illustrated and that it had twenty novel models which popped up when one opened a page? It was only years later that it dawned on me what a selfish little prig I had been towards my mother. She obviously had not been able to get what I wanted, or could not afford it, and thought that this beautiful book with its pop-up pages would have brought joy into my life at Christmas. How I have regretted my selfishness. I hope I have in some way redressed the balance since then.

After Woolworths it would be time for tea. If it were going to be a posh 'do', then Teviotdale's Restaurant on North Parade would be the venue. Usually, however, one had to make do with Ward's Café on Great Darkgate Street, where I would eat anything as long as it was chips. I still remember the dear old waitress whose privilege it was to serve us – usually my mother, Aunty Sally and me. The waitress was quite old and wished to be elsewhere, judging by her drooping eyes and forlorn expression. She looked nice though, in her black dress edged with white cuffs and trimmed with a lace neck. Her grey hair, drawn back into a tight bun, was topped with a dainty white cap and she wore a neat lace-fringed white apron. Her big handicap was her flat feet, which made toting a heavy tray quite an ordeal. But never once did she fail to deliver my chips, so I think she thoroughly deserved the sixpence tip which my mother would surreptitiously slip under the plate.

Mondays in November were especially exciting as the fair visited the town to coincide with the hiring fair, when farmers traditionally re-engaged existing farm labourers or touted for new ones. I was fascinated to see the bargaining going on, usually in the vicinity of the train station, and how some servants displayed breeches and leggings to indicate, I think, that they were adept in working with horses. I can't remember how the cowmen dressed but the farmers all wore trilby or bowler hats and fawn mackintoshes as far as I could see. However, the main attraction was the fair itself which took place in the car park beside the station, with stands extending along Park Avenue which sold all sorts of goodies. The music and the colourful flashing lights from the various roundabouts and swings were magical to us rural pre-electricity kids.

One scene from the fair still stands out vividly in my mind. My mother had put me in a magical little motor car on a roundabout and given the male attendant the penny fee for the ride, when all of a sudden I was accosted by the biggest woman I had ever seen. She towered miles above me, glaring with huge black eyes; her enormous gnarled hand stuck out as she bawled, "Where's your penny?" at me. Now, Welsh was my first language and about the only one I knew at that time – fluent English did not arrive in my vocabulary until I was about eight. I think I managed to blubber out, "Man... give penny to... " when fortunately, the other assistant arrived just in time to prevent a lynching. After that confrontation, I did not enjoy that ride one little bit.

Those idyllic, lonely days passed all too soon. My imaginary friends faded and were replaced by real ones – of both sexes. First there was Nanno Wright, a little girl who lived next door to the Royal Oak; for a long time she was my pal and 'assistant' as she was younger than I. Then there was my first 'girlfriend', Dora Jenkins, who lived in a big place called London House next to the post office. This, surely, was true love – at the age of seven. I cannot quite remember what activities we engaged in, but romance was in the air.

This was also the time of life when our immune systems

received a 'boost'. In those days, if any of the children had a contagious disease such as measles or chicken pox, we would be encouraged to play with them so that we would catch it. It was almost like collecting stamps. I don't know whether this developed our immune systems or not, but on the whole, I think I have been reasonably healthy for most of my life. I know that a lot of dirt and dirty water went down my gullet during those formative days.

The only serious medical occasion was when a few of us succumbed to pneumonia. It was a sunny August day in 1940 and we were all enjoying ourselves down by the Melindŵr stream, using boulders to make a dam. I remember that there had been a drought and the water was extremely low, so that many fish had died. Suddenly, I got this horrible pain in my side and was escorted home. My next recollection was sitting in the back kitchen with my mother, watching two tiny mice running around the bread board on the table. It's funny how these scenes remain vividly in one's mind. Eventually our family doctor, Charles Burrell, a large man with a florid, 'whisky' complexion and kinky grey hair arrived, and with one glance diagnosed the disease. I was quite lucky in that I only had an infection in one lung, whereas my friend, Gwyneira Howells, got double pneumonia. At the time, I was not sure whether to be happy or envious!

I remember the palaver my mother had to go through to cope with the disease in those pre-penicillin and antibiotic days. It involved a long period in bed and putting a tin of kaolin poultice into a saucepan of boiling water every day. When it was fairly runny, it would be plastered on to a sheet of lint, like putting jam on a piece of bread. The lint, backed by a thick layer of cotton wool, would then be strapped on to my left side. I think this process went on for weeks until at last I emerged, weak but unbowed. I mention that incident to emphasise that, although we often hanker after the 'good old days', we can be thankful for advances in many aspects of life, especially in the field of medicine.

The 'romantic stage' soon passed and Danny became my best friend. Danny was a year older than I, so he became a sort of leader in our adventures around the village. Both our families were poor so we had to create material aids to add to our enjoyment. We were fascinated with things that floated. When we were eventually allowed to go to Aberystwyth on our own, we enjoyed going to the promenade with a sixpence in our hands to seek out Mr Davies. He had spent his whole life at sea, but after retiring he had purchased a rowing-boat in which he took customers – including ourselves – for a voyage around the bay. My great thrill was to look at the shimmering pebbles as we became afloat; my whole being would be enthralled at that magic moment. Then came around thirty minutes of engrossing tales of the sea. Mr Davies seemed in his element with his black-peaked fisherman's cap, his droopy white moustache and his pipe, rowing slowly and entertaining us kids with his stories. Whether they were true or not was not important; it was half an hour of sheer delight.

In my paternal grandmother's public house, the Druid Inn, there was an old bagatelle table that had seen better days after over half a century of use. Apparently it was quite famous, and my great-uncle John used to relate tales of the times he played on it, despite his handicap. To me, however, it had potential as a raft. Danny and I unceremoniously split it in two at the hinges and carried it over to my other grandfather's 'grotto' at the Royal Oak, where all the tools and timber necessary for the conversion were at hand. I had been helping my grandfather extract some timber from the lead mine; these timbers were covered with earth and clay and had formed the base of circular 'buddles' (depressions where the lead ore was washed during the heyday of the mines in the nineteenth century). Whatever their origin, I saw their potential for making the sides of my raft. They were very rough and had a thickness of about one and a half inches. Using four-inch nails, the thick planks were fixed to the sides of the bagatelle table. Unfortunately, many gaps remained which had to be filled with huge dollops of brown plastic wood.

Once the raft was complete it looked very good, but the thick wood made it so heavy that to lift it took a gargantuan effort. However, Danny and I managed somehow and we hauled it all the way to the bridge across the Melindŵr. Under the bridge, the water was smooth and about eight inches deep – enough, we felt, for the raft to float. We thought we might be risking it a bit to introduce it into deeper water. So the raft was launched and wonder of wonders, it floated – for about ten feet anyway, by which time it was full of water. I'm afraid my attempts with the plastic wood left much to be desired. We carried it home triumphantly nevertheless, very happy but very wet.

We went on to more adventurous activities in the field of sailing. Danny's father had acquired a bicycle during the early part of the war, which put my tiny 'Gamages' in the shade. So came a period of constant nagging about having a new bicycle to replace the miniature I was now pedalling with very bent knees. I had seen my ideal model in a *Graves of Sheffield* catalogue: it had what were called 'North Road high-raised' handlebars. Eventually the wondrous machine arrived, and though I was initially disappointed in that the wheels and the handlebars were painted black (due to wartime shortages) whereas Danny's dad's bike had chrome, it was a pleasure to be able to cycle on equal terms again.

One Saturday we decided to go for a ride up into the hills to the north of Goginan. It was rather a rough day and there was a threat of rain in the air. We climbed up the lane, past Goginan Fach farm and the disused mines of Bryn Pica and Bwlch, until we were cycling amongst bare heather slopes and tufts of pale grass. Though it was summer, the dismal scene was decidedly wintry as the wind increased in force and squally rain showers buffeted our progress. We were watched from a nearby hill by a shepherd who probably wondered who these mad people were to be out in this weather. Eventually he lost interest and strode up the hill, his long coat flapping in the strong wind. We decided that we should go as far as the brow of the next hill and then turn back for home.

We reached the brow and there before us were the choppy waters of Llyn Rhos-goch (red marsh lake) which was about a quarter of a mile wide and half a mile long. On the near shore was a rowing-boat complete with oars. We looked at each other uncertainly. Should we have a go? We glanced up to see if the shepherd was still in sight, but he had long disappeared; our only company being the scattered sheep which had also lost interest in our presence.

We tentatively pushed the boat into the water and Danny, being older, assumed command. I glanced nervously at the white tops of the considerable waves and immediately regretted agreeing to this mad prank. By now we were about six feet away from the shore and already in deep water. I sat in the back of the boat while Danny took the oars. Unfortunately, he had never rowed in his life and had obviously not paid enough attention to the technique used by Mr Davies during our trips in Aberystwyth. The boat started rotating in a tight circle and there was nothing Danny could do to correct the movement. We decided to change places so that I could have a go. However, the boat had a flat bottom and our first movement almost led to it capsizing; a whole load of water spilled over the side. Eventually we managed to exchange our positions and the boat started moving in the right direction, by which I mean we were heading straight for the middle of the lake.

We were moving along quite nicely, but Danny kept staring over my shoulder at some object in the lake. I stopped rowing for a moment to see what he was staring at. There in the middle of the lake was a large log, which was spiralling slowly towards the centre. Even to my panicky mind this signified a whirlpool – and we were heading straight for it. It's amazing how, when you are in a dead panic, your mind somehow starts ticking again. The immediate question was: how to change direction? In a flash of inspiration I remembered that Mr Davies pulled on one oar. I would do the same, but which oar? I quickly calculated that if I pulled on the left oar the boat should go right. The nearest shore was to the left, so right oar it was. I closed my eyes and hoped for the best. Yes, the boat moved left. I found renewed energy with this success, and with a few hefty strokes that would have done credit to an oarsman in the Oxbridge Boat Race, we arrived on the far shore. The boat was unceremoniously dumped and we scampered for our bikes and home.

I still like things that float but I prefer to admire them from a safe distance these days.

★ ★ ★

There's a lot of talk about climate change now. Whether this is due to our so-called 'carbon footprint' getting heavier as our way of life changes, or if we are experiencing the effects of the amount of coal, coke and other dirty materials which were used during the Industrial Revolution, I'm not sure. But the weather during the 1930s and '40s seemed to be very different from today. Back then, summers seemed to be much sunnier. I wouldn't say hotter, but we seemed to enjoy long and pleasant days out in the sun with little fear of getting burnt to a crisp. Spring and autumn seemed much more recognisable: we had to wait till February at the earliest to find snowdrops peeping modestly at us; then by Saint David's Day there was a good chance we could wear leeks and daffodils. Then the leaves would start turning in September and gathering nuts would become a favourite pastime.

These days, you had better start in August if you want to beat the squirrels to them.

I am sure we got much more snow, especially after Christmas, and frosts and frozen ponds were much more in evidence. In January we were guaranteed that the little pool of water that collected at the bottom of the field below the school would be so frozen that we could skate on it – not that we had any skates, but the soles of our boots would be very smooth and shiny (and thinner) after a few early evenings of gliding over the ice a few hundred times under a frosty moon.

Then there were the periodic heavy snowstorms which we don't get very much anymore. I think the most notable storm was that of 1947, when the village was cut off for weeks and people had to struggle two miles down to Capel Bangor to get supplies. Not that a minor inconvenience like that troubled us kids in the least; that was a problem for the grown-ups. We had a whale of a time with home-made toboggans or even large trays. The favourite 'ski-run' was about two hundred yards long, from the Mount at the top of the village, down a steeply-sloping field to the cemetery of the Dyffryn Methodist Chapel at the bottom of the valley. The hill could be covered with drifts of over six feet, so that the hedges bordering the lane were mostly covered. There was an exciting little bump halfway down. Danny's dad, Rhys Evans, who worked at Blaendyffryn farm, had made a sizeable path across the field from his morning and evening trek, at right angles to the slope. We had a competition to see who could take off over this bump and land the farthest down the slope without falling off. The slope itself declined gradually as one reached the bottom, and the tops of the hedges acted as a further brake. A successful run would therefore take us conveniently into the cemetery where most of the gravestones were obliterated by snowdrifts. The occasional larger monument would still appear above the surface of the snow, so that one had to be very careful as to where one landed.

They were great days despite the cold. Our noses were red and dripping, but we were all wrapped up warm with ragged coats, caps and gloves; the luckier ones would also be furnished with scarves. Some would be equipped with handkerchiefs or pieces of rag to harness the nasal drips, while others would do the next best thing: use their sleeve. After frequent use, these would also look rather like a ski run.

Despite the good fun, something occurred during that era which has always rankled in my mind. Since supplies could not come through, except for the bare essentials such as bread (or that horrible, dirty-grey concoction that passed as bread in those hard post-war years), there came the tragic day when Davies' shop ran out of sweets. John Davies then hit on a brilliant idea which would rid him of certain unwanted items that had languished on the shelves for ages. One of these was a tin of water biscuits. To prevent the gnawing hunger getting to us after our frolics in the snow, he offered us some of these biscuits in lieu of our normal sweet ration. They were round and tasteless, with a coating of salt which introduced a modicum of taste. Anyway, they were better than nothing so we took them. But then, horror of horrors, he had the cheek to demand that we gave up our sweet coupons in exchange. We never forgave him for that; he, of all people, who was an elder at the Baptist Chapel! I think at a later date we managed to purloin a couple of bars of chocolate in revenge when he wasn't looking.

★ ★ ★

Jim was a contemporary of mine at Goginan School and a good friend. He lived at Alltygwreiddyn (*allt* can be interpreted as a hill, and *gwreiddyn* means a root, so the name of the small-holding could be translated as root hill). Jim was what I would call of true farming stock, with quite a ruddy face, rather pointed ears and pale blue eyes which seemed to have a far-away look in them at times, as if he knew something I didn't. He wasn't very academically gifted and when at school, gave the impression that he wished he were elsewhere. Nevertheless, he emanated a great warmth and I used to enjoy being in his company.

Alltygwreiddyn itself had been a notable mixed farm of considerable size in the eighteenth century and ranked with other nearby farms like Cefncoed, Troed-y-rhiw and Penbryn. Later on it had been downgraded, and when I used to visit there were just one or two cows and a few other animals on the two or three fields remaining. My father used to relate stories about his visits to the farm when two sisters, Ann and Mary, lived there. The house was very old and the walls were largely made of mud. As such, they were ideal for rats to burrow into and make their nests. Thus the sisters' beds had wooden shutters around them to keep out the draughts and, more importantly, the rats.

My aunt, Betty Ashley-Jones, remembered the sisters clearly despite being in her one hundred and first year, and related an anecdote about them. They were regular visitors at the Druid Inn and were very friendly with my grandmother. When the elder sister, Ann, died, she left the younger sister on her own in the old house. Early one morning, about three o'clock, my grandparents were woken by a loud banging on the front door. There was the very agitated younger sister, Mary, carrying a small bundle containing her personal effects. Apparently, she had been harassed just after midnight by a tramp who had forced his way into the house and terrified her. He demanded a meal and some money, but he had then been persuaded to depart. Once the coast was clear, Mary gathered up a few of her personal effects and ran the mile or so to the Druid Inn in a very perturbed state of mind. She vowed that she would never return to the farm and my grandparents were obliged to accommodate her indefinitely at the inn.

The only item of furniture she insisted on having from the old house was a chest of drawers which had been in the family for many generations. This was duly transported by horse and cart to the Druid, when Mary decided to donate the chest and all its contents to my grandmother as a token of her appreciation. On opening the drawers, my grandmother was astounded to find hundreds of little wads of paper pushed into various nooks and crannies. On unwrapping the paper, she was even more astounded to find that each wad contained coins to the value of ten shillings. The frugal sisters had wrapped their weekly pension in the paper and stashed it in the drawers. I don't know if any other treasure hoards were hidden in the house, but by the time I visited with Jim there was little sign of great wealth in the modest but comfortable living room.

Since Alltygwreiddyn was situated about a mile to the west of Goginan, the driver of the post office van would kindly give Jim a lift to the lane leading down to the house after collecting the afternoon mail from the post office. The usual driver was a man called Dai M M, a First World War veteran who had won the Military Medal during active service. If Dai was in a good mood, he would allow me to accompany Jim on the van; at other times, since he was bending post office rules to allow Jim to ride, he felt reluctant to bend the rules any further, and I would be left behind, snivelling. However, on the good days in summer, we would arrive home just in time for tea.

Jim's father was a tall, slim, rather grey-looking man who always wore a fisherman's hat pulled well down over his eyes, so it was hard to make out what he really looked like. Since he didn't talk a lot, it was also difficult to get to know him; he seemed to spend most of his time in the barn or the cowshed anyway. Jim's mother, Mrs Jones, was a very kind but rugged lady with snow-white hair and bright, pale blue eyes, one of which tended to stray a little, so that you did not quite know whether she was looking at you. She always dressed in black and was a faithful member of the local Methodist Chapel.

I remember going to Rhyl in North Wales with the Methodist Sunday School for the annual day trip. On the way home, still seventy miles from Goginan, Mrs Jones took it into her head that she would be the next person to alight from the bus. I was astonished to see her putting her coat on and collecting her bags and umbrella and then sitting on the edge of her seat, anticipating her stop.

Tea at Alltygwreiddyn was usually a very wholesome affair, with thinly-sliced bread cut from those huge loaves which were usually found on farms, with some butter and cheese or jam to add variety to the repast. Then it was out to the fields to play until it was time for me to trudge my weary way back to the village.

I remember one afternoon being at a loose end, when Mrs Jones suggested that Jim and I should go fishing in the stream across the field. We had no fishing rods but Mrs Jones, always full of ideas, furnished us with a homemade one. This comprised of a hazel cane from the hedgerow, a stout piece of string and a three or four-inch nail for a hook, which she bent using a hammer on the anvil. This she tied to the end of the string and we were ready for our fishing expedition. Unfortunately, the nails were new and glinted brilliantly in the sunlight. But we went, feeling a little bit like Tom Sawyer and Huckleberry Finn, of whom we had been reading at school.

Now I ask you, what self-respecting fish would be tempted by such a contraption? How on earth could we attach a bait to such a hook? It would need a piece of meat so large that a lion would not turn up its nose at it. There was no one around in that remote spot but even so, I felt ashamed to be associated with this charade. It was the first time I had ventured across these particular fields to the riverbank. When we arrived, I gazed in amazement at the flowing water and collapsed on the bank laughing. The river turned out to be a little trickle about a foot wide and less than two inches deep, so that the 'hook' stood proud of the water by over an inch. We hastily abandoned the homemade contraption and had more fun splashing about in the slightly deeper pools, upturning the bigger stones and catching the one-inch minnows which occasionally sheltered under them, placing them in a jam jar. When I watch TV films of fishermen off the coast of Florida going shark or marlin fishing in their high-speed boats, the vision of those shiny four-inch bent nails often comes to mind.

I have one last recollection of Jim. A lorry was delivering bags of coal to the various scattered households. In between the deliveries we took turns to grab onto the rail at the back of the lorry and get a 'tug', that is, to be pulled along by the lorry until it stopped at the next delivery point. We had reached the last three houses and it was Jim's turn to get a 'tug.' He grabbed the rail and off he went along the rough, stony lane. Unfortunately for him, the next two houses did not need coal. The lorry picked up speed and shot down the lane for about two hundred yards with Jim in tow. I can still see him with his little legs flaying wildly about, hitting the road at intervals with his steel-capped boots, creating enormous sparks. Eventually the lorry stopped to deliver more coal and Jim fell limply to the floor, more from fright than injury. I am sure it was those steel-capped boots he always wore that saved him from a much worse fate.

Jim never married and lived at Alltygwreiddyn for most of his life. He died a few years ago after a long illness and the neighbourhood lost another dear character.

So life progressed and we grew up until it was time to broaden our horizons further as we became hormone-filled teenagers.

CHAPTER FIVE

Junior Jinks in the Thirties and Forties

No IPODS, NO MOBILE phones – or phones of any sort for that matter (except for the one in the recesses of the post office) – no calculators, no television, no computers or printers, no piped water, no water toilets, no electricity! What on earth did we do? The situation seemed ripe for boredom, for vandalism, for all sorts of mischief. There were lots of old ladies and gentlemen around who could be mugged or beaten up, but this never happened. Respect, discipline and conscience seemed to be ingrained in us and controlled our general behaviour. Were we that good? Certainly not – we were up to all sorts of tricks. The occasional window was smashed as were those little china things that held the telephone wires to the posts – they were ideal targets to improve our throwing skills.

Apple scrumping was another seasonal activity. My favourite target was our own garden. It was stupid really as I could go there whenever I liked. But it was much more exciting to join the boys in this dangerous approach. In any case, it was not our trees that were the target – my uncle's apple tree only contained sour cooking apples – but those of Dei Williams, our landlord next door with whom we shared the plot. His trees contained lovely Golden Delicious apples. The adrenaline would flow as we climbed through the hedge at the bottom of the garden. Having been on the mission several times, we were dab hands at sliding through without damaging the hedge too much.

After a few raids we became rather blasé and would carelessly fill our pockets with the delicious pale green apples. Then on one afternoon raid, there was a sudden whirring noise in the air followed by a loud 'thwack'. We were momentarily stunned and looked around to discover the source of the sound. Someone happened to glance upwards and there, still quivering in the tree trunk next to our apple tree, was an axe. In a panic, we looked up to the top of the path and there was Dei Williams bounding down in our direction. Dei was a temperamental man and had obviously thrown the first thing that came to hand. Luckily I was small and managed to slide through the hedge very quickly, but I am sure that some of the larger conspirators had some serious explaining to do as to why their clothes were more torn than usual and as to where the scratches on arms and knees had come from.

Other young scamps were not so lucky. According to my old friend, Cyril Evans, who lived in the village just after the Second World War, three or four young adventurers decided to raid the Dyffryn Chapel house garden, where again the apples were very inviting. Unfortunately, this little gang was caught red-handed by someone who meticulously upheld the law by reporting them to the local policeman. The PC was very young and new to the force, so he decided to stamp his authority on the local community early in his career by issuing a summons. The poor unfortunates were dragged before the beak in Llanbadarn, on the outskirts of Aberystwyth. There was much consternation as the actions of the 'criminals' were succinctly described by the officer.

When the officer had completed his statement, the beak gazed gravely at the young culprits in the dock, then suddenly started comparing notes with them of his own experiences as an apple 'scrumper' in his youth. Then, turning to the stunned police officer, he asked whether there had been something missing in his youth, since he didn't seem to have experienced the joys of such activities. The 'criminals' were immediately declared not guilty, and the young PC was censured for wasting the court's time with such frivolities. So the young adventurers left court very happily, followed by a truly crestfallen bobby. Soon after the incident, the bobby was moved on to another part of the country.

★ ★ ★

Len Edwards was a combination of born leader and entrepreneur. He was only one or two years older than I, but he always seemed to be 'in charge'. He lived in Eagle House with Gwilym and Mary Howells; I am not sure what their connection was, but I don't think he was one of the family. All I know is that he always came up with some enterprise or other, and if there was a chance of making a few bucks in the process, all well and good.

After Len left school, he got a job as assistant projectionist at the Coliseum Cinema in Aberystwyth, known to us in our courting days as the 'flea pit'. Comfort left much to be desired – it was hit or miss whether one had a seat fitted. One would often hear a thump and a curse when some unfortunate went to sit down and landed unceremoniously on the floor. However, the films were always very good; I think that they were sent out into the wilds to test them out before being released in bigger cinemas in urban areas. But the cinema was old, as were the projectors, so that breaks in the films were very frequent. Such breakdowns would be greeted with whistles, boos and stamping of feet, and the poor projectionist had to work very quickly to splice the film together before real pandemonium broke loose.

The offending strips of film would eventually reach Len's pocket via the floor, which gave him an idea. With me as his assistant, he converted a little dry stone hut that stood the other side of the lane from Eagle House, into the 'Goginan Odeon'. He had managed to obtain an old projector – one of those 'turn handle' jobs (electricity was about thirty years away). Old sacks were obtained and hung over the many openings and a whitish sheet was hung on one wall. It was not a very flat surface, so the pictures were given an unintentional 3D effect (how modern could one get?). Then planks and old buckets were obtained to form seats for the audience of children from the village. One halfpenny was charged for entry – it was my job as front of house manager to collect these. (I never found out what became of this money. It probably went to defray expenses.) The atmosphere was rather muggy and not very sweet, as the sacks had been used for a variety of smelly jobs.

So the show would commence with a medley of snippets, mostly in black and white, leaving maybe one little snippet in colour for the grand finale. Then a photograph of His Majesty King George VI would appear on the screen and all would have to stand and give an unaccompanied rending of the national anthem. So the evening ended with everybody happy. To see actual pictures projected on a screen in those pre-electricity days was a wonder.

Len soon got tired of this enterprise and the film strips were used for a more exciting, but dangerous, activity. He found that if they were put in a bottle and the hole was stopped up with a piece of cloth soaked in paraffin, one could make a very passable Molotov cocktail. Thus, bottles were collected and a 'battlefield' was selected. Quite a crowd of youths would collect to see the show, which could be quite spectacular. I remember one of these 'bombs' failed to explode, so a young chap called John Pugh went forward to see why. He picked it up and held it to his ear to discover if there was any of the usual hissing noise. Tragically, at that very moment the 'bomb' decided to explode, leaving poor John with terrible lacerations that were to remain with him for the rest of his life. No more bombs were manufactured after that unfortunate incident.

As November the fifth approached, we all hollowed out a turnip or swede to make the traditional lantern, usually with the help of our parents. A grinning or grimacing face was etched into the side and a candle was placed inside. Then we were ready to parade our Guy Fawkes around the village in the hope that our efforts might be rewarded by a penny or two from the populace. Making a Guy was quite an ordeal: old coats and trousers were filled with straw and, if our mothers had been to Woolworths in Aberystwyth, we would have a mask of some sort. Failing that, a home-made one was concocted from a small piece of sheeting. The effigy was then placed in a home-made wagon or cart to be borne round the lanes of the village for the inspection of the natives.

One year, Len decided that making a Guy was not worth the effort but kept us in suspense as to what the alternate course of action would be. The night arrived and we assembled outside Eagle House. I remember it was a dark, moonless night with a slight drizzle, so that the bonfire would be a bit of a hit-or-miss affair. Len emerged from the house dressed completely in black, including black gloves and the trilby hat he had taken to wearing (I think the Dirk Bogarde films he regularly saw at the Coliseum influenced his way of life). We trooped down to the stone shed, now used as a coal bunker, and saw a large perambulator parked at the entrance. Len produced a black hood with eye holes which he put on before climbing into the pram. Off we went around the lanes of the village in complete darkness except for the ghostly glow of our lanterns, gaining much admiration for the wonderful work accomplished with the Guy.

Eventually, we arrived at a John Pryse's small holding and knocked on the front door. He admired the Guy so much that he decided to call his family to see the wondrous work. We all waited in the sure knowledge that a monetary reward would be forthcoming. Eventually, Mrs Pryse appeared holding a large lantern, followed by Mr Pryse holding a two-pronged hayfork which he aimed at the stomach of the Guy. I have never seen a Guy move so quickly, leaving the Pryse family falling about with laughter. We all returned home rather dejected; there was no bonfire that night and we all wondered what had happened to the money we had collected.

Once I had settled in Aberystwyth's Grammar school, I was given greater freedom. Saturday afternoons meant a trip to the matinee performance at the Coliseum. I would arrive, clutching my shilling for a programme that included a major film, the Pathe news and a serial. One serial that comes to mind was *Zorro* in the black and white days. Quite a few of us from the village would be absorbed in his adventures and would re-enact the whole drama in the field across the road from the school. Every month, this field would be the scene of a sheep mart and wooden pens were constructed to accommodate the various farmers' flocks with a large enclosed area at the end where the sheep were sold. The sheep were taken out of the pens and driven down one of two alleyways to the auctioning area. This structure made an ideal setting for our adventures. There were places to hide and great venues for the chases and sword fights we had seen earlier in the afternoon. Len, of course, had to be Zorro – after all he projected the serial in the cinema and already had the mask and trilby hat which could be punched about to roughly emulate Zorro's headgear. The rest of us poor minions had to make do with whatever articles of clothing that came to hand. However, swords were impossible to come by, so a piece of wood from a hedgerow would have to suffice.

But I had to be different. My tad-cu (grandfather) was a skilled carpenter. After a few weeks of managing like the rest of the 'hoi polloi' with a common stick, I proudly turned up one evening wielding a beautiful sword which my grandfather had fashioned out of seasoned wood. I strutted into the arena ready to wipe the floor with anyone, even Zorro himself. Unfortunately, I didn't get as far as Zorro; in fact I didn't get very far at all. At the first sweep, my trusty sword snapped into two pieces. Being made of dry, seasoned wood, it could not withstand the strength of an unseasoned stick of wood from the hedgerow. I retreated rather red in the face from the scene with probably a few secret tears of chagrin. I can't remember whether I attended any more re-enactments after that, but somehow the episodes at the Coliseum lost their charm.

★ ★ ★

Dei Pen-wal was different, both in the way he dressed and spoke. His full name was David Lewis Morgan and he was an only child. He was born in the United States but after his father's death, his mother, Mary Jane, decided to return with her twelve-year-old son to Goginan, where for many years she had worked as a teacher in the local school. So they returned to the family home at Pen-wal (top of the wall) in the Dollwen.

Whether it was to show that he was from a different environment or if it was his dare-devil nature, I don't know, but Dei did some strange things which left most of us rather puzzled. Below the school in a field beside the main road is a tree, which for some reason I was never able to ascertain, was called 'y goeden sanctaidd' (the holy tree). Well, Dei decided to climb to the top of this tree and launch himself into mid-air equipped only with an open umbrella. The tree was situated at the bottom of a slope and he at least had the sense to jump on the upslope side so that the drop, though considerable, was not quite so bad. He survived, bruised but unbowed, to carry out some other rather nefarious activities.

One evening, Tommy Bradshaw was on his way home to the Geuallt on the other side of the valley. It was very dark, but having walked home on hundreds of occasions at night, he did not need a flashlight – he knew every stone and change of slope he would encounter on the mile-long walk. About a third of the way down the steep hill to the chapel there is a recess in the hedge leading to a field. When Tommy was within five yards of this, two faint pin points of blue light emerged and moved gently from side to side, accompanied by deep breathing. The lights were at about head height and as Tommy got nearer, he could just make out a figure in white swaying gently. Tommy, who had heard eerie rumours about a ghost on the hill, was a little alarmed at the encounter but kept his head. He had never heard of a ghost with heavy breathing before. So there was nothing for it but to investigate further. He flung himself forward into the recess and grabbed the ghost in a bear hug, crashed through the flimsy gate into the field and rolled about one hundred yards down the slope until they were brought to a sudden halt by the hedge. Tommy dragged a white sheet from the ghost to discover the very white, startled face of Dei Pen-wal staring up at him in terror. Funnily enough, the ghost on the hill disappeared after that night.

Knowing about the tale of the ghost on the hill, a few of us decided to take matters a little further one evening. It was a moonlit, quiet night – a night when the gravestones of Dyffryn Chapel cemetery stood out sharply through the hedge at the bottom of the hill. The chapel itself was huge; it had been built in the heyday of mining activities when it was anticipated that an influx of miners would necessitate the building of a gallery. However, the increase did not materialise so a large empty space was left inside. One day when we had nothing to do, we found that if we shouted through the large keyhole of the chapel door, the sound would be greatly amplified in the hollow recesses. So, on this particular night we waited for an old chap – I can't remember his name, but I shall call him John Jones – to stagger his way down the hill on his way home after imbibing too much ale at the Druid Inn. As he passed the cemetery he usually rather nervously started humming a tune, probably to keep his superstitious spirits up. Suddenly the hairs on the back of his head started prickling and he broke out in a cold sweat as he heard booming from the direction of the cemetery: "John Jones, John Jones, your time is nigh. Make peace with your maker very quickly!" John took off and must have reached his house on the other side of the valley in record time, leaving us youngsters rolling about with laughter.

★ ★ ★

George and Trevor lived with their mother, Anne, in a cottage beside the main road. The house contained three small rooms: a living room, a back kitchen and one bedroom. The two brothers had to negotiate a ladder each night to sleep in the attic. The front door opened straight into the living room which had a stone slab floor and was rather sparsely furnished. There was a table next to the small window, three dining chairs, two arm chairs, one on each side of the open fire, and a cupboard against the back wall. Taking pride of place leaning against a large chest of drawers was George's pride and joy, his motor cycle. Both Trevor and George had a passion for all things mechanical and they treated the bike as their pampered baby. Any spare moment they had, the boys would be seen with a spanner or some other tool in hand, tinkering with the engine.

As mischievous kids, we would go up the main road of an evening and knock on the door of the cottage. Anne, a little rotund lady with a ruddy face and rosy cheeks would answer.

"What do you want?" she would say, peering intently at us.

"Is George in?" one kid would ask.

"George, there's a lot of 'em here to see you."

"What do they want?" George would shout from the back kitchen.

"We've come up to see your bike, George," someone would reply.

"Oh, come in, boys, come in."

We would all crowd into the little room, pushing poor Annie in front of us as George, full of smiles, would emerge from the back kitchen.

"There she is, boys. I've just been tuning her up. She sounds great now, purrs like a kitten."

"Really, George, what do you mean, she purrs like a kitten?"

"You know, she sounds smooth, not rough. Wait a minute, I'll start her up for you."

George would pull the machine upright, lift his leg over and kick the starter. All of a sudden, ornaments would rattle and smoke and noise would fill the living room. For a short time there would be pandemonium. We kids would be laughing, Anne would be crying and cowering in her chair by the fire, while George, oblivious to everyone else, would be gazing adoringly into space engrossed in the sound emanating from the machine. Children can be very cruel at times.

A few years later, I was coming home from the grammar school in Aberystwyth on the bus. It was a Wednesday afternoon, and as the bus stopped on the village square we perceived George standing forlornly, crying his eyes out. He had rather a large, round face with big blue eyes, but on this occasion both eyes were framed by the darkest black colourations I have ever seen. On his nose were two strips of Elastoplast forming a cross. Apparently, George was crying not because he had been hurt, but because he thought the nurses at the hospital where he had been taken after his accident were deliberately making fun of him by adorning his face with the OXO sign.

Since it was a Wednesday, George had had the afternoon off, spending much of it tuning his beloved motor cycle. As the road around Goginan has many sharp bends, there was no opportunity to open up the throttle until he had reached Capel Bangor, two miles down the main road. Here there was a stretch of straight road between the Tynllidiart Arms and the primary school. Sitting in his car outside the school was Mr David Miles, the county music advisor for schools, writing a report after his visit. On reaching this stretch, George decided that this was the time to see what the engine could do. The throttle was opened and the bike flew down the road. George was engrossed in the sound of the engine and was moving his head from side to side to get a better idea of the noise it was making. Unfortunately, he was so wrapped up in the engine sounds that he failed to notice the parked car standing with its brakes full on outside the school. Suddenly, David Miles found himself moving involuntarily several feet forwards, propelled by the front wheel of George's bike hitting the back bumper. Then George's head hit the round bonnet, leaving a dent the size of a football. It was a miracle that he suffered only two black eyes and a broken nose. They bred them tough in Goginan in those days!

I remember George and Trevor as good, hard-working men. George was the elder and looked a rugged, outdoor type, while Trevor, who had a severe limp, looked more gentle. Both, however, had hearts of gold and were always ready to do a favour. For many years, George worked as a coal merchant based in Aberystwyth, while Trevor, who was quite skilled with any form of vehicle engines, had a job as a greaser at a garage in Aberystwyth – those were the days when all motor cars had a myriad of nipples and joints that had to be lubricated.

When Annie died, the brothers moved from the cottage down to the end house in BrynMelindŵr Terrace, the old miners' cottages situated halfway down the steep hill from the village to the chapels. Being bachelors, the idea of keeping the premises spotless was one that never came to mind; they were quite happy as they were in their little home.

I remember my old school teacher, Miss Williams, reminiscing about them during her last months at an old people's home in Aberystwyth. Cecele and I went to visit her and the conversation inevitably turned to the old days in Goginan. Even at 95 years of age she had not lost her sense of humour. The conversation turned to her days when she would go round the houses collecting donations for the Missionary Society. "Well," she said, with a twinkle in her eye, "of all the houses I visited in Goginan, there was one which I admired very much. It was George and Trevor's house at No. 1, BrynMelindŵr Terrace. The colour scheme matched perfectly throughout the living room: everything was a lovely shade of grey!" They were great characters and their happy lives gave rise to many amusing incidents which added character to life in the village, especially after the last world war.

I always had to chuckle when George and Trevor described their weekly evening menu. Every Monday evening after work it was George's task to buy enough meat to last the week – a large leg of lamb or pork, or maybe a large portion of beef. Trevor was responsible for obtaining vegetables to sustain the pot. When they arrived home in George's car (they shunned the motor cycle in later years), the big bucket would be placed on the open fire and into it went all the ingredients they had purchased that evening. This would then form the basis of the evening meal for the next six days. They both did a good day's work and usually returned home ravenous, so that the contents of the bucket, big as it was, would not quite see them through the whole week. By the time Thursday arrived they would have to hunt for more supplies. Tins of sardines or baked beans would be added to the bucket until the next batch of goodies could be purchased.

George and Trevor worked and played hard, and the Druid Inn would be the place where they would spend nearly every evening except Sunday. One would always find George sitting on a stool at one end of the bar, with Trevor balancing the picture at the other. Everybody was fond of them, and their pint

George Richards (far right) with his brother Trevor (far left) enjoying a quiet drink along with some of their friends at the Druid Inn, Goginan. In the centre is Peter Davies, and to his immediate left is another great personality from Capel Bangor, David (Dei) Carrard. To Peter's left is the landlady of the Druid at the time the photograph was taken.

pots would be constantly replenished by their many friends and acquaintances. Thus they would end days on a merry note, but not usually to the extent that the way back down the hill would present an insurmountable barrier. However, on rare occasions, a very special night of rejoicing would lead to them imbibing more than usual. Then came the logistical problem of finding a suitable vehicle in which to convey Trevor, whose balance was severely impaired due to his rather serious handicap. George was a roadman in later life, when his wheelbarrow would solve the problem. Should this not be available, a large perambulator would serve the purpose admirably. However, George was unfamiliar with this more mobile means of conveyance, and on one or two occasions lost control on encountering the change of gradient at the top of the hill. When this occurred, both would arrive in the garden below the road in a heap, where they would be found the next morning sleeping contentedly.

The wheelbarrow would cause George further trouble during a hot summer. He was working on ditches beside the lane in the Dollwen, and decided that a cold beer would go down a treat in his lunch break. Up he went to the Druid and managed to get to the outside of quite a few beers in the short time he had. On returning to the lane, drowsiness overtook him so he had a quick nap in the wheelbarrow to revive his energies ready for the afternoon's session. It was about four o'clock before he returned to the land of the living and he was very puzzled to find himself about two miles up the valley. Apparently, a farmer had decided to tease him by wheeling the barrow very quietly for two miles up towards Blaendyffryn farm. George related the story later with much mirth.

Both brothers enjoyed life and always took these little adventures in their stride. They were a happy pair, much loved by the community. They added so much colour to the neighbourhood; after all, what would a community be without such lovely characters? Their recent passing left another void in the life of the village.

★ ★ ★

During the latter part of the Second World War there seemed to be a certain stigma and a hint of cowardice if any of us younger teenage boys went home early in the evenings. However, there was very little to do, especially in the winter, so we used to loiter on the village square inelegantly doing nothing. There were usually about five of us lingering there being boisterous, with our hard-to-control hormones causing us to make fools of ourselves with loud catcalls and whistles whenever a female of roughly our own age happened to pass.

Then at about half-past six we would be joined by a couple of Italian prisoners of war who were working at Troed-y-rhiw farm. I think their names were Marco and Angelo, and since the authorities decided they would pose no threat to the war effort, they were allowed almost complete freedom. The only feature distinguishing them from the locals was their uniform – a chocolate-brown jerkin and trousers with large, bright yellow circular patches on the thigh and the back. Being passionate Italians, they also partook of the childish bantering with their references in pidgin English to 'jig-a-jig' (sexual intercourse) whenever females were around.

There we would lounge for about two or three hours by the large red and yellow 'Craven A' cigarette advertising hoarding which was pinned to the side of Jones' wooden shop, freezing to death and absently listening to the steady thump of the motor which generated electricity for Jones' house – the only one to be so lit in the village. We were too proud to leave for the warmth of our own houses. Eventually, someone would find an excuse to go home, and very soon the square would once again be left to the stray dogs and cats, ready for the following evening's repeat performance. Even in those days teenagers could be very stupid.

★ ★ ★

Glyn Top House was another wonderful personality. His full name was John Glyn Owen Williams, and in the 1930s and '40s he lived with his mother, Edith Olwen Williams, in the first house in the former Sayer's Village – hence the name Top House. His father, John, had died a few years earlier so I was not acquainted with him, but I do remember hearing of an incident in Glyn's early childhood which literally left its mark on him. As a young boy, he used to watch his father shaving. In common with most men of the village at that time, John Williams used a cut-throat razor. Glyn, forever the adventurous one, decided to have a go at the razor to emulate his father. Unfortunately, all he did was to cut himself severely on one cheek, leaving a permanent scar.

My old friends, Gareth Jones, Gwarllan, Glyn Williams, Loveden House, Daphne Jenkins, the top shop and Danny Evans, Bryn Melindwr, obviously taken on a Sunday as all are in their 'Sunday' suits!

There were many talented people around then and Glyn was amongst the most able. He was a handsome young man with a ready, mischievous smile and twinkling eyes – they could be described as 'come hither' eyes as far as the opposite sex was concerned, with whom he was very popular. He was two or three years older than I, and good at most things. He was a brilliant elocutionist and won many awards on a national level in Wales. As such, he also excelled as an actor and with his great sense of humour it was a pleasure to see him on the stage. His soccer playing ability was to be envied; as a centre-forward for local teams a few goals from his 'twinkling toes' were guaranteed in nearly every match.

In our early youth, Glyn and I got up to quite a few pranks. I remember going on rather a dubious mission when we had little to do. Every summer, dozens of coaches came from cities in the Midlands for day trips to Aberystwyth, and on very hot days most of these would have their canvas tops drawn back to give the passengers more air. On this particular day when the spirit of mischief was very much in the air, we decided to arm ourselves with a few bottles of cold water and go up the main road to where y graig fawr (the big rock) slightly overhung the road. We climbed to the top of the rock and sat with our feet dangling over the edge. Eventually the rumble of the buses reached out ears and it was time for action. As the buses passed slowly in convoy beneath us, the bottle stoppers were removed and it was 'bombs away'! We emptied the contents of each bottle on the poor passengers below and were much amused to hear their squeals and the frantic rush for rain jackets. When the water ran out, we thought of using the only other source of 'water' available to us, but I think we refrained from utilising that commodity at the last moment.

I don't think I often saw Glyn on a bicycle, but in his late teens he acquired a motor car, if the machine he got could be credited with such a name. It was a very small Austin Swallow with two wheels in front and one at the back. It had been around for years before Glyn acquired it and I think most of it was ready to retire before it arrived in Goginan. However, it went, and whenever there was a gradient in its favour, went very well. It had one fault: the brakes left much to be desired. One had to apply them at least a hundred yards before the point where one wished to stop. This was of course years before the ideas of MOT certificates and all that nonsense came into force.

I remember the day when Glyn was summoned to attend his driving test, which in those days was held in the little coastal town of Borth, about seven miles to the north of Aberystwyth. An early departure from Goginan was essential to ensure that the vehicle would arrive in good time. Glyn waited nervously beside his car for the driving inspector. Now, if I tell you that sitting in the passenger seat of the Austin Swallow was really only suitable for slim people, I do not exaggerate. I was thin and weighed about nine-and-a-half stone at that time and I can only describe sitting in the car as very snug. The examiner finally appeared from the office and poor Glyn almost fell over. The fellow was enormous – at least 23 stone. When he saw the vehicle, he blanched, and looking in alarm at Glyn, enquired as to whether he was actually expected to sit in a toy car. Eventually, after much huffing and puffing, he managed to squeeze his enormous frame in, though quite a proportion of his body spilled over onto the driver's seat. Glyn managed to get in on the driver's side but had to sit sideways. After much revving the poor little engine managed to pull the heavy cargo off the kerbside. After less than a hundred yards the car gradually came to a halt and the examiner tried in vain to get out. After much pushing on Glyn's part the deed was accomplished and the test ended as quickly as it began, with the

examiner waddling back to the office, wheezing and muttering comments about ridiculous toy cars under his breath.

The next time, Glyn managed to pass his test with a much slimmer examiner. I am sure that he was 'allowed' to pass, because when the brakes were put to the test, 'emergency stop' was something of a misnomer. But the examiner did not want to go through the ordeal of another nightmare trip in that car.

However, the little car did us great service in our courting days. Nearly every Saturday night it travelled the seven miles to Aberystwyth's hostelries like a trooper with few mishaps, though there were one or two on the homeward journey. These were the days before drink-driving laws were introduced, and though one could not describe our condition as anywhere near being inebriated, we would acquire that happy state of mind where mishaps were taken in one's stride and in no way regarded as a major hindrance.

One late evening, Glyn was in a merry mood and accompanying our gentle folk duet by swaying the car rhythmically in and out of the cats' eyes in the middle of the empty road. As luck would have it, our singing was interrupted by a loud hiss as the near-side tyre punctured. We pulled to the side and came to a halt after about twenty-five yards (the brakes had been much improved by that time). Changing the wheel was out of the question; such was Glyn's confidence in his little motor that to carry a spare wheel would be an encumbrance. At that time of night there was no garage open, in fact there were no garages at all in the area. We reached the consensus that Glyn should remain in the driving seat while I perched on the back bonnet with my legs each side of him so as to keep the weight of the car off the ailing wheel as far as possible. We covered the remaining five miles in this extremely uncomfortable position. When we eventually limped into the village, we struggled out and were dismayed to see an oval wheel *sans* tyre or tube. Still, it got us home and for that we were very thankful.

One evening a few weeks later, we ventured in the car all the way to an eisteddfod at the village of Pontrhydfendigaid (the bridge on the beautiful ford) where Glyn was going to compete in the Champion Recitation competition. About halfway between Goginan and this village there is rather a steep hill called Rhiw Gaer (fort hill). Due to the delicate nature of the brakes, Glyn decided that a gentle descent would be propitious; thus we descended at about twenty miles an hour. Suddenly, we observed in the dim light of the headlamps a wheel rolling in front of us down the slope. The car continued for a short distance and then started tilting towards the middle of the road with a shower of sparks as we made a two-point landing. Fortunately, no significant damage was done and after a search on our hands and knees in the moonlight we managed to locate three of the four nuts which held the wheel in place and the wheel itself, lodged in the hedge about fifty yards down the hill. By this time, Glyn had managed to acquire a jack so the wheel could be replaced using the three screws. We very

slowly and carefully reached our destination in time for Glyn's competition and he managed to win second prize. I'm sure he would have won except for that unfortunate incident.

★ ★ ★

Our wireless at home was a Cossor, a popular make in those days. It had a polished rectangular brown casing with a fretted piece in the front covered with a brown cloth where the voices and music came from – a wondrous mystery which I eventually discovered to be the loudspeaker. Underneath were three little brown knobs: one to switch on, one to control the volume and one to change the sounds (later to be deciphered as stations). I think we had the Home Service, the Light Programme and a very exotic station called Radio Luxembourg. The machine probably produced myriad other sounds, but those were the ones I remember. Then there was a little square in the middle that lit up when the wireless was switched on; that too was magical in the pre-electric days.

There were some very good programmes such as *Forces Favourites* and *Workers' Playtime* with excellent light and varied music which I think would liven people's mornings if they put them on again. There were variety programmes, especially at weekends, like *The Hippodrome* and *In Town Tonight*. All the traffic of London would screech to a halt each Saturday night to listen. I was very impressed as a child with the man who shouted 'Stop!' and everything would go quiet.

Then there was the sport. How we anticipated a boxing match, or a soccer or rugby international for weeks before the event. During a football match we had to get the *Radio Times* and turn to the page that contained a grid map of the pitch, each grid having a letter of the alphabet. In this way we could visualise the movement of the ball as Raymond Glendenning, that wonderful commentator with the handlebar moustache, would describe the play, while a disembodied voice would intone "G4" or "F2", so that we could follow the play on the chart.

What I did not understand was the name 'wireless'; it was full of wires – I still haven't really grasped that anomaly. What I did know was that it needed three batteries to make it work. There was a huge rectangular battery called a 'dry battery' which cost a lot but lasted a long time; then there was a small thin battery with lots of holes in the top into which wires were poked – this was the grid battery. Finally there was the wet battery. I was familiar with this one: it was a heavy glass affair with a red and a black knob on top onto which more wires were attached. Inside was a liquid which bubbled at intervals and sometimes gave a feeble hissing sound. This one only lasted a week before it had to be charged.

Every Monday morning, we children who attended school in Aberystwyth would queue up to wait for the bus with one of these wet batteries in tow. I am sure the driver and conductor were in fear and dread when the hordes mounted the steps of the bus armed with these lethal weapons. I think it took us a bit of time to realise, despite dire warnings from my mother and uncle John, that the bubbling liquid was acid which burnt and corroded anything it touched. Nearly every trip would echo to the thump of one of the monstrosities falling over, leaving a little bubbling puddle on the floor. The poor conductresses with their 'hennaed' legs – a pencil stripe down the back to emulate real stockings – did their best to control the situation, but it was a losing battle. On arrival in Aberystwyth we all trooped to the 'Primrose' garage in Cambrian Street (now 'Cheap Charlie's Discount Stores') where the batteries would be left on charge for a week. On Friday evenings we all lined up with our sixpences to pick up our possessions and carry them back home, sure in the knowledge that we would be guaranteed a weekend of delightful aural entertainment beside the blazing fire in the yellow glow of the paraffin lamp. Those were the days!

CHAPTER SIX

"But she's already had a clock…"

I THINK I MENTIONED THAT my main motive for writing this book was the inspiration I gained for my life and career from the inhabitants of the Melindŵr valley of my childhood. The more I think of it the stronger that belief becomes, especially when I think of the people who were so instrumental in my upbringing.

My mother was Olwen Evans, or Olwen fach (little) as she was popularly known due to her rather diminutive size. She was born on 22 November 1899, the youngest of three girls to William and Margaret Jane Evans, in the village of Pen-y-bont Rhydybeddau (literally 'bridge end at the ford of the graves'). However, when Olwen was ten, the family decided to move across the intervening hill to the Royal Oak in Goginan. Her father, William, was a blacksmith working in one of the silver-lead mines. He now decided to combine this work with running the Royal Oak, which catered largely for the miners from neighbouring valleys.

Olwen attended the school in Goginan and found herself sitting next to a young boy of her own age who was rather lucky in that he could surreptitiously copy some of her work. That boy eventually became my father. She was a brilliant student – so much so that in her last year at school a special class was created to cater for her abilities: Class X7. However, as she was the youngest, Olwen had to leave school at the age of 14 and be the Cinderella who stayed at home to help with the domestic chores.

I recently browsed through headmaster David Herbert's log in the archives at Aberystwyth, which he had faithfully kept through his forty years' tenure at the school. His entry for 23 April 1914 included: "Olwen Evans left school today, a very gifted student who merited further education, had family funds permitted…" This was the only occasion I could find where he had actually mentioned a pupil by name in such a context. It made me feel so proud.

At the beginning of World War I in 1914, the manpower of the village was depleted as many left to join the forces. Olwen, to her chagrin, was co-opted to deliver mail to outlying farms, a round trip of upwards of eight miles. The trek was probably much longer because she had such a nervous disposition that the sight of a horse or a cow in a field would cause her to make a wide detour.

Her work started at seven in the morning when she had to turn up at the village post office and sort out the letters and parcels for delivery. She would therefore have to leave home at 6.30. Imagine a day in mid-winter in say, January or February 1915: bitterly cold, damp and it might have snowed all night. The path across the disused mine would be very treacherous in the dark before the winter dawn, especially the very narrow part where it traversed the spoil heaps. Then started the daily trek from the village up the valley-side and through the woods in a south-westerly direction. Eventually, the path would lead to the top of the windy ridge where the first farm, Lluest, was situated about a mile from the village. Another footpath then took her across two or three fields to Cefnbangor farm, overlooking the Rheidol valley. She then turned eastwards and followed the old ridge-top road which once took the stage coaches to Rhayader before the A44 was constructed early in the nineteenth century. A series of farms followed with picturesque Welsh names like Llwyn-y-gog, Hafodau, Bwa-drain, Penrhiwlas and Penbrynmoelddu – eleven hilltop farms in all, each between half a mile and a mile apart – not an easy task for a fourteen-year-old girl in all weathers. To make matters worse, each dwelling had a daily newspaper which the post girl had to deliver. The round usually took her about four hours to complete, depending on the number of detours or the time taken to free herself from snowdrifts or other hazards.

Returning to the village often wet through, her next chore of the day was to 'do' for her grandmother Sarah Jane Hughes and crippled son John, in a small cottage. I knew that cottage well since I was born and spent my early days in it. With its uneven flagstone floor and nooks and crannies it was not an easy house to keep neat and tidy.

Early afternoon saw her home at the Royal Oak for another session of cleaning and washing more stone floors after the revels of drunken lead miners the previous evening. How she hated cleaning the black-leaded grates and steel fenders encrusted with spittle and worse. But she endured all in the knowledge that she would soon get a few minutes to practise on her beloved piano before the pub doors opened for the next night's revelry. Music was Olwen's saving grace. The whole family was musical. Her mother and older sister Sally had beautiful soprano voices; her eldest sister Lillian was quite a phenomenon with the loudest and strongest contralto I have ever heard. Her father William and her uncle William Henry had tremendous bass voices, especially William Henry. He served as a regimental sergeant-major during the First World War and in the post-war period became the anchor of the bass section in the village choir.

One time the choir was due to perform Handel's *Messiah*. However, on the night of the performance there was a terrible snowstorm and less than half of the choir, many of whom lived on outlying farms, managed to arrive at the venue. Those who made it were nearly all tenors or sopranos – the only alto was my aunt Lill and the only bass was my great uncle, William Henry.

The outcome was an excellent rendering of the *Messiah* with an almost perfect balance of voices!

One November morning in 1912, my grandmother became unwell – so sick that she found herself unable to fulfil the weekly 'do' for a wealthier neighbour, a Miss Saycell, who gave piano lessons. Olwen was called to deputise for her mother in the task. She timidly knocked on the back door and explained the reason for her visit, after which she was shown inside to what, in her mind, was a small palace. Having cleaned the bedrooms and kitchen she eventually opened the door to the 'holy of holies': the parlour. There in all its glory stood an upright piano complete with shiny brass candlesticks. Nervously, she polished the woodwork and then hesitantly lifted the lid to reveal the gleaming ivory keys. She hesitated again and looked around the room. Her finger gently touched one of the keys; she jumped at the sound and was hooked.

There followed months and months of cajoling from Olwen, who ran errands and did everything she possibly could for her parents. Then one day, a cheap upright piano complete with brass candlesticks arrived on the back of a local farmer's cart – the result of her parents' extra toil and hardship. That was not all: her mother's good work was appreciated by Miss Saycell, who promised Olwen six months' piano lessons, much to her delight. Life in 1912 was suddenly good for Olwen: she had her piano and her lessons showed that she was a very gifted young lady in the field of music.

In 1914, however, matters suddenly took a turn for the worse. Olwen's abrupt departure from school caused her endless dismay, especially since her best friend Lizzie Williams, the daughter of the village carpenter and coffin-maker, landed a place at the grammar school in Aberystwyth. Despite her private moments of utter despair, she continued to undertake her tasks as post girl and domestic with fortitude.

Olwen Evans at her organ

At the end of her six months' tuition, Olwen was deemed a competent pianist. Since Jezreel Baptist Chapel lacked an organist it was decided that she should fill the post, necessitating her attendance at three services every Sunday. To her proud parents it seemed like a reward for the sacrifices they had made to acquire the piano, so poor Olwen had no option but to do as she was told. How the butterflies in her stomach had a field day during those early services! It was a daunting task as the standard of choral singing at those services was very high and she felt that everyone in the congregation knew much more about music than she did. Every wrong note brought the dread sensation of her father's eagle eyes boring into her back.

Since 1897 it had been a Good Friday tradition for the chapel to hold an eisteddfod. I could never fathom the connection between events which had occurred nearly two thousand years before and the eisteddfod. But there it was, and it continued uninterrupted through two world wars until it finally ceased in 1964. I mention this because our family seemed to play a dominant part in its running. My great uncle John Hughes made a good job of being secretary for more years than I care to remember. He used to write to at least ninety good citizens each year in the hope that they would patronise the event with their donations. Then, at the end of the show, he would write to each individual in his laborious long hand, thanking them for their contribution and giving them a blow-by-blow account of what had occurred: who had won each competition, how many singers entered for the champion solos, how many choirs had entered and any other incident of interest. Now that's what I call devotion to duty.

My grandfather William always dressed up to the nines for the event, proudly displaying his official silk rosette which was usually a dusky pink. His white hair was always beautifully brushed and 'brillianteened' so that the front stuck up in a quiff. His job was to be a sort of master of ceremonies, summoning competitors to the stage in order. This duty would normally be performed by the secretary, but since my great uncle was crippled all his life and could only move with the aid of crutches, he could only watch with eagle eyes as my grandfather served as his deputy on stage.

My mother was horrified to learn that as the chapel organist her duties extended to being official accompanist for this event, even though she was barely 15. How she wept with trepidation at the prospect of having to accompany a variety of musical pieces, often at first sight. Singers came from far and wide since everybody in those days had Good Friday as a holiday. Many had wonderful voices and would present the poor girl with operatic arias. Some even had the temerity to ask her to transpose a piece a tone or semitone up or down, should they feel that their voices might struggle. One can only imagine what hell a teenager with only a few months' tuition would go through on being presented with such a situation. These events started at one o'clock in the afternoon and would often continue until two or three the following morning.

Rehearsals began weeks before the event. These occurred twice a week in the chapel vestry and all the village choirs would take turns. At four o'clock in the afternoon it would be the turn of the children's choirs. Then came the ladies' choir for a couple of hours. The ladies would then have to wait for the male contingent to arrive. This could take some time as their journey would take them via a pub to ensure that their vocal chords were suitably lubricated for the occasion. Thus my mother would be lucky to see home before about eleven at night. But then there would be a knock on the door. Standing there would usually be Margaret Ann Morgan the Bank, a large lady always dressed in black, wondering if Olwen could go through the contralto solo she was intending to enter. There was also the horde of men, women, boys and girls whom my mother had to put through their paces once or twice a week in their efforts to bring their vocal contributions up to scratch.

The great day finally dawned! Not to be left out, the remainder of the family would perform a variety of menial tasks. My aunt Sally and 'aunty' Maggie were in charge of refreshments. This meant a trawl of households for the loan of spoons and knives (cups, saucers and plates all suitably inscribed with the chapel logo in pale blue were already available at the vestry). Each piece of cutlery was identified with a piece of coloured thread or wool bound around the stem so that they could be returned to their rightful owners.

The ladies always dressed in white blouses, black skirts and the inevitable variety of hats. There would be the usual pre-festival gathering to make sandwiches, usually meat or fish paste or ham, and cakes and pastries had to be provided. This would produce the usual rivalry as to who presented the best quality fare. On the day, long trestle tables were erected and two large boilers placed on the fire, with one of the villagers making sure (for a small fee) that boiling water would always be at hand. Cups were filled and passed down the line while plates of goodies were placed at strategic positions on the tables.

I believe the first small efforts were held in the Baptist Chapel itself but as the event grew, a special building was erected in the field next to the chapel cemetery. This was a substantially-sized building called the pavilion which could hold up to six hundred people. The ground naturally sloped gently downwards so everyone had a good view of the stage. The problem was that the building was made of corrugated iron sheeting. There were two double doors as I remember: one at the back and one at the front by the stage, and about four smallish sash windows on both sides. The idea of cleaning these windows was often forgotten, and as this was the only annual event in the building they were covered by layers of cobwebs, thus minimising their effectiveness. To make matters worse, wartime saw the necessity to cover them with black cloth, making the interior very gloomy.

Funds would not allow expenditure on adequate seating, so the 'hoi polloi' had to sit on low planks set on stakes driven into the ground. For the more respectable members of the community, my grandfather (whose task as blacksmith and carpenter was to maintain the edifice) had cemented a series of shallow steps on one side of the central gangway on which were placed about six rows of long benches with the added luxury of being furnished with backs. Apart from the concrete steps, the remainder of the floor left much to be desired. To prevent erosion the mud floor was covered by a thick layer of pebbles and gravel, making any movement between items sound rather like a horde of holidaymakers tramping over a pebbly beach.

Another disadvantage of the building was its outer layer of

corrugated iron. Since the event was always held at Easter, April showers were always a risk. If such showers took the form of hail, the impact of the stones on the roof would drown out all proceedings within. During such occasions the audience would sing popular Welsh hymns until the tempest subsided. Sometimes the disruption would be man-made as the children, bored with certain items, would drag a stick along the length of the corrugated side of the building.

Before the evening session began, the twilight furnished by the windows was replaced by the illumination of about six small paraffin lamps which gave about as much light as there is in a cinema when the film is showing. This didn't help discipline as the evening wore on. It was holiday time and curious revellers from the local pubs would turn up and create quite a rumpus until PC Jones appeared, his silver buttons glinting in the twilight. This were the days when policemen commanded a bit of respect.

The stage was a substantial size, extending right across the lower end of the building, and was illuminated by better quality lamps. In later years I recall the introduction of several Tilley lamps which provided adequate lighting, but proceedings had to be halted occasionally in order to pump them up. The stage had a magnificent backdrop of a wonderful woodland scene painted in oils by Mr Baxter, a local artist, made all the more wonderful in that he suffered badly from the St Vitus' Dance syndrome.

Despite the obvious drawbacks of the venue some wonderful competitions in song, elocution, literature, poetry and crafts were enjoyed by the audiences. Choirs came from many of the local villages and from Aberystwyth. There was a great rivalry between the local choirs and the Aberystwyth choir, whose members regarded themselves as of superior quality as they came from town. Great would be the jubilation if a lowly village choir managed to topple the giants. The town choir's conductor, Richard Evans, was a colourful character who was very physical in his conducting. On more than one occasion the Tilley lamp hanging at the centre of the stage received a huge wallop from his flaying arms and swang precariously for the remainder of the choir's rendition.

Choirs were something special, as was being a member of one. Male voice choirs would arrive via the Druid Inn in fine voice (in their own eyes). To signify their membership, a copy of the music would be prominently displayed sticking out of the top pocket of their jackets so all would know that here was someone very important. Sometimes they sang as a group inspired; at others, standards left much to be desired, maybe due to the beer.

Once, the Goginan Male Voice Choir gave a rendering (or rending) of an old popular piece, 'Comrades in Arms'. The adjudicator complimented the choir on their fine singing, but my mother knew better. During the performance, the choir had twice dropped a semitone as they sang, but my mother, knowing that they were singing flat, had transposed the accompaniment twice so quickly that the adjudicator had not spotted the deception.

All in all these events were a great success, as the length of time they continued uninterrupted testifies. Once my great uncle, grandfather and mother grew too old to continue, proceedings very soon came to an end. But it was an event in the life of the village of which I was proud to be a part.

Music had been an integral part of village life for a very long time. When I was very young, I was fascinated by the array of musical instruments that were stashed away in what my grandmother called the 'lumber room' at the Royal Oak. There were two bass drums, a side drum and various brass instruments. I knew that the only person in the family who had any instrumental expertise was my mother, so it was obvious that this wonderful collection had no practical part in the family. Eventually I gleaned that they had been part of the equipment of the Goginan Brass Band which had been a *tour de force* in the lead-mining days. In the 1940s and early 1950s one of the big drums was used by the Aberystwyth branch of the Army Cadet Force.

My mother's skills as a pianist and accompanist were constantly in demand over the years. Weddings and funerals were regular engagements. I used to have a go at the little Mason and Gamlin American organ which the chapel had purchased, but my valiant efforts produced very irregular hooting noises which rather jarred even to my own ears. My mother on the other hand produced these beautiful mellow sounds and her feet hardly even seemed to move on the pedals. Her playing of the 'Dead March' from Handel's *Saul* during funerals was so poignant and soulful that I still recall the emotions which were roused among all who had the privilege of hearing it.

One of my mother's ongoing activities was accompanying the village choir. This choir, apparently the longest running group of its kind in the Aberystwyth district, was made up of all sorts of people of all ages, from about sixteen up to eighty and beyond. There was no audition to join; if anyone thought that he or she could sing they were in. Most of those who joined were very good and had a good grasp of the traditional way of reading music at the time: tonic solfa – doh, ray, me, fah, soh, and so on. They had all learned to read this form of notation either with Mr Herbert at school or under the auspices of the chapels when tonic solfa schools were held in the vestries on certain evenings. The sounds produced were rather varied; one or two had quite unique voices which could in no way blend in with the remainder. Their voices were usually quietened by placing a large person in front of them or else they were told to shut up and mouth the words. As a child, I had to be prepared for my mother's absence on one rehearsal evening a week if a competition was in the offing, though the regular rehearsal used to be held on Sundays after the evening services in the chapels.

Around 1930 the village choir decided on a new venture. A

Goginan's young people's choir in 1925, conducted by Hugh M Evans.

The cast of the 1930s production of 'Y Trwbadŵr'.

new Welsh operetta called *Y Trwbadŵr* (*The Troubadour*) had been composed by JT Rees, a well-respected local composer from Bow Street. The story was based on the amorous adventures of a fourteenth-century poet called Dafydd ap Gwilym (David son of William) who was born in a little cottage called Brogynin near Penrhyn-coch. He worshipped at Llanbadarn church where, according to legend, the priest saw more of the back of Dafydd's head than his face, as he preferred ogling girls in the congregation to concentrating on the sermon.

The opera was written especially for a school in Tregaron, but the choir in Goginan under their conductor of the time, Hugh M Evans, the local post master, decided to break the usual pattern of choral singing by tackling this new work. The first performance was given in the pavilion, where the beautiful woodland backdrop adorning the stage during the eisteddfod was painted for the operetta.

My mother provided the accompaniment, and also did so when it was resurrected after World War II. This time, I had the privilege of taking one of the minor principal roles. Many of the cast in the original performance were still young enough to take the same roles after the war, a gap of about eighteen years. Llywelyn Bebb, a farmer and leading light in the musical life of the village for years, took the leading role of Dafydd ap Gwilym as well as being in charge of the musical side of the production, while my aunt Betty Ashley-Jones took the leading soprano role of Morfudd on both occasions. She is now over a hundred years old but she still vividly remembers those wonderful performances.

In 1948 there was a shortage of materials for making costumes due to the war, so there was a lot of scraping together of old clothes which could, with hard work and a stretch of the imagination, be construed to represent fourteenth-century dress. Luckily the woodland backdrop had survived the damp conditions it had endured for eighteen years and was very adequate for the performances given in various village halls. But when the show was taken to the King's Hall in Aberystwyth there was no way that our usual scenery would be adequate for the large stage. So the show had to be put on using green drapes and one solitary coniferous tree, a vital part of the plot, which had to be propped up centre-stage by a step ladder. I remember that this post-war production was directed by the Welsh Baptist minister of the time, Joseph Morgan. He also took over direction of the Goginan Male Voice Choir for a time, though in this case his enthusiasm far exceeded his musical ability.

In August 1938, the Baptist Chapel elders decided in their wisdom that it was time to reward sister Olwen Evans for her years of devotion free of charge as church organist. After much deliberation, a clock was bought, suitably inscribed to honour the occasion.

Village life was largely dominated by the activities of the chapels. Denominational rivalry came to the fore on Sundays between the Methodist Chapel – with its superior numbers but slightly inferior musical prowess – and the smaller Baptist Chapel which had good singers who sang the hymns with gusto (much to the chagrin of the Methodists). This rivalry brings to mind a tale which a former Welsh comedian, Ryan Davies, told me. A Welsh sea captain was marooned on an island rather like Robinson Crusoe. His eventual rescuers were very impressed with his abilities in building a beautiful, fully-furnished log cabin on the island. Before leaving, he insisted that his rescuers should accompany him to the top of the hill dominating the island. On reaching the summit, they were surprised to see two buildings standing next to each other in the valley below.

"What are those buildings, Captain?" they inquired.

"Chapels, boys, chapels," the captain proudly replied.

"But why two chapels, Captain?"

"Well," he replied, "do you see that one over there? That's the one I don't go to."

Here is another example of 'churchianity' as a dear friend of mine, Evan Mason Davies, called it. My mother lived next door to her good friend Lizzie Williams who was organist at the Methodist Chapel. They had been brought up together and were very good friends until it came to Sundays, when Olwen became Mrs Evans and Lizzie became Miss Williams. It was also a tradition in the village that in good summer weather both congregations would go for a walk along the main road after the evening service, except that the Methodists would walk along one side of the road and the Baptists along the other, and never the twain would meet!

During World War II my mother was faced with additional obligations in the music world. It was the custom to greet servicemen and women coming home on their first leave with a 'welcome home' variety concert. Here they would be presented with the products of the village ladies' knitting group: scarves, socks, balaclavas and so on knitted in the various colours of the forces – khaki, air force blue and navy blue. In the early days of the war such events occurred weekly or fortnightly and it was my mother's task to provide an hour or so of entertainment. We lived in a very small house at the time – two up and two down – and on two or three occasions each week the front room would be crowded with up to fifteen children of all ages, including many of the evacuees. Each child was put through his or her paces. My mother would spend so much time, not just on producing a good sound from them but on the interpretation and meaning of words – a lesson which has stood me in good stead over the years when I have taught music in schools and directed operas.

Olwen provided her services for another twenty-six years, which brings me to the title of this chapter. In 1964, one of the more observant brethren in the chapel realised that their organist had held the position without payment since 1914, a period of fifty years. After the evening service one Sunday, a special meeting was convened so that the question of sister Mrs Evans' golden jubilee could be discussed. The general consensus was that something should be done, but what? Then came the memorable comment: "But she has already had a clock!" There seemed to be no answer to that. It was eventually decided that £50, one pound for each year of service, would be a fitting tribute. She continued as organist for another twenty years after that. The development of cataracts in both eyes impaired her vision so much that in the last four years of her service she played hymns from memory. Once the minister had read out the first verse of a hymn, as was the custom, she had recalled a tune of suitable metre for the accompaniment.

Olwen was a bit of a creaking door – she had lots of little ailments – but it would take something very drastic before she would deign to visit a doctor or even take an aspirin. Once, however, alarm bells were set ringing in my mind when she looked at me and said: "I wonder if you would drive me down to town to see Doctor Roberts?"

Fearing the worst, I immediately dropped what I was doing and rushed to find my car keys.

"What's the matter, Mam, are you ill?" I asked.

"Good Lord, no, I'm fine. It's just that I hear he has broken his leg and I wanted to go down to see how he was."

She suffered a stroke on Christmas Day 1984 and was committed to hospital for the last few weeks of her life having lost her speech and the use of her left hand. But her love of music prevailed. My profession meant that I had to be in London for the week but I would travel to Aberystwyth every weekend to be with her. Fortunately for me, a friend of many years, Menna Bassett, who lived near Aberystwyth, would visit her nearly every day. As they listened to Welsh music together on the radio, especially Welsh hymn singing, my mother would play the accompaniment with her right hand on Menna's forearm.

An unsung heroine? I like to think she was and that she fulfilled what I sense to be the true meaning of service to music. But then again, she was rewarded with £50... and a clock!

CHAPTER SEVEN

My Dad, Evan

THROUGH NO FAULT OF our own, my father Evan Richard Evans and I were comparative strangers throughout the formative years of my life. The depression of the late 1920s and early 1930s meant that regular local work was very scarce, so he had to travel to London to seek employment. We did not really get to know one another until 1942 when he returned home after thirteen years' absence; before that the only chance we had to get acquainted was during his annual fortnight's holiday.

My father was born in April 1900 at the Druid Inn to David

and Annie Evans, the fourth of their eight children. At school at the age of ten, he met the girl he would marry in 1929. On leaving school he worked locally until his early twenties when he sought work in South Wales like many of his contemporaries. I must confess

My father, Evan, making himself useful, painting the windows of Dei Williams' house, Bangor House, ably assisted by Lizzie Williams, the teacher, and under the watchful eye of the dog, Spot.

that I never bothered to enquire as to what he did during this time, but my uncle Dan told me that for a time he was a sparring partner for Jimmy Wilde, the 'Tylerstown Terror', once the world lightweight boxing champion. I never even knew that my father could box; he always seemed such a gentle man.

He returned to Goginan in the late 1920s and formed a romantic attachment to my mother. However, the economy was still weak and regular work was extremely hard to come by. He therefore had to seek temporary work where he could find it. For a time he worked on building roads in Lovesgrove, about three miles west of Goginan, for which he received a weekly wage of £1. 16s. 8d. When that work ceased, he had to seek odd jobs such as grave-digging at a rate of eight shillings a grave.

Unemployment must have been a humiliation for him and my mother, made worse by having to seek two signatures certifying that he was out of work for the allowance of ten shillings a week dole money. It was therefore understandable that the promise of work in the furniture department of Bon Marche in Brixton should cause him to leave home. His weekly wage was £3, from which he had to pay for his lodgings with a dear old lady, Miss Lumsden, and send money home to sustain my mother and myself. The other regular communication was the weekly brown paper parcel containing dirty washing!

I found some of my epistles to my father among my mother's memorabilia a few years ago and was quite taken aback as to how forward and greedy I was when about six years old. I wasn't demanding small things either. My list included bicycles, chemistry sets (at six!) and aeroplanes, but no books; reading was not my favourite hobby.

Very rarely, my father and I had a short telephone conversation. However, matters had to be pretty important to warrant the palaver of preparing for such an event. First, one had to give notice to the local village post office so that a call could be booked. Then, I think my father had to be notified so that he in turn could book a time to receive the call in a London post office. When the flustered conversation eventually took place, all the crackling and changes of volume made it seem like talking to someone in space.

My father was not exceptionally tall but he was well-built and obviously very strong, for his work in the furniture department of the store demanded moving some very heavy items. He always used to relate the time when he had to deliver a piano to a house in Chesham Bois where Monty Banks, husband of the famous singer Gracie Fields lived. When the lorry arrived at the house, the three crew members were instructed by Monty to take the piano up to the second floor. Unfortunately, the stairs curved and were too narrow. So it was decided that my father, being the strongest, would carry the piano on his back while the other two would try to keep it steady. Eventually, after much huffing and puffing the task was completed without mishap, for which my father received the princely sum of sixpence as a gratuity. I think this insult bothered my father much more than the effort he expended.

He remained working in London throughout the early years of the war despite the almost daily interruptions of bombing during the Blitz. He recalled coming home early to his lodgings one day to notice a hole in the roof of the house. Inside, he found Miss Lumsden sitting in her chair in the lounge, calmly knitting. He looked around the room and discovered another hole in the corner of the ceiling. On enquiring as to what had happened, Miss Lumsden calmly replied, "Oh, that thing came through the ceiling." She pointed to the fireplace and there, to his horror, he saw an unexploded bomb. Apparently, she had picked the bomb up and put it there.

My father returned home in 1942 and was almost immediately appointed foreman of a group of workers that was laying telephone cables between Aberystwyth and Llanon, about twelve miles to the south. This entailed his staying in lodgings during the week, but at least we could be together as a family at weekends.

When this project came to an end, my father decided to try a career as an insurance salesman with the Pearl Assurance Company. He was given a rural area with a wide radius of about fifteen miles from Goginan. In the early days he borrowed my bicycle to cover the considerable distances to isolated farms. At that time there was quite a lot of poverty and many of the contributions amounted to about one penny a week. It must have been laborious and frustrating work for him, as very often he would arrive at an isolated farm or cottage in the hills only to be told that the occupiers could not afford the premium that week but would pay double (usually two pence) the next week. His days were very long: he would leave home at about eight o'clock in the morning and not return until about seven or eight in the evening, so that my mother and I would get rather anxious as the hours passed, especially on winter evenings. Then came the considerable time needed to transfer data from his notebook to the ledgers each evening.

Eventually, he moved up in the world and purchased a 1926 Sunbeam motorcycle with square tank, carbide lamps and solid tyres. It was wartime and petrol was scarce, but the bike worked very well on a mixture of petrol and paraffin. How it functioned I don't know, but I never remember an instance when the machine failed him. I do know that it had not been taxed since 1938! People, including the village bobbies, were so fascinated by this ancient machine that trivia like missing licences and tax plates went unnoticed. The only unreliable features were the lamps. To obtain light, water had to be poured onto the carbide, but no warning was given when they were about to give out. Luckily the bike was not capable of great speeds, otherwise there could have been a disaster on the country lanes.

My father on his rounds in his work as an insurance agent. The newer motor cycle replaced the historic 1926 Sunbeam which he used for several years without mishap.

I only remember the lights giving out on two occasions when I was riding pillion. One was when we were riding along what we called 'the flats', where the road to Aberystwyth follows the flood plain of the River Rheidol. We had no water so we improvised. I had to answer the call of nature, so what better place to deposit it than in the carbide lamp? It worked wonderfully! The same thing happened another time as we were approaching Llanbadarn Fawr, a mile or so from Aberystwyth. We were climbing the little hill towards the village square when we were left in darkness. Who should be standing on the square but the village policeman. Immediately, out came the notebook and my father was charged with riding a motorcycle *sans* lights.

"But, Constable Jones," protested my father, "the light just went out as we were coming up the hill."

"A likely story," replied the officer, "what I see is that you have no lights, and that is good enough for me."

"I'm telling you the truth. If you don't believe me, give me your hand." Before the policemen knew what was happening, my father grabbed his hand and placed it flat on the red-hot surface of the carbide lamp. I'm sure the whole village heard the policeman's howl. The outcome was that my father was let off with a warning.

Eventually, the toll of the long hours out in all weathers and the stress of keeping financial accounts accurately after the day's work led to my father suffering a severe heart attack which left him partially disabled at the age of fifty-six. However, being idle did not suit him and he managed to get some part-time employment which kept him occupied but still gave him time to pursue his varied interests.

There was a big project going on in the 1950s and early 1960s to construct hydro-electric dams at various points on the River Rheidol. My father was employed as night security officer at the administrative complex, initially five miles to the east of Goginan at Ponterwyd, and subsequently in Cwm Rheidol (Rheidol Valley). The work was not at all onerous and it gave him a chance to indulge in one of his hobbies: fishing. He used to lay lines in the river during the night and collect the spoils before he returned home in the morning.

Most of the labour involved in the construction of these dams was undertaken by Irish workers whose social activities certainly added interest to local life. Many of these Irishmen would move into a camp in the foothills of Pumlumon in the late summer or early September and not be seen again until Christmas Eve. Then they would appear at the door of the George Borrow Hotel in Ponterwyd before opening time, standing quietly in a row not speaking to anyone. The doors would open and they would troop in and stand by the bar quietly drinking Guinness after Guinness, until one by one they would slide down the side of the counter to the floor in a drunken stupor. One of their mates would then drag them out into the cold night air where they would slowly become sober enough to move back in for another session.

The workers who lived in the lower camp in the village would spend Saturday night revelling in Aberystwyth, and many were the bottle fights before the night was out. The last bus from Aberystwyth to Ponterwyd left at half past ten and most would endeavour to catch it rather than face the twelve-mile walk home. PC Pugh would invariably receive a phone call warning him of the rowdy conditions on the bus. When it arrived in Goginan, he would be ready on the village square to oust all the drunken 'Paddies' out of the bus. Then he would get on his motorcycle and herd them like sheep along the road for the last five miles to Ponterwyd. Some of those who had imbibed too much during the night would fall by the wayside, but invariably one of their pals would lie down with them at the side of the road to ensure that he would wake up in time for the bus that would take them all back to Aberystwyth for early morning Mass.

I remember taking my father to Cwm Rheidol one Christmas Eve to start his evening shift. I had chosen a very inauspicious time as on the way back I found myself travelling behind one of the jeeps conveying workers to Aberystwyth for a night out. The festivities had obviously started earlier in the afternoon and were continuing in the back of the jeep. It was all I could do to avoid the hail of beer bottles and cans that came hurtling from the open back of the vehicle. How my windscreen was not smashed, I'll never know.

My father was an excellent fisherman in the Welsh tradition of going after the fish rather than sitting on the river bank. Nearly every week during the fishing season, he would spend some of his free time on the banks of the Melindŵr stream and bring home up to twenty small trout, all around seven to eight inches in length. These would be gutted and fried to give a supper of delightful taste. On his days off he liked me to take him by car well up into the Pumlumon foothills and drop him off about four miles from civilisation. He would charge me to pick him up at the same spot no sooner than eight o'clock in the evening, then walk another six or seven miles further up into the hills along the river banks.

His other great interest was cooking, a blessing for my mother whose culinary talents were more basic. The kitchen was too small to prepare any lavish meals, so he hit on the idea of buying a good-sized shed where he installed a Calor gas oven, a table, a cupboard and an easy chair so that he could indulge in his culinary pleasures. The variety of dishes that he produced was amazing, even in the stringent times of war. His double-barrelled shotgun also came in handy; the occasional rabbit pie would adorn our table.

Once, when I came home from London for a holiday, an incident occurred which puzzled me and continues to intrigue me even now. I had the notion of cleaning my car before returning to my lecturing post. The vacuum cleaner, one of those cylindrical models, was kept in the corner of the shed where my father spent much of his time along with our dog. I retrieved the machine and noted that there were one or two potatoes deposited at the entrance of the cylinder. I removed them and carried the cleaner to the back door of the house so that I could connect the plug to the power source. Suddenly, even before I had switched it on, the machine started to judder violently in my hand. I was about to look inside the cylinder when the largest rat I had ever seen came out and ran away across the road. It had evidently made a nest inside and judging from its size was about to produce its offspring. I hated rats before, but ever since that incident I have had a real fear of them. This rat was either very brave or very foolish to cohabit with a human being and a dog!

My father was a very mild-mannered, gentle man brought up in the traditions of the Church in Wales. He attended St Matthew's Church in Goginan regularly during his childhood, along with his family. In later years, he joined my mother at Jezreel Baptist.

He was a great story teller. I vividly remember those he used to tell me during his two weeks' annual holidays from London when I was a toddler. One was about an old sailor and his parrot, who lived in a log cabin by a lake. Their adventures were very exciting. Each Christmas when he came home, I would ask for the adventures of the sailor and his parrot, and woe betide if the story varied one iota from that of the previous year. Very often one would see a gang of village youths standing in a huddle, only to find my father in the middle telling them some story or other. Indeed, he told me many of the anecdotes which I relate here about some of the old characters, so I am thankful for his contribution in perpetuating the memories.

My father suffered a second heart attack when he was seventy-two and died in 1972. Though we did not see a lot of each other in my early years, I think our later acquaintance more than made up for it. I am thankful that he was there for me for many years and that I had him as my father.

CHAPTER EIGHT

Uncle John

M ANY OF GOGINAN'S INHABITANTS during my childhood had a marked effect on my life. One was my uncle John Morgan Hughes. In fact he was my great uncle, and I just called him John. He was born in 1883, the youngest of five children born to John and Sarah Jane Hughes. On leaving school at the age of fourteen, he went to London to work in the dairy trade, which seemed to be a long-standing tradition for young Welsh people from the local area. Unfortunately, he was given a damp bed which resulted in him contracting hip disease. There was little that could be done at the time to counteract it except to lock the hips. He was therefore severely handicapped and could only move with the aid of crutches for the rest of his life. But did that stop him carrying on with his life? Indeed not; even if his body was handicapped, his mind was alert and capable. His intellectual powers were great and he used them to the full.

His father John Hughes was born in 1843 and was a mining engineer at the local silver-lead mines. However, when the mines in the locality closed he decided to emigrate in search of fame and fortune in the gold mines of Colorado along with a good friend of his, William Garland. His wife Sarah Jane (1851-1929) stayed at home in Irfon House in Goginan where she looked after her handicapped son.

John Hughes' influence on his son was significant in many ways – none more so than in his almost fanatical allegiance to the Odd Fellows Friendly Society of which he was a devoted

Four generations. My great grandmother, Sarah Jane Hughes, John Hughes' mother (left) with one of her daughters, Margaret Jane Evans, my grandmother, of the Royal Oak (right). Standing is my mother's sister, Sally Davies with her daughter, Megan, as a child.

member for most of his life. The full name of this society is the Independence Order of Odd Fellows Manchester Unity Friendly Society – quite a mouthful. It was once quite a significant part of Goginan, especially when the lead mines were in full swing. I therefore make no apology for including a history of this society which helped ordinary working men and women of the village in many ways before trade unions and welfare services came into being. I found it very interesting!

The society's roots can be traced back to 587 BC during the Israelites' exile in Babylon. Many of the exiles banded together into a brotherhood for mutual support. This was maintained by the many who were later taken to Rome by Nero and served in the Roman Army under Titus Caesar. The idea spread rapidly through the Roman Army and was taken by them to Spain, Portugal and France. The brotherhood reached Britain in the twelfth century and became the basis of the guilds which regulated markets and trade. Its earliest name was the Merchant's Guild; this represented all members of a particular trade in a town.

With the expansion of trade, individual trade guilds sprang up, responsible for the training of craftsmen. Three separate degrees of membership were introduced: the Apprentices (trainees), the Fellows (wage earners) and the Masters (trained business owners), all controlled by a Grand Master, one of whose functions was to examine the work (masterpiece) apprentices submitted to prove their skill. By the thirteenth century there were guilds in all cities and towns, and in many villages. They usually met in churches – the only buildings large enough to accommodate them – until some of the more prosperous guilds erected their own building, the Guildhall.

By the fourteenth century, splits were occurring in the welfare of the guilds. On completion of their courses, Fellows normally progressed to the rank of Masters but numbers had increased to such an extent that the existing Masters were afraid that their position and the welfare of their businesses would be threatened. They therefore tried to exclude the lower circles by making deliberateley expensive uniforms and livery or regalia a pre-requisite of entering the guild. The Fellows then set up the Yeomen Guilds in opposition to the Livery Guilds. The Yeoman Guilds eventually became respectable but as there were usually insufficient numbers of a particular trade in a village or small town to form a single trade guild, the Fellows of several different trades would combine to form a guild known as Odd Fellows. Landowners and bosses often saw these guilds as a threat as they could rise up against injustices and oppression. On the other hand, clubs for mutual help could reduce the demands of the Poor Rate, a tax which landowners were obliged to pay to help local paupers.

John Hughes, with my father to his immediate left and another well-known inhabitant of the village, Henry Morris. I don't know who the young man with the cat is!

The Tudor period was one of mixed fortunes for the guilds. Henry VIII took the opportunity to reduce their power when he broke away from Rome. He confiscated all the assets of the guilds because they were in close affiliation with the Roman Catholic Church. Also, the Statute of Apprentices passed in Elizabeth I's reign took the responsibility of training apprentices away from the guilds, leading to further suppression. This in turn resulted in the loss of financial and social support for ordinary people.

This fear of the guilds continued into the eighteenth century when membership of a society became a criminal offence. The events of the French Revolution at the end of that century put fear into the upper classes, leading to further suppression of the guilds in case they should instigate a similar event in Britain. Guilds were forced to become secretive: passwords were required for entry to clandestine meetings and prospective members (usually confined to immediate family or close friends) were closely vetted.

In 1810 the Odd Fellows in Manchester became dissatisfied with the general conduct of the original order and broke away to form the Manchester Unity with better organisation and new rules. This became the Odd Fellows of today with benefits such as travel warrants and free lodging for any member who had to travel to find employment. The order also introduced standard protection policies to help members with the financial burden of visits to doctors or hospital treatment.

In the early nineteenth century, persecution of the Odd Fellows tailed off and numbers grew as the order became more prosperous. However, the deportation of the Tolpuddle Martyrs in 1834 for being members of an illegal friendly society brought a new panic. The Odd Fellows' Annual General Meeting of that year abolished the ancient tradition of the oath, replacing it with an 'obligation' in order to evade the penalty of the law. This change without consultation caused the American order to split from its British counterpart at what was already a delicate period in relations between the two countries after the American War of Independence.

The Industrial Revolution saw a great migration of workers into the factories of the towns and cities. In the days before the advent of trade unions and the National Health Service, the Manchester Unity Order became the largest and richest friendly society in Britain and still offers social involvement, care and support as well as financial benefits.

My uncle never ceased to amaze me with his meticulousness as secretary of the local branch and in observing all the ceremony attached to the fortnightly meetings in his house. He used to stand at his desk for hours, carefully entering all the financial inputs in about seven or eight enormous ledgers. How these meetings – with an attendance of about eight members – demanded such a plethora of statistics, I never could understand; in any case he would never divulge any information. What amazed me even more was the way he packed these ledgers into two big brown paper parcels once a month and carried them by fastening them somehow to the hand grip of his crutches. He would climb a steep quarter of a mile with them up to the main road to meet the Aberystwyth bus. Then came another half-mile walk from the bus stop to the Grand Master's house. He was such a small, frail man but he had great strength in his shoulders and hands.

My father was also a member of the order. Once he fell sick and my uncle watched him like a hawk. He saw my father taking a bucket out to the garden shed at quarter past eight in the evening. The next morning he gave my mother a stern warning that if he ever again caught my father out of doors after eight (especially if carrying a bucket), his sickness allowance of ten shillings a week which he received from the Odd Fellows would be stopped forthwith and my father would be summoned before the committee for censure.

What really reminded me of the Odd Fellows and my uncle's devotion to the society was a little pocket knife which he gave me a few years before he died. One blade was broken but it had never been out of his possession since the time it had been given to him by his father. What I fancied about it was the handle: it was a lustrous brown and yellow with three joined links, the symbol of the Odd Fellows, and the names 'John Hughes. Rico. Colo.' on the hilt. What these last two names meant I had no idea, but they led my wife and me on an unexpected adventure.

We had decided to go for a multi-centre holiday to the United States which would set us back to the tune of £4,000. Luckily, Thomas Cook was running a raffle and, wonder of wonders, I won – so the holiday became a freebie. We commenced our trip by visiting Cecele's parents in Houston, Texas. Her father, a retired commercial airline pilot, decided to give me a taste of the West by taking us to a rodeo. The lights dimmed on the vast arena and a spotlight picked up a beautiful young blonde lady in white cowboy 'duds' riding a magnificent white horse and carrying the American flag. She was greeted with thunderous applause as she rode around the arena. She eventually came to a halt in the centre. The crowd was hushed as the lights dimmed in the arena and all rose to their feet, hand on heart as the strains of the American national anthem 'The Star-Spangled Banner' filled the air. It was very moving – until the spotlight which illuminated the flag in all its glory began to move sideways and downward... and stopped on a steaming pile of horse shit! I glanced sideways at my father-in-law who was shaking with suppressed laughter. Nearly everybody else kept their eyes staring at the flag, now in twilight. It seems most Americans, lovely people though they are, do take themselves very seriously, so it was nice to see that at least my father-in-law and the spotlight operator could look on the lighter side of life.

We continued on our trip and eventually landed in the town of Durango, Colorado – once a cattle town but now catering for skiers in winter and tourists in summer. I was looking at some road signs and lo, there it was: Rico, one of the names on my great-grandfather's pocket knife. We visited the local university and looked up the name in microfiches of newspapers from the turn of the nineteenth and twentieth centuries. We found references to my great-grandfather and his friend William Garland. It seems that John Hughes had purchased part of a gold mine in the Colorado hills and had named it 'Goginan'! His name was missing for the next four years, but in the papers of 1903 he appeared again as the conductor of the local choral society, along with the titles of some of the choral pieces they sang, which the Goginan choir also used to sing. I wish I had taken more notes on this nostalgic encounter, but to me it was a very moving moment.

We hired a car and drove to the little town of Rico. It was uncanny how similar the valley was – with steep wooded slopes and the small river – to parts of Cwmystwyth around Pwll Peirian where my great-grandfather had apparently spent considerable time before emigrating. Rico is now a ghost town largely run by Mexican immigrants or Indians. It must have been huge once; I found out that there were four or five different Odd Fellows' lodges when my great-grandfather was there.

We managed to locate the chapel where he used to worship and have choir practices. By coincidence we had arrived in the town during the very week that the chapel was celebrating its centenary. Unfortunately, because of the celebrations, the register for the cemetery plots had been taken away for inspection, so we decided to look for any signs of his grave. The cemetery was overgrown and we had to fight our way through the tall grass in heat over 100 degrees Fahrenheit. We were both dressed in trainers and shorts despite Cecele being taught by the Girl Guides in New Orleans to avoid places where scorpions and rattlesnakes might be located. We survived, but the search was to no avail. Then, as we sat exhausted outside the local hotel, we realised that since my great-grandfather had been alone in the town, there would be no one to place a memorial stone on his grave. However, I felt comforted that at least I had trodden the same paths as he did over a hundred years ago. John Hughes died in 1911 in Cortez, Colorado without ever returning to his native Goginan as far as I know.

My uncle John's fastidiousness in his work with the Odd Fellows was mirrored by his devotion to other causes. I have already mentioned his long-standing work as secretary of the local eisteddfod, a task which he undertook very efficiently for well over forty years. It was due to his energy that it continued uninterrupted through two world wars. After World War II, social activities received an impetus with the return of the younger members of the community who had been on active service. My uncle served as secretary in the formative days of the local soccer team and the annual sports day.

On the death of my great-grandmother in 1929, my mother had moved in to look after John. My father had left to find work in London, so John helped my mother in the task of making me a reasonably decent human being. Being an only child, the odds were that I would be spoiled rotten, but this was not to be. I remember John telling my mother when I was getting on for five years old and at the demanding stage: "Olwen, if you say 'no' to the boy, it means no." I think that lesson has stayed with me all my life.

Being disabled meant that John would conduct the business of the house in meticulous fashion. Each morning, once my mother had assisted him in dressing (the top he could manage, but the trousers, boots and socks presented a problem), he would hobble his way down the narrow stairs and, with the aid of the table and chairs, make his way to the fireplace which she had cleared of ashes the night before. The old cast iron grate would always be gleaming with black lead polish and one could see one's face in the brass handles of the oven doors. Being a proud man and the man of the house, John insisted that it was his job to light the fire every morning. He very neatly scrunched up the newspaper into almost perfect spherical balls and placed them with precision at the base of the grate so that the ventilation from below would be perfect. Then came twigs and small blocks of wood (which once a week he would manage to cut into equal lengths with his billhook) and the small coal. Usually, depending on the direction of the wind, the fire would light immediately – this was vital to the beginning of the day as the kettle would have to be boiled for breakfast. Then came the performance of making the tea. Boiling water was poured into the empty pot and left for precisely three minutes for the pot to warm up, then the tea was placed in the pot which was then taken to the kettle (never the other way around). The tea was left to stew for exactly five minutes. So the day went on in an orderly fashion according to his own mental time-table.

Once breakfast was over, his next duty was to go down to the garden which he shared with the landlord next door. Located just inside the gate, which he would unlock every morning, was the village pump. In return for this daily duty he was given a concession on the peppercorn rent which he paid for the little four-roomed house where we lived – I think the annual rent amounted to about half a crown. It was also his responsibility to see that this gate remained padlocked every New Year's Day to retain the legality of ownership. Then he would proceed for his daily visit to the *ty bach* (the little house) – also called the 'House of Commons' since everybody sat there! This was a particularly good toilet as it was built by the landlord, David Williams the carpenter. Every Tuesday morning my uncle cut the previous week's *News Chronicle* into rectangles of exactly the same size to be used as toilet paper. These would then be hung on a nail in the toilet and I spent hours reading snippets and sometimes articles about world affairs and sport (no wonder I became a teacher!).

John devoted one morning a week to cleaning the brasses. There were ornamental brass and copper kettles which had served the gentry in Hafod mansion in the nineteenth century, and several brass candlesticks of various sizes and shapes. This task would take upwards of three hours but they would be glistening when he was done with them.

One of his great feats was to organise the garden which extended down the side of the valley. To reach it, one had to negotiate a very steep and uneven path. How he managed to get down, I don't know, but once there he would get rid of his crutches and use the long-handled spade instead. With this he would shuffle along and create perfectly straight troughs. My mother or I would then plant the seed potatoes under his eagle eye. God help us if a potato strayed from the straight and narrow, was not an equal length apart or was placed upside down according to his judgement. He would then cover the potatoes and prepare perfect beds for the sowing of the various seeds. We were sure of a good crop of vegetables every season.

Another autumnal task which he performed to perfection was to wash and dry all the apples from the garden. Each one would be inspected for any blemishes and carefully wrapped in newspaper for storage in a dry compartment in the shed.

Much of his day would be spent in reading the paper, doing any chores within his capability and entering data into his Odd Fellows ledgers. I seldom saw him reading a book except expositions on Scripture which he faithfully read on days approaching Sunday, so that he could argue from a base of knowledge in Sunday School.

Sunday was devoted entirely to Jezreel Baptist Chapel. There were three services each Sunday: at ten o'clock there was the morning service with a sermon; at two in the afternoon was Sunday School for three Sundays, while the fourth was devoted to a communion service; then at six o'clock there was the evening service with another sermon. Every Sunday my uncle, with me in his trail, would trek down the steep hill three times to the chapel in the valley. If ever there was a devoted Christian, my uncle fitted the bill admirably. How he managed to negotiate that steep hill, sometimes as steep as one in five, I don't know. Coming up the hill at the end of the service, he would often have to reverse on the steepest parts. But he did it in rain or shine. I don't know how he endured the hard wooden seats of the pew either; due to his disability he had to half lie with his head resting on the vertical back of the pew and the top of his legs against the edge of the seat.

Jezreel was one of the prettiest chapels I have ever seen. There were two doors, one on each side of the pulpit and the big seat where the deacons or elders sat, so that if anyone came in late they would be exposed to the stares of the congregation. The pews, which were beautifully painted in lightly grained varnish by my grandfather William Evans, radiated up the steps in all directions from the centre where the organ was situated. Thus

The minister's view of his congregation at Jezreel chapel, Goginan.

the pews were all of different lengths to cater for the various sizes of families.

My uncle and I had a small pew in the front to accommodate two people and there he would lift me on to the wooden seat during the hymn-singing where I would conduct the singing at the mature age of five (I cringe at the audacity of it now). I must say, though, there was some very good four-part singing of those wonderful old Welsh hymns. My uncle, who had a good baritone voice, would very often get the *hwyl*. I used to watch him as the end of the last chorus of a hymn was approaching. If the hymnbook started to move up and down to the beat, it was a sure sign that he was going to repeat the last chorus. Then my little arms would move more expansively and energetically to indicate to the congregation that the repeat was imminent! My grandfather across the way, however, would close his eyes if he got the *hwyl*. These antics used to annoy me intensely as I grew older as I was in a hurry to get out of the place. The morning services were

John Hughes with his dog, Spot.

tolerable since I knew they would be fairly short as the resident minister in my early childhood, the Reverend David ap Morgan, had to walk about three or four miles over the hill to the next valley to conduct a service at two o'clock at Cwmsymlog Baptist Chapel.

Afternoon Sunday School was a bit of a cattle market. After a sedate little hymn, a reading and a prayer, the superintendent would give the signal for everyone to move to classes according to age groups. There were quite a few children attending, so we were given the largest triangular pew which was located in the far corner of the chapel up the steps. There we could observe and pass comment on people's hats or demeanour as well as creating our own mischief. I am sure God gave those meetings a miss. I used to watch John pontificating very warmly in his class which contained most of the elders of the chapel including Richard Mason the butcher and John Davies the village shopkeeper, among other notables.

Jim Jones from Capel Bangor – a rather grey man with rather a grey voice – was one of the deacons at the chapel. He was also a *codwr canu* (precentor), whose role was to lead the singing in the days before places of worship had organs. Now that the chapel had had an organ for at least forty years, I thought his role was a bit superfluous. However, I soon found out he had other duties to perform.

I was baptised at Bethel Baptist Chapel in Aberystwyth where the floor of the pulpit could be removed to expose a huge bath in which I was completely immersed in water. (In my mother's time, baptisms used to be conducted in the Melindŵr river. The river would be temporarily dammed to form a pool of decent depth for the purpose; in my time we had the added comfort of warmed water.) It came to my turn and the minister, clad in huge fishing waders, got me by the scruff of the neck and dunked me backwards into the water. When I arose dripping wet, there was no great white light and no sign of a white dove but just the grey voice of Jim Jones singing a hymn unaccompanied in a minor key. I felt that there couldn't have been much rejoicing in Heaven at the saving of a sinner on this occasion.

Teatime at Irfon House was quite special because my uncle would invite Jim along. We always had red jelly, pink blancmange and custard which Jim, for some reason, insisted on eating with a fork so that the operation took rather a long time. This was done under the watchful eye of my uncle's dog Spot, a wild black and white mongrel full of energy who took my mother at a pell-mell rate down to the bottom of the garden every evening. He had a very funny habit which Jim learned to his cost on his first visit to tea. Spot, who was quite a size, would sit next to any stranger invited to a meal at our house. If the stranger reached over for a utensil or a jug, Spot would reach up and very gently grab the person's wrist in his jaws, then glance at my mother and not let go until she gave the go ahead.

Six o'clock would see us all back in chapel. I did not relish those evening services as they went on a bit. Also, the light from the paraffin lamps in winter did nothing to raise the spirits. These lamps were very pretty; there was a chandelier of sorts containing four globed lamps in the centre, with several similar lamps scattered

The Reverend Dafydd ap Morgan, minister of the chapel for over thirty years.

on carved poles around the room. The light they gave was warm and glowing but dim, which possibly explains my aversion to low-level lighting in later life.

The usual schedule for the evening service was an opening hymn followed by a reading, then another hymn followed by a prayer which could go on for up to fifteen minutes (I always felt these were more of a performance than a genuine prayer). Then came another hymn followed by a sermon which could be up to forty minutes or even an hour if the minister lost control of things. They always followed the same pattern: a quiet steady start, then a turn of the knob for louder volume and a little bit of Bible thumping and shouting (we really were sinners). Then came the *hwyl* intoned in a minor key, prompted by occasional 'Amens' or 'Halleluiahs' from the deacons, before the storm subsided towards the end. Then came the notices, followed by (horror of horrors) all the kids filing out to sit on the long bench behind the organ to recite the verse which had been painfully drummed into our heads at Sunday School. The creeps would recite a long verse which drew beaming smiles from the august gentlemen in the big seat; others would give a short, sharp, two or three-worder such as 'Jesus wept', drawing black looks and frowns from the big seat. Then a last hymn and out.

After supper round the paraffin oil lamp on the table, the wireless would usually be switched on for such weekly serials as the old variety show *The Hippodrome* (or was it 'Happidrome'?) with Mr Lovejoy, Ramsbottom and Enoch as the regulars. I remember the highlight being Enoch doing a tap dance! Still, if Archie Andrews the ventriloquist's dummy could have a show on the wireless, why shouldn't Enoch have a go? These shows were most enjoyable, as was the series on the lives of Gilbert and Sullivan. No wonder that I have always sung, produced and directed their operas.

John had his regular visitors. Many of the old ladies who brought their water pots to fill at the village pump would pop in to have a chat with him. My favourite was Marged Ann Llywelyn with her deep violet-tinted glasses, as she always bought me sweets. Then there was William Defi Bradshaw who was a deaf-mute. I was fascinated with the animated silent conversations he had with John, which went on for hours until the fingers and hands got a bit weary and it was time for the pipes and the Ringer's Shag to come out and pollute the room.

So John lived out his useful life. He died in 1968 at the age of eighty-six and was buried next to his mother in Jezreel cemetery. The village was poorer for his passing. He was a great influence on me, especially in that he gave me a firm grounding in the 'do's and don'ts' of life.

CHAPTER NINE

Dan Jones

O NE OF THE MOST remarkable and memorable personalities to have lived in Goginan was Dan Jones, a quietly spoken, mild-mannered man with a ready smile. I am very grateful to his nephew, Mr Tegwyn Jones of Bow Street, for allowing me to include some of his reminiscences of Dan, and also to Mrs Tegwen Jones of Talybont, next to whose family home in Goginan Dan lived for many years.

Dan was born in Goginan in 1888 in a small terraced house called Y Guallt (which could be translated as 'the pleasant hillside'). According to Dan this was a poor lead miner's cottage, typical of the time, consisting of three small rooms, two downstairs and one upstairs which was reached by means of a removable ladder. Such houses would often accommodate five or six children.

By the time Dan was a lad, most of the local mines had closed because they became uneconomic to run. Goginan mine had closed by 1886, two years before Dan was born. However, mines were still working in the next valley to the south. And at the age of fourteen, Dan started work at Lefel Fawr (the big level) in Cwm Rheidol. Every Monday morning before four o'clock, Dan would begin the five-mile journey over the hill to work, carrying a loaf of bread. His wage amounted to six shillings a week (one shilling a day), of which one shilling and three pence would go on board and lodging with potatoes and soap thrown in, according to the custom of the time. Landladies certainly did not make a fortune from this arrangement, as butter and ham cost one shilling a pound and bacon ten pence.

Dan described the miner's life, along with that of his family, as being a continuous struggle to survive from day to day. The average wage of a lead miner at that time was around fourteen shillings a week. Conditions in the mines were atrocious and unhealthy with a lack of fresh air, smoke, the constant drip of water from the roof of the adits and of course the long trek to and from work, often over mountains in wet and windy conditions. In winter especially, miners' wives were faced with the daily task of providing dry clothing for their husbands. This entailed drying work clothes in front of the fire each evening so that the atmosphere became damp and permeated with the unhealthy smells of the lead mine. In many cases, miners had to leave home well before dawn for the walk to work. Their wives would make them a packed lunch, possibly a small pie prepared the day before, then they would ready their five or six children for school. The miner would drag himself home as late as eight o'clock in the evening. The unsavoury conditions at work would inevitably create bronchial problems resulting in loss of breath, which in turn often led to a relatively short period of ill-health followed by an early death.

The social and working conditions which Dan experienced made him very conscious of the exploitation of the working classes which

Dan Jones as a young man.

had been prevalent for many centuries in local agriculture and industry. His feelings of injustice were further strengthened when he saw conditions in Canada and the United States. where a miner's wage before the First World War was sixteen shillings and eight pence a day, compared with the three shillings and four pence the Welsh miner received. His discontent was further inflamed when he visited Russia to survey working conditions with his close friend TE Nicholas, a dentist in Aberystwyth. (I remember visiting Mr Nicholas with my father when I was very young and being told to sit quietly in the back garden by the bird bath, and to shout when the fishes appeared! At the same time Nicholas struggled to extract a tooth from my father's mouth in the little garden shed where he conducted his business). During their visit to Russia they found that profits were largely shared amongst the workers in various ways, such as full pay during sickness and a pension amounting to half of one's income. He saw some of the profits being used to modernise, expand and ventilate the factories, to provide creches for children and a holiday home on the Black Sea coast. He also noted that miners would be compensated for working in dangerous conditions with shorter hours per shift, a practise unheard of in Cardiganshire lead mines during the nineteenth century. Considering the contrasts which they observed, it is easier to understand why Dan and Nicholas became members of the Communist party. Nicholas paid for his political beliefs during the World War II by being incarcerated, and the authorities kept a very close eye on Dan. During the war, he worked in a reserved occupation ploughing fields for local farmers, and his was the first tractor I ever saw with a protective hood of his own design and construction to protect him in all weathers.

Adults tended to look rather askance at Dan for what they regarded in the early days of the war as his unpatriotic beliefs, but we children saw him as a popular character and a source of

Dan Jones engaged in one of his favourite hobbies, fishing the Melindŵr near the site of his birthplace, Ty'n y Graig.

Dan Jones with his young assistants, Byron (left) and Geraint Howells.

entertainment. He had erected a workshop in a field just below the main road where we would often congregate to shoot his airguns at metal caricatures he made of all the Nazi leaders. The evening would end with a rendering of 'The Red Flag' in Welsh, though we had no idea of the significance of what we were singing. I have a small photograph somewhere of us all giving the Communist clenched fist salute, though I must have insulted the party by clenching the left instead of the right fist. Dan gave the clenched fist greeting whenever we passed on the lanes in the village.

In later years his eyesight failed and he had to wear tinted wrap-around spectacles which his neighbour, Mrs Sal Howells, found very useful when peeling onions! He also became increasingly deaf, much to the embarrassment of his nephew Tegwyn, whom he would accost in a very loud voice in the public library reading room in Aberystwyth on the evils of reading such rubbishy Tory papers as the *Daily Mail* and *Daily Express*. He also discouraged me from reading these papers and told me to try and get my hands on the *Socialist Worker* instead.

Dan was certainly a unique character who, notwithstanding his rather unorthodox political views, made an enormous impression on the village. But it was his fund of anecdotes and reminiscences on social life in the nineteenth century that I found most interesting. He published these just after World War II in a booklet entitled *The Memories of a Labourer*. I enquired of Tegwyn Jones as to how this publication came about and was fascinated to hear how Dan managed to publish the booklet himself. Apparently, he kept one room in the house aside for his paraphernalia, which included an old Adana printing machine. I don't know anything about printing but having looked at pictures of various Adana letter presses, I can only guess at the colossal amount of work Dan and his two young assistants, Byron and Geraint Howells, had to undertake to produce the booklet's forty-three pages. Everything had to be done by hand, requiring great concentration to select each individual metal letter type (which incidentally are back to front) and carefully insert each letter on to what was called a composing stick. The completed words would then have to be separated by a blank metal block. Then I imagine the whole metal block or frame would have to be inked – a very messy and unforgiving task in my experience. A piece of paper would be carefully placed on to the block frame and a hinged plate called a platen would be pressed down on to the paper to produce the typed surface. Of course, if there was a misprint or spelling error, the offending metal letters would have to be lifted out using something like tweezers, I assume, and the correct type re-inserted. Then the whole process would have to be repeated! The booklet itself is fascinating, but when one thinks of the physical and mental effort that went into its publication, it becomes a wondrous accomplishment.

In honour of their hard work, I would now like to include some of Dan's reminiscences from *The Memories of a Labourer* (in my own words).

Dan notes that wall ovens were an integral part of the domestic scene, especially for working class families which relied on cooking their own bread. They were situated within the chimney breast to one side of the grate, close enough to make use of the same flue as the main fireplace. On bread-making days a fire was lit within the wall oven for about two hours prior to cooking. Then the fire was removed and up to six large elongated tins containing dough were put in. Fire-bricks would retain the heat long enough for the bread to be perfectly baked. Sadly most of these fireplaces have been removed in the interests of modernisation, but I am sure one would still come across a few in older farmhouses.

In pre-wireless days, the clock on the mantelpiece was one of the most important pieces of furniture in the house. If it stopped for any reason, there would be a minor crisis until it was repaired by Thomas the Clocks. He would arrive early in the morning armed with his silk bag containing all his magic instruments. He spent most of the day delving into the innards of the clock until the instrument was revived. The fee was always ninepence and his food.

The garden was a vital part of a miner's home, well stocked with all kinds of vegetables to provide a major part of the family's diet. Vegetable soup – *cawl* or *potes* in the local dialect (pronounced pot-ess) – was a staple diet. Even in my childhood in the 1930s, Saturday was *potes* day. This had a basis of a small amount of meat or just a bone to give it flavour, then all sorts of vegetables were thrown into the pot.

In the nineteenth century, peat was often the only source of fuel which the miner could afford. It was cut during the summer in the bogs which were widespread on the surrounding hills, and stacked up to dry. In autumn the miner would borrow a horse and cart from a local farmer to carry the fuel home where it would be stacked close to the house. In return the miner would use some of his spare time to work for the farmer.

Life was very precarious not just because of the dangerous and unhealthy conditions the working men faced in their various occupations but also due to the very low standard of living, brought about by low wages. Such stringent conditions gave rise to much uncertainty and lack of confidence, so that superstition was deeply ingrained in society. This came to the fore in times of crises such as sickness or the death of a domestic animal in a poor household. Such was the insecurity that the bad luck was often blamed on someone putting a curse on the family or bewitching them in some way. This would drive a member of the stricken family to visit a conjuror or magician who usually dwelt well away from any other habitation, often in a lonely and bleak spot up in the mountains. The isolation added to their mysticism.

Dan relates an intriguing story about an old miner called Edward who, late one evening on returning from work, found that his heifer was very ill. It died the same day. The next day the sow refused to eat. So the following Saturday, Edward left his home armed with the conjuror's pay – half a crown. On the road he met an old friend who, on being told his mission, warned Edward to keep quiet about the unfortunate events and since the conjuror was supposed to be a seer to let him do all the talking. Usually when one arrived at the house, the conjuror would invariably be away and the wife would ask preliminary questions as to the reason for the visit. The unwary client in his distress would open his heart and tell all, while the conjuror would slip into the back kitchen and eavesdrop. Then when he eventually emerged, he would confidently and mysteriously relate the problem. In this case, however, Edward refused to answer any questions, much to the frustration of the conjuror. Eventually, Edward had to reveal the reason for his visit. The conjuror gave him a piece of red paper in an envelope with instructions to draw the paper over the animals' backs every morning and evening. Edward then wanted to know whether someone had bewitched him.

"It is very likely," replied the conjuror, "being that two animals of different breeds have been struck."

"Who is it?" asked Edward.

"I won't tell you," replied the conjuror.

"If you don't tell me," said Edward, "then I won't pay you."

"Then I shall put another curse on you," threatened the conjuror. "You will not leave this house the way you came!"

"Very true," replied Edward, "I came in facing you, but I shall leave with my bottom towards you."

"By the time you reach home, there will be horns growing on your head!"

On the way home, Edward's hands found their way to his head several times to see if there was any sign of the horns.

Rather than going to the more expensive conjuror, many rural folk would visit old crones, usually well over eighty years of age. These old ladies would charge a shilling for their services. The reason for a visit was usually illness, which was invariably diagnosed as some form of heart disease. A member of the family would visit on behalf of the patient. The old crone would perform a ritual involving a ball of wool, usually blue in colour. She would unravel lengths of wool from the ball and while the process was going on, the patient was supposed to take a turn for the better as the wool was measured out; then the customer had to take the length of wool home.

When I was young, I often noticed horseshoes nailed to doors with their prongs pointing upwards. I always thought it was a symbol of good luck but superstition said they would weaken the power of a curse. Whether these superstitions had any credence is doubtful, but the fact that some were still in evidence even when I was a child was proof of their influence in the past.

To serve the needs of the village during the nineteenth and much of the twentieth centuries, there were a number of service occupations. Apart from the miners who extracted the lead and silver ore underground, there were male labourers on the surface and ore dressers, mainly women and children. Local farmers employed several male farm servants to work with livestock. Domestic labour of both sexes formed a significant proportion of the labour market on farms and in the homes of the mining agents. Then there was a great variety of commercial specialists: butchers, carpenters, stonemasons, builders, blacksmiths and shoemakers, to name but a few. Later in the nineteenth century, innkeepers, schoolteachers, policemen and clergymen appeared.

Carriers formed a vital service in the transfer of machines

to the mines and ore to the railway heads or to Aberystwyth, the seaport. I remember William Hope with his cart and his horse, Blossom, in the 1930s. William was a carrier of sorts who travelled between his home in Llywernog near Ponterwyd to Aberystwyth every Wednesday, I think. I once had a ride with him on his cart; how that came about I don't know, but the significant feature of that journey was that poor Blossom suffered very badly from flatulence and rhythmically farted with every step she took. I recall William becoming very flustered and chastised the poor horse with, "Manners, Blossom fach, we've got visitors aboard!"

I vaguely remember my grandfather speaking of Isaac y Bank, so I was grateful to glean some more information about him from *The Memories of a Labourer*. Isaac and Margaret Davies lived in a cottage on top of the hill overlooking Goginan, called Y Banc (the bank). Apparently he was a rather short, dapper man, always dressed in a home-spun woollen suit, a blue flannel shirt decorated with a little embroidery and a flattish hat similar to those worn in the past by vicars. His visage was completed by a small beard on his chin.

Early every morning Isaac would place his three shire horses, Captain, Lion and Dragon, between the shafts of his huge wagon. Dragon was a high spirited horse and often grabbed Isaac's shovel hat and threw it in the air before the day's work began. Then they began the rough six mile journey up the mountain to a lead mine called 'Y Camdwr' where the labourers would load the wagon with two to three tons of lead either for delivery to the harbour at Aberystwyth or later, when the railway arrived, to the village of Llandre.

To prevent the wagon rolling backwards should the horses stop for a break on a steep hill, Isaac had designed a steel roller which was attached by chains to the wagon so that it rolled behind one of the back wheels. When the horses stopped, the roller would prevent the wheel from rolling back, giving Isaac time to place a stone behind the other wheel. He also had a device to prevent the wagon going out of control when descending steep slopes; this was a steel sole which was tied to one of the shafts of the wagon. Before descending the slope, the sole was placed under one of the front wheels, thus locking it. One horse was left in the shafts while the other two would follow behind.

Having delivered his load, Isaac would start on the homeward journey, but usually slaked his thirst at one of the hostelries on the way. In the meantime the horses, knowing the way home, would continue on their journey before Isaac eventually caught up with them. If Isaac had left it a bit late in leaving the pub, Margaret would have to open the gate of their property at about ten o'clock at night to let the horses in. Isaac's working day lasted some fourteen hours and his pay amounted to five shillings per ton of lead carried.

Eventually old age and sickness forced Isaac to give up his beloved profession and he died very soon after retiring. He and his wife were buried in the cemetery of Jezreel Baptist Chapel. Unfortunately, only a grassy mound marks the final resting place of one of the best waggoners of his age.

It was obvious that Dan revered his grandfather John Morris Jones, not only for his expertise as an engineer in the lead mines but also for his dignity and self control with respect to the tyrannical domination the moneyed employers exercised over the common workmen of the nineteenth century. Two stories related by Dan concerning the fortunes of his grandfather could well serve as magnificent plots for adventure novels.

The first involves John as a young man discovering some lumps of lead in a mountain stream one day while he was fishing. This, incidentally, was often the way in which many large mining projects started. His expert eye suggested the potential for a considerable source of the mineral at this spot and, when

the weather improved toward summer, he returned armed with
pick and shovel to prospect for more. He realised that the source
of the water coincided with a course of lead which gave signs
of being a rich vein. Though the site was remote, he had been
observed digging at the source and very soon, as happens in
rural areas, the rumour spread through the district like wildfire
that John Morris Jones had discovered a rich vein of lead. The
rumour reached the ears of a captain of one of the local lead
mines who, unknown to John, secured the rights to look for
and exploit the source by the following spring. This mine was
worked for years and produced a great wealth of the mineral.

The story does not end there, however. During the late
summer of that year while the captain was busy opening this
mine, John planned his revenge. He remembered that there was
another little mountain stream rising about half a mile further
up the mountain. Having visited the stream on several occasions
while fishing, he knew very well that there was no sign of any
lead present at this site. Once again he was spotted and very
soon afterwards received a very stern warning from the captain
to keep well away as he had the rights to this area too. John
returned to the spot under the cover of darkness armed with
some lumps of lead. When he arrived, he pushed several lumps
of the lead as far as he could into the source of the stream; other
lumps he distributed here and there along its upper course. He
kept a couple of lumps and a few days later decided to visit a
local inn for a pint of beer, knowing full well that other old
miners would be there. Eventually the conversation came round
to the affair between John and the captain. After a time the pitch
of the conversation was lowered as John divulged to the listening
group that he had discovered another rich vein at a source about
a mile away from the existing one. To prove his discovery he
clandestinely produced the lumps of lead from his pocket. By
the following week the captain was employing two men, then

four, then several more spent weeks blasting the surrounding rocks for signs of this elusive lead, to no avail.

John spent much of his weekends as a young man fishing in the foothills of Pumlumon. On Saturday afternoons he would be seen heading for the hills, armed with his fishing rod and a package containing bread, salt, lard and bacon. He used to keep a frying pan stashed away on the mountain to cook any trout he caught. On Sunday afternoons before returning home, he would cover the pan with lard and place it upside down in its hiding place to keep it in good condition. He spent Saturday nights in a cave and always carried his great coat to keep warm at night. He also kept a small stack of peat in the cave to provide a fire and a small candle made of pig's fat to help light it.

This preamble leads to the second story related by Dan. One evening, John's fishing had taken him farther than usual up into the hills and the sun was already setting over the sea in the west before he decided it was time to return to his cave for the night. But before returning he spent some time in the silence of the evening, disturbed only by the occasional bleat of a lonely sheep or the bark of a fox alarmed by the intrusion into its habitat. He sat down by a small lake and filled his pipe with colt's foot leaves. When dried, these made an excellent store of tobacco. Suddenly he noticed an unnaturally dark hue which extended in a broad streak across the shallow floor of the lake. He removed a clod of earth on the shore and struck the dark patch with a stone. He immediately realised that he had hit upon a vein of pure lead.

The discovery left him perplexed as to what to do. He eventually decided to seek help from a young Welsh doctor for whom he had worked on several occasions doing odd jobs and who he knew took a great interest in local mining affairs. On his arrival at the doctor's house after walking several miles, he was greeted with warmth and provided with a good meal and drink as well as a box of real tobacco. On being told of the discovery, the doctor enquired as to whether John had divulged the information to anyone else. John replied that he, the doctor, was the first to know. The doctor urged him to tell nobody else and that he would go with him the following Sunday. Before he left, John mentioned his idea that they should develop the project together and thus share any income which should ensue. The doctor, however, though he was grateful to John for his faith and trust in him, would not come to any conclusion until he had seen the lead for himself.

The following Sunday morning the doctor arrived in his horse and carriage and, as they moved off up the mountain, presented John with a beautiful pipe and a box of tobacco. The morning was happily spent smoking and drinking from the bottles of ale that the doctor had brought with him. Eventually they reached a small cottage on the hillside where they left the horse and carriage. They proceeded on foot along the rough pathway following the river towards its source, stopping on occasion to take sips out of the silver flask which the doctor produced, a rare treat for John who could not afford such fine spirits. Eventually they reached a large isolated stone standing by the stream. John removed a clod of earth and the doctor was overawed at the rich vein of lead that was revealed. The doctor then sat down and produced a beautiful meal from the hamper he carried, followed by bottles of ale and several pipes of tobacco. This was undoubtedly the best day of John's life.

For a long period the doctor was pensive and a frown clouded his features. Eventually he gave voice to his doubts as to the real worth of the discovery in terms of its location.

"Should this be sited in Goginan or Ponterwyd," the doctor observed, "we'd have a very valuable asset, but here we are almost on the roof of Wales. Who would be prepared to risk money on such an isolated spot, and who would be willing to work in such harsh conditions?"

"But we have other mines locally in similar situations," argued John.

"You are quite right," replied the doctor, "but every one of those is close to a road; here we would have to cross miles of rough territory to reach this site. However, I'll take a little of this lead with me as a sample."

John's disappointment was palpable and he refused any further offers of drink. After walking down the mountain towards the carriage in gloomy silence for a long period, the doctor offered John three guineas for the discovery. John refused the offer and insisted that they should agree on the partnership which he had proposed earlier – that the doctor should apply for the right to exploit by taking out a 'take-note' and that John would exploit the vein initially using a pick and shovel. To this the doctor disagreed, stating that with his experience of such matters the project would be doomed to failure.

Before reaching the carriage, the doctor upped his offer to five guineas. Once again John refused and the doctor indicated that this was the end of all discussion on the matter. John saw all his dreams and aspirations vanishing and, in desperation, decided to accept the offer of the five guineas. The doctor immediately produced a notebook from his pocket and on a page that already contained some writing asked John, who could not read or write, to make his mark (a cross) at the bottom of the page. The driver of the carriage signed as a witness. Despite the disappointment, there were scenes of jubilation in John's household that evening at the sight of such gold on the table all at the same time.

Within six months a company started work on the project on top of the mountain and John Morris Jones was one of the first workers there. There was a rumour that the doctor had sold the rights to a company for two thousand pounds. The work became one of the wealthiest projects in Cardiganshire.

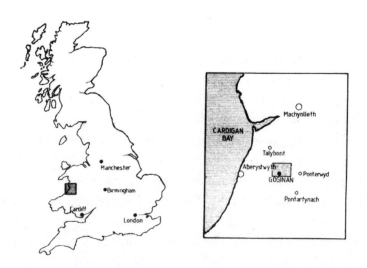

Fig. 1. Location of the Goginan Mines in Mid Wales

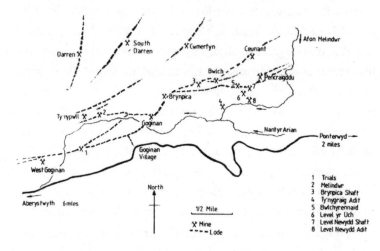

Fig. 2. Location of mine workings & lodes in the Goginan District of Mid Wales

reminisced harshly as to how that Sunday turned from being the happiest in his life to one of utter despair. On many occasions he would trudge up to the lake where he originally discovered the dark shadow. He would kneel on the shore and see the reflection of his own face looking back at him – the true reflection of the poor miner.

Despite being a communist, Dan's upbringing in a religious family never really left him and every year an anonymous donation appeared in the ledgers of the Dyffryn Methodist Chapel funds. Reflecting on his experiences in life and the obvious exploitation of the common working man during the nineteenth and early twentieth centuries, I can quite understand why he should feel his convictions so strongly. Dan died in the 1960s and was buried in Dyffryn cemetery, but he and his little book left a great legacy behind and I was proud to know him.

CHAPTER TEN

Silver and Lead

WHEN I PERCEIVE THE tranquil and peaceful atmosphere which seems to permeate Goginan today, it hardly seems believable that this was once a bustling, thriving community where hundreds of men, women and children strived for long hours in all weathers and conditions to extract the precious ores from the Silurian and Ordovician shales, grits and mudstones that make up the strata of the hills around the Melindŵr valley. But it was these very structures and the ore contained in them that made the name Goginan famous in mining circles over many centuries.

In 1986 Simon Hughes produced a wonderful and detailed treatise entitled *The History of the Goginan Mines* which contains a comprehensive study of the development of Goginan and the surrounding mines throughout the centuries, and I am grateful for his assistance and advice in preparing this section of the evolution of the village.

As with all industry, the progress of mining can be erratic with periods of boom interspersed with periods of decline as ore-rich lodes near exhaustion and new extracting methods are developed. However, according to Hughes, the Goginan area proved to be an exception since production continued almost uninterrupted from the advent of the Society of the Mines Royal in the 1560s right through to the beginning of the twentieth century. The Society was formed on 28 May 1568 to administer all the mineral ore mines in the country that were owned by the Crown. Queen

Elizabeth I was interested in the potential mineral wealth of her realm as iron was needed for munitions and silver essential to replenish the royal coffers. Thus the lead mines in Tudor times were worked mainly to obtain the silver associated with lead.

The Goginan mine includes four mines all within two miles of each other. These are Goginan, Pen-y-graig-ddu (the head or top of the black rock) two miles to the north-east, and between them two smaller mines, Ceunant (steep valley) and Bwlch (the gap) – all developed along a rich vein of lead and silver (see maps). Goginan produced a considerable amount of silver but Cwmsymlog, about two miles to the north, produced more initially. Much of it was transported to London at the end of the sixteenth century.

This period put the area's lead mines on the industrial map and landed gentry began to take control away from the hands of local people. The wealth gleaned from the labours of the impoverished and ill-treated workers lined the pockets of enterprising individuals and benefited communities in other parts of the country. One of the first entrepreneurs who came to the area was Sir Hugh Myddleton, son of Richard Myddleton, the governor of Denbigh Castle in late Tudor times. Sir Hugh was a successful goldsmith and businessman based in London and a close friend of Sir Walter Raleigh. He managed to lease some of the main lead and silver mines of Cardiganshire, including Goginan and surrounding mines, for a rent of £400 a year. The venture was so successful that he made a profit of £2,000 a month.

One of the main problems in exploiting the area's lead and silver ore was the high water table resulting from the wet climate of west Wales. To combat this, Myddleton introduced water-wheel-driven pumps so that deeper-lying deposits could be reached. He also undertook a project to improve London's water supply. The project, commenced in 1608, involved the construction of a 38-mile-long canal from the New River Head reservoir in Hertfordshire. The New River, as the canal was called, was finished within four years. However, the project cost Myddleton more than he anticipated and he was forced to become a surveyor in later years to supplement his income. He died in rather straightened circumstances in 1631.

Myddleton was succeeded in his mining enterprises by a more adventurous character called Thomas Bushell, a close friend of Francis Bacon, the English politician, philosopher and essayist. Bushell was a very competent engineer who expanded on Myddleton's efforts. He supervised the cutting of three new deep drainage adits (horizontal or near-horizonal passages or tunnels cut into the hill) in Goginan below the flooded base of earlier workings. These were essential to get rid of ground water – an ever-present inconvenience.

The silver Bushell produced was sent to the Tower of London for minting into coins. This journey was both dangerous and expensive, so in 1637 he applied for permission to establish a mint at Aberystwyth Castle. Permission was granted and the mint produced silver coins marked with the Prince of Wales' feathers on one side and an open book, the Aberystwyth mint mark, on the other. The denominations of these coins were a half crown, a shilling, sixpence, a groat (four pence in old money), three pence, two pence and a half penny. The mint, which commenced its work in 1639, was moved to Shrewsbury in 1642 but was then relocated to Furnace (a village about twelve miles north of Aberystwyth) for a very brief period in 1648.

Bushell was an enterprising man but was very unpopular with the local gentry since he was an outsider reaping the benefits of the area's mineral wealth. Matters came to a head in 1642 when Pryse of Gogerddan estate engaged in industrial sabotage. He stopped up many water courses – essential for the working of the wheels – with rubble, threatened and intimidated miners and other workers, and held unnecessary courts of enquiry at times which would necessitate miners to be away from work.

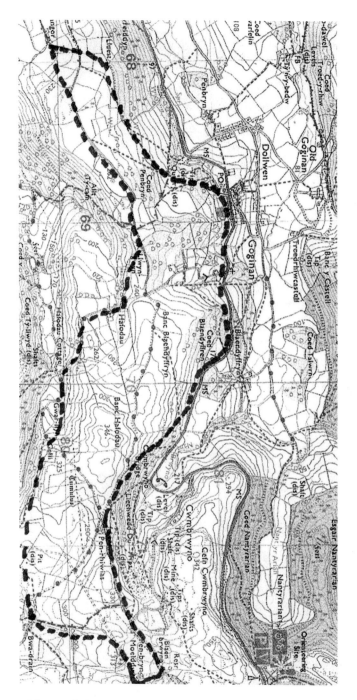

Olwen's daily post round in 1914

Penbryn Garm, Goginan. The home of Lewis Morris in the mid eighteenth century and possibly where Oliver Cromwell stayed for a short period during his forays in the region of Aberystwyth castle.

John Roberts, the present owner of Penbryn Farm, at the back door of his home. Though well into his eighties, he completes a full day's work in the running of the property.

Troed-y-rhiw farm, Goginan. An excellent example of the long house, where the livestock were once kept in the one end of the dwelling. To the right is seen the tithe barn. The Melindŵr stream flows across the field in the foreground, and in the left-centre of the picture where the trees reach the river bank there was, in my childhood, a waterwheel which provided power to the buildings. I believe that this was the original 'Goginan Fawr' which could have given its name to the village.

The Melindŵr Valley, looking west from Nant-yr-Arian towards Aberystwyth.

The Pavillion, venue for the annual eisteddfod and performances of 'Y Trwbadŵr', with Jezreel chapel house and the vestrey (the first little Baptist church in 1829) in the foreground.

Goginan silver-lead mine as it was in the early 1930s, with the 'Royal Oak' and the waterwheel housing in the background.

Jezreel Baptist chapel in 2007.

The interior of the chapel in 2007.

The Dyffryn Methodist chapel in 2007.

The interior of the chapel in 2007.

St Matthew's Church, Goginan, in 2000.

St Matthew's Church, Goginan, in 2007.

Marie enjoying a joke with my wife, Cecele, during Marie's one hundredth birthday party at the Deva old people's home in Aberystwyth, while Betty (ninety-eight) is deep in conversation.

Betty celebrating her hundredth birthday.

The Druid Inn, Goginan.

My grandmother, Annie, outside the Druid Inn with her daughters, Marie (left) and Betty (right) in the late 1930s.

…Aberystwyth was the distant 'Mecca'… Whenever I looked west down the Melindŵr valley, I would experience a certain joy; the sky always seemed lighter and bluer, for just around the corner a couple of miles down the valley, one would be nearing Aberystwyth…

The first Methodist chapel in Goginan, opened in 1843. In 1865 a larger chapel was erected, and the original building became the chapel vestry. With the closure of the larger chapel, this building has once again become the chapel.

A nineteenth-century photograph of Goginan lead mine showing Jezreel Baptist Chapel in the foreground and the Wesleyan chapel at what is now Troedrhiwcastell farm.

The Melindŵr Valley and its environs, taken from the Ordnance Survey One Inch 'Old Series' sheets, surveyed between 1791 and 1874.

Aerial view of Goginan mine taken in 1985.

Level yr Ych (A) and Level Newydd (B) as they look at the time of writing.

The entrance of John Taylor's incline completed in 1838, now preserved as a memorial to mining activities in Goginan.

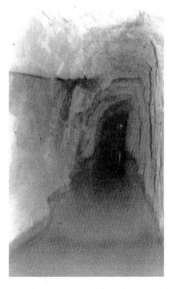

Level yr Ych: one of the last levels worked in the Goginan area. Photograph by Simon Hughes.

William Waller's adit, which emerges near Troedyrhiw bridge in Goginan. The water emanating from it is the purest and coldest I have ever tasted.

Goginan: The main road in 1900.

Goginan: The main road in 2007 (note the absence of people).

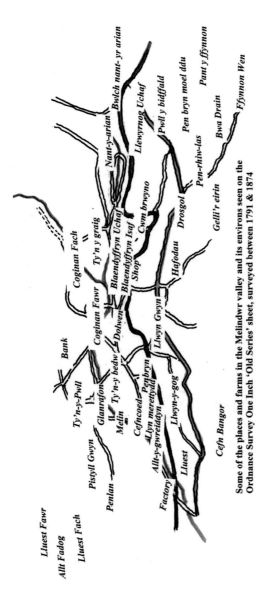

Some of the places and farms in the Melindwr valley and its environs seen on the Ordnance Survey One Inch 'Old Series' sheet, surveyed between 1791 & 1874

It is interesting to note that no mention is made of Goginan village except for the work 'Shop' somewhere near the site of St Matthew's church half a mile or so east of the site of the present village. I would think that this issue was published very early in the nineteenth century as farms like Troed-y-rhiw and Troedrhiw-castell are not mentioned. Is it possible that Troed-y-rhiw could once have been called Coginan Fawr? More recent maps show what is here called 'Bank' as Goginan Fawr. Also note that, apart from the mention of 'lead veins' to the north-east of Coginan Fach, no other mention is made of the silver-lead mines. Also some old farms like Pistyll Gwyn, Llyn Merettydd and Gelli'r eirin no longer appear on later O.S maps.

━━ The route of the trunk road A44 built in the early nineteenth century

〰 The old ridge road used by early stage coaches from Aberystwyth

Eventually, the frustrated Bushell had to complain to the Society of Mines Royal and Pryse was bound over to keep the peace on a bond of £500 never to hinder mining operations again.

Bushell made a lot of money from Goginan and Bwlch mines which he used to help King Charles I in his battle with Parliament. He lent the king £40,000 and clothed the Royalist army. He also formed his own regiment from the miners under his charge and maintained them throughout most of their losing battle. The end of the Civil War led to the rule of Oliver Cromwell, who saw the revenue gleaned by Charles from the lead mines as a perpetual thorn in his side. Cromwell invaded Aberystwyth and blew up the castle. It was said that he also destroyed much of Goginan mine but there is no real evidence for this. There is also a legend that he spent a few nights at Penbryn farm in Goginan. With Cromwell's victory, Bushell fled, leaving his partner Edward Goodyeare in charge. (Goodyeare was a Parliamentarian, making it even more unlikely that Goginan mine suffered any damage at Cromwell's hands.) Bushell turned his back on business and lived as a recluse in the Isle of Man.

During the turmoil created by the restoration of the monarchy there was not much activity in the Cardiganshire mines except for general maintenance. However, one important event towards the end of the seventeenth century was to have a very marked effect on the way lead mining would proceed. A rich lode of lead was discovered near the surface of Gogerddan estate (at Escair-hir, east of Talybont). Sir Carbery Pryse who, along with other Cardiganshire gentry, was still steaming over the injustice of the wealth on his land being taken by the Crown, refused to let this new discovery undergo a similar fate. His stand led to the Mines Royal Acts of 1688 and 1693 which ended the Crown's ownership of the mines. Apparently, Pryse was so elated that he rode from London to Gogerddan in forty-eight hours to spread the good news which was greeted by celebratory bonfires on the hills above the county's lead mines.

The Acts created a spirit of wild speculation with many people buying shares in mining ventures. The Company of Mine Adventurers was formed by an ex-collier called William Waller and Sir Humphrey Mackworth. Waller was a bit of a firebrand who had been previously engaged by Sir Carbery Pryse; it was he who had encouraged Pryse to take his petition to parliament. Sir Humphrey Mackworth, a mine owner from South Wales, was a brilliant businessman.

The Mine Adventurers began working in Goginan in 1698 and by 1701 four mines – Goginan, Bwlch and Pen-y-graig-ddu, along with a new mine called Bryn Pica (see map) – were in operation. The Adventurers had put up £1,000 to buy the lease. The silver content of all these mines was excellent, with 44 ounces of silver per ton of ore. Unfortunately, as with many speculative ventures of the time, the company was dogged by fraud and embezzlement scandals. Waller was accused of mismanagement and failing to realise the mines' potential. Even though he was responsible for excavating over 8,000 feet of new adits and shafts, the total value of ore production was just £400. In 1709 Waller was dismissed.

The Goginan mines were adversely affected by the economic depression of the early eighteenth century. However, a man named Lewis Morris tried to revive their fortunes in the mid eighteenth century. Morris was born in Anglesey in 1701, the oldest of four notable brothers who were known as 'y Morrisiaid of Fon' (the Morrises of Anglesey). He was a great patriot, historian, scholar, poet and map-maker. who spent much of his early career mapping various parts of the coast of Wales. He was very interested in Celtic remains and was an authority on the Welsh language. In 1763 he published a book of poems entitled *Y Diddanwch Teuluaidd* (The Family Entertainment).

In 1742 Morris was appointed deputy steward for the Mines

Royal at a period when the fortunes of Crown properties were at a low ebb. In 1744 the Crown issued him with a warrant to produce a correct survey and plan of Cwmwd y Perfedd – the area containing most of the lead and silver mines of Cardiganshire – and to demarcate the boundary between Crown property and that of local gentry. His task was not made easy by the locals who resented any representative of the Crown. In 1745 Morris wrote a letter complaining that two of the area's foremost landowners, Thomas Powell of Nanteos and Thomas Pryse of Gogerddan, were being very obstructive towards his attempts at a survey.

As part of his work for the Crown, Morris also had to locate other sources of ore. In the 1750s while working a mine at Esgair-y Mwyn on bleak moorland near the village of Ffair Rhos, he was arrested by a group of armed miners led by two magistrates, Herbert Lloyd and the Reverend William Powell, who maintained that the mine was on private land. Morris was carted off to Cardigan jail where he languished for a time until the government released him. The dispute raised doubts as to the integrity of Morris' accounts and records and led to his dismissal in 1756. The Mine Adventurers' lease ceased towards the end of the eighteenth century.

While working for the Crown, Morris lived in Allt Fadog near Capel Dewi but was romantically involved with Ann Lloyd, heiress to the small estate of Penbryn in Goginan. In 1757 he moved to Penbryn and produced a family of ten children. Morris had a dark complexion, was ruddy and stout but suffered from asthma, gout and bouts of depression. He was not a pleasant person, being proud, boastful, scornful and having a fiery temper. He died in 1765 and is buried in Llanbadarn.

Apart from the contributions of Lewis Morris there are few decent records of the development of the lead mines during the first half of the eighteenth century. In 1760 wealthy entrepreneur Chaunsey Townsend, who had financial interests in South Wales and London, took over the lease of Goginan mine from the Mine Adventurers. There is a dearth of information about this period but it is known that by 1810 the mine was worked by Job Sheldon and Co.

By the 1820s the mine had passed into the hands of a Mr Evans of Ponterwyd Hotel. Evans had little interest in the project and, having neglected the mine for a time, he passed it on to Matthew Francis for £30! In 1836 Goginan, along with Bryn Pica mine, was sold by Francis to John Taylor and Son, but Francis retained a twenty-five per cent share. The two parties thus began a long and turbulent relationship. Francis certainly had a flair for business. At the outset of Taylor's control, shares were issued at £5; by 1838 they had appreciated in value to a stupendous £420, giving Francis around £10,000 profit on his investment in two years.

Even so, Goginan was not the most efficient of local mines – that honour went to Cwmsymlog. Taylor ordered Francis to install second-hand machinery in Goginan which included a 34-foot diameter waterwheel from Cwmsymlog and a 19-foot wheel from Cwmystwyth. The palaver involved in moving these wheels by horse and cart can only be imagined. Taylor and Francis also had ambitious plans to sink deeper shafts and longer adits and by the 1840s Goginan became very productive with an output of over 1,000 tons per annum. In 1841 a steam engine was installed for crushing the ore as well as a 45-foot waterwheel for pumping water.

However, cracks were beginning to appear in the partnership. Taylor mistrusted Francis as he often made ambitious forecasts but always had an excuse if there were any shortcomings, such as faulty machinery or the vagaries of the elements. Eventually Francis was dismissed and his place was taken by John Taylor junior and his brother-in-law, George Fossett. Taylor continued to look for areas to expand in other sites such as Bwlch-yr-enaid, Level yr Ych and Level Newydd, all to the immediate north and east of Goginan. His fortunes, however, were mixed.

Matthew Francis continued to live in Goginan, probably smarting at the advances made in the mine without his guiding hand. He worked as a consultant and supervisor both locally and abroad; such was his enthusiastic approach that work was readily offered to him. In the mid–1840s he was joined by his seventeen-year-old brother Absolom, who initially lodged at the Druid Inn but later lived in Rose Cottage, a detached house overlooking Goginan mine. Absolom was trained at the Truro School of Mines and publishd a book entitled *A History of the Cardiganshire Mines*.

In 1847 Matthew Francis formed the Bwlch Consolidated Mines Company and became its general manager. Bwlch mine had been neglected by the former lessees but Francis saw great prospects for it since it was sited so close to the thriving Goginan mine. He bought powerful pumps and winding and dressing machinery for his new project. However, he was handicapped by a lack of water and had to approach his rival for access to the Blaen Melindŵr reservoir which supplied Goginan mine. Taylor was a gentleman and in 1848 allowed a leat (water course) to supply Francis' 40-foot wheel with water. For a time output was up to 50 tons a month but then declined, forcing Francis to abandon the project.

By now, Goginan was employing 700 staff and over 7,000 tons of concentrate (almost pure lead ore) were produced in five years. The crushing mill was reputed to be the largest in mid-Wales. There were up to fourteen wheels of various sizes and new shafts were sunk down to nearly 150 fathoms (900 feet) below the surface. In 1849 over 1,100 tons of concentrate were dressed and sold for over £16,000; running costs had amounted to about £12,000 and the so-called mineral lords received their cut of just over £1,550 leaving a profit of around £2,700. This allowed dividends of £35 a share to be paid out. In 1850 Goginan was still producing an average of 23 tons of concentrate a month.

The latter half of the nineteenth century was a period of speculation, with local companies being given auspicious names in order to attract the capital of prospective shareholders. In 1850 Francis, with partners JJ Atwood (a solicitor from Aberystwyth) and Absolom Francis, launched the West Goginan Mine Company and carried out work at Cefn Coed and Ty'npwll but with little success. The company name was then changed to The Troed Rhiw and Cardiganshire Consolidated Silver/Lead Mines. Francis and Atwood engaged in such nefarious practices as sending unrepresentative ore samples to smelters. Atwood was adept at pressurising smelters for quick settlement of cash transactions.

It seems that Francis and Atwood let their ambitions run riot and speculated wildly, running up debts with many of their suppliers. John Hayward, a wealthy businessman from Devizes in Wiltshire who had a senior position on the board of directors and seemed to be the only honest participant in this speculative and back-biting saga, was left to pay the bills. He was quoted as saying how he "abominated the accumulation of bills." Three rather dubious and aggressive shareholders – Mr Trevethic, Mr Law and JP Thomas – scorned Hayward's honesty and contrived to oust him from the board. Eventually Thomas, with the connivance of Law and Trevethic, managed to acquire a majority share holding in the company. Thomas gave Hayward a chance to retain his senior position on the board by offering him some of his shares at grossly inflated prices. Hayward was left over a barrel and had no option but to accept.

Relations between Francis and Taylor remained very strained, as shown in various letters between the two published in the *Mining Journal*. Taylor approached Francis through one of his captains, James Paull, with a view of re-opening operations at Bwlch-yr-enaid and Level Newydd works, but to no avail. However, James Paull retained an interest in the Level Newydd mine.

1865 was a very lean year for Goginan mine with only 100 tons of concentrate sold. This decline continued and the mine only produced ten tons a month in 1875 but its saving grace was that each ton was producing 24 ounces of silver. It is likely that Taylor withdrew from activities at Goginan mine in 1877. In 1879 less than 100 tons of ore were raised in Goginan, realising a mere £1,164.

One thing that can be said for Francis is that he knew how to sell himself. His penchant for producing glowing reports of his activities led to work overseas. In 1869 he visited Bilbao in Spain on mining activities. There he was taken ill and died.

In 1875 the Bwlch Consuls Mine ceased operations to be replaced by the Bwlch United Mining Company in 1878, but no ore was sold before 1880 despite the services of the very experienced specialist, Captain Nicholas Bray. In 1880 a new company called The Goginan Silver Lead Mines Limited was launched by John Kitto and Son and included in the directorship were Captain Nicholas Bray, John Kitto, Dr Evan Rowlands the village doctor, and Captain J Bonsall of Fronfraith (I recall my father speaking of them). Captain James Garland of Cwmsymlog mine (related to the William Garland who accompanied my great-grandfather to Colorado) was employed as adviser. However, the paltry £12,000 investment was insufficient to make a great difference to the mine's development. Nevertheless a compressor was bought to power the pneumatic drills.

This new enthusiasm for Goginan prompted Absolom Francis to form the Troed-y-rhiw United Mines in 1880-81. This venture was not very successful and survived for a very short time. In 1883 the name was changed to the Cardiganshire Consolidated Silver-Lead Mines Limited and involved John Kitto in association with Absolom.

Many factors mitigated against any great success for the mines in the 1880s. Machinery and equipment were expensive and a water supply was costly. Water used by Goginan mine was brought by leat from as far as Talybont (about ten miles away) and rent had to be paid to the landowners whose lakes or reservoirs were used. In the case of Goginan, eighteen landowners had to be paid rent, at a total cost of nearly £150. Costs were exceeding profits by several thousand pounds, and by 1886 the Goginan mine was doomed. Original share values had dropped from £1 to seven shillings and sixpence.

One of the major causes of the recession was the availability of cheaper lead and silver in Spain, Australia and South America which made the local ore uneconomic. The government brought in a bill to nationalise all mines in the hope of stopping cut-throat competition amongst shareholders. The bill was met with great opposition from the Victorian gentry and capitalists; people stopped investing in the mines. Shares in Goginan mine were suspended in October 1886 and never re-appeared. The mine itself was closed and flooded to adit level. Absolom Francis died in 1891 and was buried in Capel Bangor church cemetery.

The early part of the twentieth century saw an attempted revival of some of the sites. In 1909 Henry Glover leased the East Goginan mines: Ceunant, Pen-y-graig-ddu, Level Newydd and Bwlch-yr-enaid. The lease ran out after eight years and little is recorded as to the amount of work done in that time. The sites were then leased to George Heath and Wallace Henry Paull, son of James Paull. The company was called the Melindŵr Mines Development Syndicate Ltd with registered offices in Birmingham where Paull resided, but a local address at 'Ivy Bank' – a house in Llanbadarn. Paull decided that £7,000 would be sufficient to commence the development of Level Newydd. There was also interest in re-working the 73,000 tons of waste at Goginan mine for any remaining ore.

By now, geological surveys had been conducted which gave a more accurate picture of conditions and prospects. It was found that Paull's £7,000 was in no way adequate for re-development; £50,000 would have been a more realistic figure. However, operations continued apace and the 1920s saw their heyday, especially at Level Newydd. Geological surveys suggested that a 6,000 foot crosscut should be dug, beginning on the banks of the river Melindŵr and working roughly north-westward. This would tap several valuable ore veins in virgin ground. Unfortunately this so-called 'Ty'n-y-graig crosscut' was never begun. Simon Hughes has little doubt that had this cross-cut been dug, it would have developed into the largest mine in mid-Wales and one of the principal silver producers in the United Kingdom.

Despite infusions of capital, the economic problems of the 1920s spelt the final demise of lead and silver mining in the Melindŵr valley. Attempts to continue were made by merging Melindŵr Mines Limited with Cwmystwyth. This was unsuccessful and by 1922 Melindŵr Mines Limited was in liquidation. However, Paull would not give up and managed to get the Dunlop Rubber Company mildly interested for a time but this effort again met with failure. Even as late as 1935 Paull was striving to raise money for one more attempt. He died sometime during World War II and his estate, including his mining interests, were left to his sister and daughters. Eventually the rights were forfeited and the last vestige of mining activity in the area died with him.

Now little or nothing is left except for William Waller's adit whose outlet lies next to the bridge over the Melindŵr stream at Troed-y-rhiw farm, and Taylor's Incline which has been preserved as a monument to the past. There was a little renewed activity during the very late 1940s and early 1950s centred on Taylor's Incline but it came to nothing. Most of the mine is now under green grass. I am tempted to say, "How green is my lead mine." It looks prettier now but a very big part of what gave the village its life has gone.

Many people and places benefited from the wealth gleaned

from the rocks around Goginan: Sir Hugh Myddleton's New River provided water for London; Thomas Bushell was financial benefactor to King Charles I; Matthew and Absolom Francis, John Taylor and John Kitto all made money from their enterprises by fair means or foul. Look at the industrial history books and you will see pictures of these august entrepreneurs. But what of the real producers of the wealth, the workers? How are they remembered, if at all, in the annals of history? "Does it matter?" one might ask. After all, they received their wages if they produced a good day's work. Conditions weren't great but tolerable in the circumstances and most of them were able to work until they were about thirty-five or forty before becoming 'unproductive' so why should they complain? I can quite imagine such idle thoughts going through the minds of the bosses now and again as they took a break from scanning the revenue returns for the month or leisurely reading the *Mining Journal*.

It's probably true to refer to the lead miners as fodder for the capitalist gentry. As Dan Jones mentioned in his book *The Reminiscences of a Labourer to the Youth of Wales* a miner's life was much cheaper than buying a machine. Ventilating machines cost a lot of money, so miners had to breathe in the noxious dust of the previous shift for eight hours at a time. The situation was aggravated by the introduction of drilling machines. Holes had to be drilled upwards so that water would not collect in them; this process produced so much dust that for a time the workers could not see each other. Later drilling machines, however, injected pressurised water into the hole thus eliminating the dust and so making conditions more tolerable.

All in all, Goginan mine was relatively safe judging by the very few accidents that were recorded. Nevertheless the potential hazards were numerous. Entry into the mine was either by descending down the vertical winze (shaft) by ladder. One can imagine the danger of such a descent with little light and slippery, wet rungs with possibly a covering of frost or ice in cold weather; one slip and the fall could be several fathoms. The other, and often more favoured means of entry where practical, was by means of inclines such as Taylor's; this would be a longer but relatively safe means of reaching the vertical shafts before descending further. The miner would then be faced with a trek of maybe a mile along the tunnel before reaching the ore. There was always the possibility of a rock fall from the roof of the tunnel and one had to endure the constant drip of freezing water which permeated the rock joints.

The blasting of the rock was another potential hazard; powder could be unreliable and go off unexpectedly before the miners could retreat to a safe position. One can imagine all sorts of dangers facing these people every time they ventured below ground. Health and safety was very much neglected until the Kinneard Commission of the early 1860s appointed inspectors to visit the mines and look into conditions. Even then accidents occurred, as experienced by a distant ancestor of mine, Henry Boundy, who died by falling into an unfenced shaft on the night of 24 October 1880.

What was the financial gain for facing such danger? Dan Jones mentioned a wage of one shilling and sixpence a day as an average wage for a miner in the mid nineteenth century, and four pence a day for girls working in the surface sheds. In some cases miners would be paid according to the amount of lead they produced. Whatever the wage it was a pitiful sum, especially when one considers that each miner had to pay for his candles at eight pence a pound; he would go through about two pounds of candles a week. He also had to pay for the powder he used underground, again at about eight pence a pound. In less prosperous times he might also have to contribute to the price of sharpening his drills. As the fortunes of the mines started to decline in the 1860s miners could not even rely on being paid regularly and could not afford to hire solicitors to fight their cases.

The following story gives some indication of how little value was placed on miners' lives. On 26 July 1850, John Blyther, a 22-year-old miner of Cornish extraction was returning to his mother's cottage in the company of Michael M'kan, a 32-year-old Irish miner who was lodging with them. It was a hot afternoon and tempers were frayed after a long shift. The two got into a heated argument which turned into a fight. Blyther, being the younger and more agile man, struck M'kan two or three times before the older man managed to retaliate with a blow which knocked Blyther to the ground. The blow must have landed on a vulnerable spot because within ten minutes Blyther was dead. M'kan was arrested and taken to Aberystwyth Gaol. The incident appeared as a five or six line column in *The Cambrian*. Strangely, this was the only time the incident was mentioned in the paper. There was no follow-up of the trial or any mention of a sentence being passed. Obviously such a tragic event amongst common miners was so trivial that it did not merit any further discussion – such was the value of a miner's life in the nineteenth century.

Before closing this chapter I would like to take you back on an imaginary visit to a fairly typical family of miners in the village and spend a day in their lives.

It was five o'clock on the morning of 12 February 1868. The wind blew in gusts, slashing a mixture of hail and sleet against the window panes of the small bedroom. Thomas Trevellyan turned over and was woken by a bout of coughing. He struggled into a sitting position, gasping for breath. It had been one of those restless nights which seemed to occur with increasing frequency this winter. His wife Mary stirred and moaned in her sleep; it was amazing that he had not woken her but her long, arduous days usually meant that once she dragged herself to bed she would immediately fall into an exhausted sleep.

Thomas was thirty-five, very frail and sallow of complexion.

His days as a lead miner had come to an abrupt end the previous October when a slip on the ladder taking him down to the bottom of the shaft had resulted in a broken tibia. He was hauled back to the surface, placed in a horse and cart and carried home to his little cottage about 200 yards up the creek from the mine. There his mates helped Mary to put him to bed. The next day he was visited by Doctor Rowlands, the mines' doctor who, after a cursory glance at the wound, shook his head and glanced sadly at Mary, saying that Thomas's working days were over. The wound was tightly bound and complete rest was ordered.

Matters went from bad to worse as the damp conditions in the house resulted in Thomas succumbing to pneumonia. After a long and critical period, Thomas took a turn for the better but was left with a weak chest and a hacking cough caused by long periods of working in dust and smoke underground. The mines' captain visited the family on one occasion full of verbal sympathy and left £3 on the living room table next to the Bible as a form of compensation, promising that they could live in the cottage for the foreseeable future.

Thomas lay back exhausted after his bout of coughing and gazed at the window curtains flapping in the gusty breeze; he made a mental note to stick some more paper in the cracks. His attention was drawn to the noise of movement in the loft above. His seventeen-year-old son would be getting up from his straw pallias (mattress) to get ready for the seven o'clock shift at the mine. He heard the sound of voices; it was Philip trying to wake his fourteen-year-old sister Rachel. Due to Thomas's incapacity, Rachel had been forced to leave Goginan school at the age of thirteen to bring a little more money into the family coffers. John Bradshaw had offered to employ her in the dressing sheds. He was a kindly Irishman who, after twenty years valuable service underground, had been given the responsibility of supervising the women and girls who dressed the lead ore on the surface. Rachel's mother, who was a good Roman Catholic, had approached him in desperation.

Eventually Philip's feet appeared at the top of the ladder, the only means of access to the loft. The tallow candle he carried in his left hand threw enormous dancing shadows on the dingy walls of the living room; he was followed by a very sleepy Rachel. The candle spluttered as a sharp gust of sleet-sodden wind rattled the front door.

Rachel shuffled slowly to the far corner of the room where a small bowl contained cold water; she shuddered as her fingers broke through the thin sheet of ice that had accumulated on its surface. Summoning her courage, she quickly splashed some water on her face – at least it made her feel more awake. Meanwhile Phillip put on his hob-nailed boots; he peered at the sole and noticed that two of the nails were missing from the left boot – he would have to be extra careful as he climbed down the frost-covered ladder in the shaft. They had a quick breakfast of bread and dripping and made ready for the trek down the rocky path past the big water wheel to the mine.

Phillip checked the tin box where he kept his candles and his lunch of bread with a little meat left over from the previous night's meal. He did the same for Rachel and noticed as she struggled into her boots that the right sole was coming apart. He made a mental note to try and repair it that evening and to try to find the money to buy her another pair when the monthly market next came to the village. They both put on their worn overcoats and Phillip put a sack over Rachel's head and shoulders to protect her from the worst of the weather. As they stumbled down the path she kept close behind her brother, whose broad back shielded her from the worst of the elements. She entered the ore dressing room, glad to be out of bitter cold outside.

Rebecca Pengelley was a Cornishwoman who had come to Goginan with her husband, Isaac, in 1852. Since he had succumbed to emphysema ten years earlier at the age of thirty-nine, Rebecca had worked in the ore dressing mill. During the last two years she had been put in charge of the girls who worked there, some as young as eleven. She greeted Rachel with her usual cheeky grin and gave her frozen hands a quick rub; Rachel liked Rebecca and regarded her as a sort of second mother.

The previous day, Rachel had been in the picking shed. Here the ore was raked through a hole over a grating where loose dirt and mud was sprayed away by water. Then the ore landed on a large table where it was sorted out according to its lead (or galena) content. Rachel's job had been to pick out all the lumps of pure lead that needed no further dressing. It had been a cold job handling the newly-washed lead cobbles. Today her job moved her farther down the mill where she sat on a bench and picked up lumps of largely barren rock which had some lead adhering to them. She was given a cobbing hammer which she used to separate the ore from the barren rock. Further down the floor, some ladies used large, flat bucking hammers to crush the lead into lumps smaller than one and a half inches diameter – the maximum size accepted by the roll crushers. These looked rather like a large version of the mangles which Rachel's mother used to wring moisture out of clothes on washing day. The work was tedious and incessant; the eight-hour shift seemed interminable to Rachel and the other girls – and all for four pence a day!

Meanwhile, Philip had reached the section of the shaft where a level had been dug horizontally away to the right. He stepped carefully off the ladder and onto a small platform. He adjusted the candle on his hard hat; at least here it was burning fairly brightly in an upright position, indicating that the air was reasonably clean. This would soon change once the drilling began. About sixty feet (ten fathoms) below him there was another level; between the two the bedrock contained veins of rich ore.

Philip, along with his twenty-year-old pal John Paull and

'Paddy' O'Driscoll, a 45-year-old Irishman, walked along the irregular floor of the level for a distance of a mile and a half in the wan light given by the three candles. Water continually dripped on to their hats and shoulders and before long they all felt chilled as it slid down their necks onto their backs. Suddenly the candles started guttering and their breathing became increasingly laboured as the tunnel began filling with dust, which became denser the further they went. O'Driscoll gave a grunt as his hat came into contact with a lump of rock jutting out of the side of the tunnel. What little conversation that occurred centred on the news that the price of shares had suddenly tumbled and the rumour that pay would be withheld for the foreseeable future.

At last they reached their place of work where a winze (shaft) had been sunk to the level beneath. The neck of the winze had been blasted away and looked like a huge funnel, acting as a chute to carry the extracted ore down to the trams waiting at its base. The trams carried the broken ore to the main shaft where it was transferred to huge buckets called kibbles; these were hoisted to the surface by the water-powered winding gear.

At the top of the winze the dust – a product of the earlier shift – was very thick and the three men vigorously shook sacks in a futile attempt to clear some of the choking substance. The previous shift had drilled the shot holes and blasted a large portion of the ore, a process known as 'stoping.' Since the ore was being excavated from above, the holes had to be drilled downwards. This meant that there was always a danger of the holes filling with ground water. Therefore, dynamite was the explosive used since it was not affected by water, though it was a skilled and complicated process in that a detonator was required to trigger off the charge. The three miners spent much of their day throwing the resulting broken material down the winze to the waiting wagons below.

Low-burning candles gave a good idea as to when the shift was drawing to an end, indicating the time when new blast holes would have to be drilled at strategic places. As yet the only way to drill the holes was by means of iron borers struck with a heavy hammer. The three miners took it in turns to hold the borer and wield the hammer – a rather tedious and tricky task in the restricted space and semi-darkness. O'Driscoll, with his greater experience, would select the places for drilling and set the dynamite before they all retired to a safe distance. Once it was detonated, the miners would try to retreat as quickly as possible before the noxious fumes could enter their lungs. Thus would end another eight-hour shift; then came the long trek back to the main shaft and the tedious climb back to the surface – all for between two and three shillings a day!

Education in Goginan

I N 1964, GOGINAN'S DYFFRYN Methodist Chapel celebrated its centenary. To mark the occasion a booklet was published which mentioned a Lewis Jones who lived between 1728 and 1809 in Hafodau, a small farm near the old coach road. Jones was a philanthropist who established a very prosperous school during the latter half of the eighteenth century at Llwyngwyn, a short distance from the farm.

As many as sixty children attended and education was closely associated with the religious principles of the time. Jones himself was an Anglican and is buried in Llanbadarn church cemetery but his pupils came from all denominations and many became pillars of the Methodist community. Jones' estate had a value of £200 – quite a sum in those days. He specified in his will that the interest on one half of this would be shared amongst the local poor on 26 December each year, while the interest on the other £100 would be devoted to furthering their education.

In the early nineteenth century, the Goginan Lead and Silver Mining Company promoted by John Taylor and Son established a school by renting a room from one of the nonconformist chapels near the mine – I would presume this was Dyffryn's vestry as Jezreel Baptist's vestry was too small. Pupils were drawn from miners' families and the children of captains and superintendents of works who were all Cornishmen, thus the lessons were conducted in English. There seem to be conflicting assessments of the valley's wealth during this time. The Commissioners painted a picture of a very prosperous and expanding mining industry benefiting both the proprietors and people of the village. However, the Reverend Owen Owen spoke of much poverty and that the schoolmaster, who often had to rely on gratuities from shopkeepers and local farmers, received a total annual income of £28 – with only £10 coming from the mining company. The head teacher's comment to the Commissioners was, "I give them quite as much instruction as they give me payment for."

Throughout the nineteenth century there seems to have been a close association between the leading figures in the mines and the social and educational fabric of the village. The names of Absolom Francis, a leading mining official and Doctor Evan Rowlands, the mines' doctor figure prominently in records of many of the social functions towards the end of that century.

The first mention of Welsh education in Goginan this author could find was in the 1841 census. John Roberts of Pistyll Gwyn (white well), a small holding on the northern slopes of the valley, taught small groups of probably both children and adults in local farm houses as there was, as yet, no school building in the village. It is possible that such education would be associated with the Sunday School and would involve the teaching of the basic rudiments of reading and writing through the medium of Welsh. John Roberts was possibly the noted hymn writer whose pseudonym was 'Ieuan Gwyllt' and is known to have connections with one of the largest farms in the valley, Blaendyffryn (the head of the valley).

As the lead mines expanded in the middle of the nineteenth century, boys between the ages of twelve and fifteen were either obliged to work underground or on the local farms. Thus there was little or no opportunity for education except at Sunday School. Non-conformist ministers and the Church in Wales clergy used their churches to teach adults to read and write, so church furniture often served a dual purpose. In St Matthew's, a local church (now sadly closed), the backs of the pews were hinged so that they could be turned over to serve as desks during these classes.

Parents could send their children to Aberystwyth for a private education but only those such as mine managers, prosperous shopkeepers or the owners of the larger farms could afford to do so. Fees amounted to ten shillings a quarter for a curriculum which included reading, writing, arithmetic, English grammar, geography, history and Latin. Then there were more advanced courses in the classics, Euclid, book-keeping, astronomy, land and mine surveying, map and chart-making, navigation and higher mathematics, for which the fee charged amounted to one guinea a quarter. There were also unusual courses given at sixpence a lesson, such as Hebrew and, at a fee of £1 a course, phrenology (the study of brain function) and mesmerism!

The increased pressure for educational facilities in rural areas led to many more village schools. Goginan's opened on 18 January 1865 with sixty-six pupils. It was officially called the Goginan British School. It was opened under the auspices of locally appointed committees which were supported by local gentry, the Diocesan Education Fund and local subscription.

This was a turbulent period in Welsh history with many popular risings such as the Rebecca Riots and the anti-enclosure riots which were rife in Cardiganshire. This led to questions in Westminster as to why the Welsh were so lawless. The conclusion was reached that the continued existence of the Welsh language was to blame. In 1846 William Williams, MP for Coventry, carried out some research into the role of Welsh in education and the following year a report was published. It caused a furore, especially the sections in which the report's commissioners made disparaging remarks concerning the morals of the Welsh. Author RJ Defel called it the 'Treachery of the Blue Books' – a reference to the Saxon's 'Treachery of the Long Knives' against the Britons.

The report, written largely by three monoglot English barristers, found that the provision of education in Wales was very poor and that the use of Welsh was largely to blame. They concluded that the moral and material condition of the people would only improve with the introduction of English as the sole medium of education.

It was thus very fortuitous that the Sunday schools took over the teaching of Welsh reading and writing to both children and adults. They could be regarded as the forerunners of the adult education system. Sunday schools also encouraged the publication of religious books in Welsh, such as expositions on Biblical texts. However, since they were beyond the means of many locals, book clubs were created so they could be paid for in easily affordable instalments. William Davies, a tailor and draper, formed such a club at the Druid Inn with subscriptions of two shillings and sixpence per month. When subscriptions amounted to thirty shillings, the member could purchase a book. A similar club was opened in Goginan by John P Jones, a watchmaker and jeweller of Pier Street, Aberystwyth.

This period is associated with the most hated symbol of English oppression in Welsh schools: the Welsh Not, or Note. This was a wooden block or plaque with the letters WN printed on it. Any pupil speaking Welsh at school would be humiliated by having to place this block around his or her neck. The block was then passed on to the next pupil caught speaking Welsh. This continued throughout the day until the end of school, when the last unfortunate pupil wearing the block was punished. I do not know whether this was used in the early days at Goginan School but I do remember my grandfather telling me it was present at his school when he was a boy – it was certainly used in Cardiganshire at that time.

The first principal teacher appointed at Goginan School was Thomas Hughes Parry, a certificated Teacher of the Third Class (whatever that meant). During the first year a sewing teacher, Louise Williams, was also appointed – these people probably worked at the first Methodist chapel which also served as a school.

Events farther afield had a profound effect on the influx of population into the village. The cholera epidemic in Cornwall and Devon in the 1830s saw the movement of workers from the declining tin and copper mines to similar occupations in the growing lead and silver mines from the early 1840s to the 1850s. There was also an increase in Irish workers escaping from the Potato Famine of the 1840s. It is interesting to note the changes in the composition of pupils at Goginan School between the 1840s and the 1870s and relate them to the population changes during the same period.

Number of schoolchildren at Goginan School, 1841 to 1871

Year	Number of scholars	
	Boys	Girls
1841	not listed	not listed
1851	47	56
1861	54	88
1871	132	119

Population growth and the origins of the inhabitants of Goginan, 1841 to 1871

Year	Pop	% growth	Inhabitants born in				
			Cardiganshire	Cornwall	Devon	Ireland	Elsewhere
★1841	694	–	542	66 (approx)	–	–	12(approx)
1851	1,151	71	894	112	20	46	79
+1861	1,311	14	1,158	30	7	30	86
=1871	1,342	2	1,206	46	14	7	69

★ *The 1841 census was vague as to the origins of the inhabitants but it is likely that most incomers were of Cornish origin.*

+ *Note that the number of Irish immigrants equalled the Cornish element.*

= *The decline in growth for 1861 and 1871 was in keeping with the decline in the fortunes of the lead mines.*

The rapid increase in the population between 1841 and 1851 resulted in the employment of three teachers – two of local origin and Jane Pearce, a 32-year-old from Cornwall. By 1861 there were three different teachers (one, Owen Prys, remained at the school for 30 years) and a boy scholar had been added to the staff to assist with basic teaching. By 1871 there were two more pupil-teachers: John Sullivan (fifteen years old) and William Evans (fourteen).

During this period, several strange surnames appeared on the school register such as Bradshaw and Bray (Ireland), Trenwith, Francis, Garland and Boundy (all of Cornish origin) and Ball and Paull (Devon).

Records of the work performed at the school show that

education was basic and concentrated on the 'three R's': reading, writing and arithmetic. On their first day at school, pupils were tested in reading and classified accordingly. During the first week in 1865 there were further tests in mental arithmetic and the formation of letters. There followed further tests in spelling and multiplication and division for the older pupils.

Music was also important and at least one song was learnt every week, such as 'Come Away Sweet Love' by the sixteenth-century composer, John Dowland, 'The Last Rose of Summer', 'Men of Harlech' and 'Land of my Fathers' (probably in English). For the girls, needlework and sewing classes were soon introduced. Physical exercise took the form of drill in the playground: running on the spot, standing at attention and arm swinging. Regimentation seemed to be the order of the day.

From the beginning, discipline was maintained to a high standard and the main punishment seemed to be detention after school for offences such as stone throwing, lateness and fighting. Behaviour was also monitored outside the school grounds and any reported cases of rudeness or other types of bad behaviour were dealt with accordingly. There seems to be no official record of corporal punishment but I am sure it was used on occasion.

Inspections by members of the management, local dignitaries, representatives of the British and Foreign Schools Society or Her Majesty's Inspectors, were frequent. Letters were sent out in English and Welsh to parents stating that every child on the school books was expected to be present. Inspectors scrutinised the premises and the teaching but also contributed to the learning process in various ways, such as exhorting the children to greater effort. On special occasions, local dignitaries might present pupils with small presents such as a new halfpenny. Any child who had not attended school for a minimum of one hundred days in the school year would be barred from any such treats. Fees were collected regularly and bills sent out by the managers if parents went into arrears.

The emphasis throughout was on a good basic education and good behaviour both in and out of school. There were few frills except the occasional half-day holiday and it seemed that end of term holidays were extremely short. In 1865 for instance, Easter holidays only lasted from Good Friday to Easter Monday.

Towards the close of the nineteenth century, the decline of the lead mines led to a corresponding drop in pupil numbers and attendance figures. Average numbers attending school had dropped from between 80 and 90 in the 1860s to about 60 in 1871. On 15 May 1891 there were 37 pupils at school out of a total 66 on the register. A frustrated attendance officer, appointed to deal with the problem of absenteeism, blamed the small salary for his lack of diligence.

There was also discontent amongst the staff. A headmaster's wage in the 1890s was seventeen shillings and sixpence a week plus a house, whereas pupil-teachers could earn £1 a week for less work. On 11 September 1891 headmaster P Jones left the school citing three reasons for his departure: the small salary, unhealthy housing and a disagreement with a vindictive HMI.

Throughout the nineteenth century there were no reports of the school being closed for any reason, but in January 1908 there was an outbreak of whooping cough which caused the school to close until 13 March.

A significant date in the life of the school was 15 November 1909, when a young man who had received his training at Carmarthen College was temporarily appointed as headmaster on the death of the previous incumbent, James Evans. His name was David Herbert. He soon proved himself, was given permanent headship and went on to teach at least two generations of village children, serving the school and the community for forty years until his retirement in 1949.

Now that we are moving into the twentieth century and closer to my own experience, let me give a brief description of the school and its environs. Whatever can be said about the Victorians and their concepts of education, they certainly built their schools to last. Goginan school building still stands as firm as it did when built in 1878. It is a sturdy stone structure, facing south, with gables at both ends. The eastern gabled end, which contained the smaller of two rooms, housed the infant section. This room had a fireplace and two enormous windows facing north and south which let in abundant light at all times. However, since the base of each window was at least five feet off the floor, it was impossible to be distracted by anything that occurred outside.

The main body of the building contained what we called the 'big room.' It was at least forty feet long and about fifteen feet wide with six fair-sized windows (again at least five feet off the floor), four of which faced south, while two at each end faced north. For practical purposes this room could be divided into two by a partition, the upper part of which was made of glass panes. In the centre of the north side was a fireplace next to a small dais on which stood the headmaster's desk.

Between the main room and the gabled ends, passages ran from the two entrances where the cloakrooms were situated. The western gabled end consisted of the headmaster's house, which to us children from our little hovels looked very grand, but it was open to the wind and rain rushing up the valley and was forever subject to damp and some repair or other.

The school stands out like a beacon when one approaches the village along the main road from the west. When I was a child it was painted a rich golden yellow and could be seen for miles. It always puzzled me, even then, why the school was positioned on a very sharp bend in the main road, some distance away from the village itself. The distance could be explained in that the inhabitants of the village would be spared the shrieks and whoops of the children at playtimes while still being within sight, but the corner position took longer to fathom. Obviously, the road in the 1860s would have had little or no traffic to create a hazard. In later times when motorised traffic increased, the entrance to the school yard was recessed to give some semblance of safety from the road.

Behind the school was a large walled area which served as the school playground, and situated along the farthest wall of this area were the toilets, one for the girls and one for the boys, rather primitive bucket toilets as I remember. I don't think the word 'conveniences' was at all apt, as one had to spend a long time preparing oneself for the journey in wet and windy weather and even then got soaked to the skin. They were certainly not convenient for anyone caught short!

In 1905 my father became a pupil at the school, to be followed in January 1910 by my mother when her family moved from the next valley to take over the Royal Oak. Apparently they shared the same desk in the 'big room' at the age of ten. I don't know if this pleased my father, as he did not quite possess the intellectual abilities of my mother. Her favourite facetious comment at home was to remind my father of David Herbert's comment: "Look at Olwen Evans' work next to you, Evan Evans. Aren't you ashamed of yourself?" It did not deter him too much, however, as they were married in 1929!

The general format of education in the early twentieth century had not changed significantly from that of the nineteenth. The emphasis was still on giving pupils a firm grounding in the 'three R's'. Geography and history were important in the curriculum, especially that concerning Britain and her Empire. Important dates were committed to memory, while geography was largely of the 'capes and bays' variety, where names also had to be memorised.

I'm not sure how much Welsh was formally taught at Goginan around the turn of the century, but in Wales generally there had been a great decline in the speaking of the language, especially since it was thought to adversely affect British unity in the face of crises such as the Boer War in South Africa. However, Welsh continued to survive in the more mountainous regions – away from the lowland coastal areas in North and South Wales where English influence was strong. Its revival in schools was probably helped by the appointment of Sir Owen Edwards as Chief Inspector of Welsh Schools in 1907, and later with the creation of the Urdd, the Welsh League of Youth, in Aberystwyth. By about 1908 Welsh was being taught at Goginan.

In November 1901 a new assistant teacher joined the school. His name was Abraham Pierce and he used to cycle the two miles from Capel Bangor every day. According to my father, he could be very strict – so much so that the boys sought revenge by coming to school armed with pins. At the end of the school day as the boys filed down the corridor where his bicycle was parked, the pins would emerge and find a target in its tyres!

On 15 December 1913 my father left the school, having passed the Labour Certificate Examination. Then on 13 April 1914, my mother had to leave due to domestic circumstances, thus thwarting what would have been an excellent academic career according to the school record of the time. The following day, her more fortunate good friend Elizabeth Williams was granted a place at the County School in Aberystwyth. In 1923 Elizabeth joined the school as an assistant teacher and continued to serve until her retirement, thus giving stability and continuity to the education pattern through much of the early part of the twentieth century.

My first impressions of the Rŵm Fach (little room) are rather vague. I think I remember my mother handing me over to Miss Williams; luckily I knew her well as she lived next door. But on this day everything was strange and big. She looked enormously tall, the room looked huge and the ceiling seemed miles above me. I felt very small and lonely. The desks were quite small, brown and long; each desk could accommodate six or eight pupils and were arranged to form three sides of a rectangle around the large coal fireplace. I remember looking up at the flower pots (with geraniums) that lined the window sills several feet above our heads. On the tables were a plethora of crayons, coloured paper, pencils and plasticine (or clay as we called it then, but it was only in one dull grey colour). The walls as I remember had the letters of the alphabet in lower and upper casing – this was going to be serious learning! However my time in the little room proved to be pleasant.

Every morning after taking the registers, Mr Herbert would appear to have a little *tete-a-tete* with Miss Williams, always holding a newspaper in front of them. I remember Jim Jones crawling on his knees to ·peep under the paper to see what was going on and tumbling about on the floor with laughter at what he saw – what it was we never knew!

For many years I have had very funny dreams. In most of them I have been travelling to strange places and invariably getting lost. I've often wondered why this dream recurs. Could it be due to one experience I had whilst a pupil? I think it was 1936 or 1937 when Miss Williams took all of us on the bus to Aberystwyth to see *Snow White and the Seven Dwarfs*. I think it was the first animated film in colour and it was showing at a special matinee for children at the Coliseum Cinema, a theatre I came to know very well in my courting days. I remember sitting right on the left end of the front row next to Miss Williams. What an experience – not sitting next to Miss

Williams but the film with all its colour and magical music.

Incidentally, it seemed the custom at that time to put me on the end of a row. I don't know if it was because I was such a small wimp whose little bottom could be squeezed into the smallest space, but I have two photographs of the schoolchildren celebrating what might have been the Silver Jubilee of King George V in 1935 and the Coronation of King George VI in 1937, where I am clinging on to the edge of the chapel step, sitting on the right cheek. They had the good sense to move me to the other end for the next picture so that the left cheek had the same treatment!

But back to *Snow White*: I don't know how it happened, but the next thing I remember was crying my eyes out on the street, completely lost. Someone must have found me and taken me to the bus station where I was reunited with the rest of the children. I cannot remember whether I was annoyed or ashamed at getting lost then, but even now I often get nagging fears of not being able to find out where I am. Maybe I need to see a psychiatrist!

Even at that stage, the basis of our education was reading, writing and arithmetic. I still have some exercise books full of addition and subtraction dating back to 1937, each sum headed by the name of an animal or bird; thus we learnt to write and do calculations in one fair swoop. I must say I was quite a clever little boy then as most of the sums were right!

Such lessons were interspersed by activities like paper streamer making or using clay. I also remember something we called 'Picatatin'; I think this was where we had semi-circular serrated pieces of cardboard and somehow, using a framework of wool, the whole operation eventually came out as a tea cosy for my mother, of lemon yellow and mauve stripes (yuk!) There followed another contraption made up of a cotton reel with four little nails hammered into the top. Using the same lovely

King George the Fifth's Silver Jubilee, 1935.

The Coronation of King George the Sixth, 1937.

colours, we wove a long strip by way of the hole in the reel. This could then be coiled and sown together to make a base for the teapot.

I loved the action songs we performed in class. I recall one where Miss Williams was the hen and we were chicks – the words went something like:

'O dewch yn awr fy nghywion bach am dro i chwilio am damaid…'

(Come now my little chicks for a walk to look for titbits of food…)

We sang the chorus which consisted of 'Chick, chick, chick, chick, chick' as we shuffled around the desks, following Mother Hen. It's been seventy years since we performed this, but it must have made an impression that was retained over the years and probably steered me into theatricals in later life.

We did get some relief from our work with occasional visits. One that remains in my mind was that of a black lady dressed in the flowery clothes, headdress and numerous beads which, I assumed, these ladies wore in the deep south of the United States. She told us about life in the cotton fields of the Mississippi Delta and sang folk songs like 'Old Folks at Home' and 'Steal Away to Jesus.' For years I yearned to visit this romantic part of the world with its huge cotton plantations, warm climate with plenty of sun and blue skies, the big Mississippi river meandering to the sea and all the workers swaying while they sang these beautiful songs. When I finally got there a few years ago I found it was nothing like that: it was hot alright, but so steamy and uncomfortable with pesky flies everywhere that I was glad to get out. Sometimes it's better to dream!

The other pleasant occasion was when a local dignitary would visit and give us a shiny new halfpenny, exhorting us to greater efforts. Then there were the tea parties on such occasions as a royal jubilee or a coronation when we were all presented with cups and saucers or mugs with the royal visage on, all kindly donated by some local dignitary like Miss Mason, who lived in Bow Street but was a regular visitor to our Baptist chapel. They were great days.

Moving up to the 'Big Room' was quite an event. Now we sat at big desks to take two pupils; these had hinged tops and an inkwell (big mistake). Discipline and education became more serious, as did regimentation. Being a chapel-going community, the day began by singing the Doxology – 'Praise God from whom all blessings flow...' – then came a bout of reciting the tables and some mental arithmetic. Multiplication and long division were exercised daily. On Tuesday morning after playtime came an essay or composition in Welsh. The same occurred on Thursdays, except this time in English. We went home for lunch. As I lived for a time in the Royal Oak about a mile away, I went to my aunt Sally for a glass of lemonade (I still have the glass) and some chips. I don't think Jamie Oliver would have approved, but I am still here and fairly healthy. Then back to school for the afternoon session which ended at four o'clock, if one were lucky.

Tuesdays and Thursdays were the terror afternoons, for it was then that the morning's essays were publicly marked. Each victim was summoned forward to stand by Mr Herbert's desk, which stood on a small dais. He was a slight man with a balding head and pebble glasses which were so thick that he could use them as rear view mirrors, making nowhere safe from his gaze. Many an unsuspecting miscreant's hand felt the sting of the cane made of hazel wood which he wielded so expertly. I never felt it because I was a bespectacled little goodie. Despite his rather small stature, he had a very strong and dignified persona which all respected and feared.

On these afternoons, he would position the 'victim' between his desk – where he sat on a high stool, making him even more

threatening – and the blazing coal fire which scorched one's nether regions. He would then proceed to read the literary creations slowly and deliberately with pregnant and ominous silences whenever his eyes savoured a spelling or grammatical error, which were frequent. Then came some vitriolic observations which caused the poor victim to shrivel even further so that the flames of the fire incinerating the posterior became infinitely more acceptable than the verbal torture from the front. Things didn't end there, because at four o'clock while the goodies would be allowed to go smirking home, the sinners would be retained to write out each spelling error, usually forty times, before being released. Does this sound cruel and rather sadistic? By today's standards I'm sure it does. But I have never felt any remorse or embitterment at the way we were taught. I pride myself now on making very few errors in spelling or grammar in either English or Welsh and my tables are top notch!

We did have some relief and enjoyment. Drawing and music was a regular feature on the timetable, as was physical exercise in the playground, weather permitting, and games like rounders

and cricket on Friday afternoons in spring and summer. I always remember that if anyone was fortunate enough to score more than twenty runs in cricket (hitting the ball over the playground wall into the nettles the other side counted for four), it was time for demon bowler David Herbert to step up to the crease and bowl his unplayable 'daisy cutters'.

Reading was very much encouraged and each month the town library would send up a box of books of all kinds in both languages which would be allocated to each pupil for a week.

There were the occasional visits by other people to break the pattern of work. The nurse would make her periodical visit to check for nits and lice. The absence of running water and any effective means of heating water meant that hygiene possibly didn't get the attention it deserved. Another occasional visitor was the doctor who used psychology to calm our nerves before moving round with his spatula and making us say 'Ah'. He was a tall, rather rotund man with a bald head and glasses. He would draw our attention to the blackboard where he drew an egg wearing a pair of glasses; we had to guess whom he was drawing. Shouts of 'Doctor Jones!' seemed to break the ice, so that he could proceed with his grim task.

Talking of doctors, most of the diseases at that time were exogenetic: mumps, measles, chickenpox and so on. It was always the custom to send us to play with anyone who had caught them so that we would be infected as soon as possible to strengthen our immunity systems. It seemed to work, considering the amount of dirt and dubious water that went down out gullets.

World War II brought some significant changes. Posters began to appear on the walls of the room showing pictures of various kinds of bombs and grenades which one might find lying around, and what to do about them. Other posters entitled 'Careless talk costs lives' also appeared to remind us to keep our mouths shut. Fire buckets and stirrup pumps appeared in one corner of the room and I believe some form of adhesive webbing was stuck to the windows. In the event none of these features came into use.

Then in 1940 came the evacuees from Anfield, in those days a poor district of Liverpool, which necessitated adjustments to the school timetable. At first the school was divided into two four-hour sessions. In the mornings, school began at about eight o'clock and continued until about noon; then the afternoon session lasted from about one o'clock until about five. The local children attended the morning session while the evacuees, who had their own teachers from Liverpool, attended in the afternoons. Then came a rethink. Whether this was due to getting up very early or working late, I don't know. However, it was decided to make use of the partition in the 'Big Room', so that the evacuees took the west side while the home team stayed in the eastern end. Playtimes became a bit of a battle-ground when each side would raid the other's entrance porch. Luckily the home side had Howard Jenkins; he was a big lad and acted as a very efficient battering ram! On the whole, however, each side got on with the other quite amicably and after a time the evacuees assimilated very well into village life. As the fortunes of war changed, most of the evacuees returned home, though one or two decided to remain and adopt the Welsh way of life, even as far as learning and speaking the language.

In July 1943 midday meals were introduced and the section vacated by the evacuees became our restaurant. Before that time, to keep our scrawny bodies and souls together, we used to be given a third of a pint of milk ladled out of a huge basin into our mugs by Mr Herbert; later this was succeeded by the issue of a Horlicks tablet each morning at playtime. The school meals provided a distraction as the bigger boys (despite my puny four-stone-something body, I was included in this category) had to set up the folding tables and chairs ready for lunch. The meal was pretty basic: some form of meat, usually mince (which hid a lot of dubious ingredients) with potatoes and gravy, followed by pudding. I must say that, as a child, I jibbed at most foods, relying mainly on potatoes and milk – hence the physique. But a few weeks of this fare and I was eating anything put before me.

The addition of these meals to school life brought forth another welcome activity. My friend Hedd Jones and I were appointed to carry the bin which held all the leftovers of the week down the road for about half a mile to a pig farm. This invariably took most of Friday afternoon by the time we had stopped to collect various berries or nuts. However, Friday afternoon lessons were largely cancelled in favour of collecting National Savings for the war effort and this was the time Mr Herbert and Miss Williams devoted to doing the books while all the children crowded into the 'Big Room' and got up to all sorts of nefarious mischief (I think Mr Herbert mellowed a lot during this period).

In 1944 my turn came to take the scholarship examination for entry into the grammar school in Aberystwyth. There was a lot of heart searching and not a few tears as this ordeal approached. I must say that, though Mr Herbert was a stalwart with his cajoling and some veiled threats of dire consequences should I fail, I owed so much to the guidance of my mother during these trying times. Though thirty years had elapsed since she left school, her knowledge of English and Welsh grammar and arithmetic was such that she would have performed a damn sight better than I did!

We had to write two essays, one in English and one in Welsh, in the morning session in the big hall of the grammar school. True to form, muggins proceeded to write two essays in English. The afternoon session was a bit of an ordeal as intelligence tests were introduced for the first time as a result of the 1944 Education Act. All these figures and numbers one had to compare and make some sense of were quite a mystery, as there had only been one prototype available to give us a clue of what was expected. This was followed by mental arithmetic and an arithmetic paper which was made up of mostly written questions which one had to understand before working out an answer. However, wonder of wonders, I passed. Even more astonishingly, I passed well enough to be eligible to enter a further examination which, if passed, would result in the award of a closed scholarship of thirty pounds if one went on to enter university.

So ended my association with Goginan School. Mr Herbert retired in 1949 and was succeeded by Miss Kate Rowlands, a lady who was native to the village. She was succeeded by a number of other ladies, one of whom was an old grammar school colleague of mine, Mrs Mary Elizabeth Thomas (nee Jones). Eventually, dwindling numbers sadly brought about the closure of the school.

How would I sum up my education at Goginan School? My first reaction is one of thankfulness. It was not entertainment but good basic learning which has served me so well right throughout my subsequent career in education. Not only did it teach me the basics of knowledge, it taught me how to learn. Having suffered the slings and arrows of so called progressive and enlightened methods of education in the late twentieth century, I am proudly old fashioned enough to believe that, without grasping the bread and butter of learning – the tables, spelling and grammar – a child is at a terrible disadvantage in later years. I don't think I knew of any child in my time at Goginan who could not read or write with beautiful handwriting.

However did we manage without calculators, computers and the new all-singing, all-dancing electronic white boards? I am not for a moment decrying these wonderful inventions; I am sure they are an invaluable aid for preparing children for the modern world, but there are such happenings as power cuts. I only wish that there was more personal communication between teacher and pupil as we had when we were children, without the intervention of a machine – we get too much of that in the home with that monster the television dominating domestic life.

Ah well! Time to get off my old-fashioned hobby horse. Thank you Miss Williams, thank you Mr Herbert and thank you Goginan School for giving me such a good start in life.

Religion in Goginan

B EFORE WE DELVE INTO the history of religious activity in the
Goginan area, it might be worthwhile to look at the changes
and developments which have occurred in the religious life of
Wales in general, and then relate such changes to those that have
developed locally over the past three hundred and fifty years or
so.

The end of the Civil War in the late 1640s led to the establishment
of a Protestant Republic under the leadership of Oliver Cromwell.
One of the first acts to be passed in 1650 was the Act for the Better
Propagation and Preaching of the Gospel. This in turn created new
schools which taught children to read and write. Unfortunately,
the teaching was through the medium of English which was of
little use to the children of Wales, who had little or no knowledge
of that language. Also, during the Civil War, Wales was almost
entirely Royalist.

With the restoration of the monarchy in 1658 a series of measures
against Nonconformist sects were passed which was collectively
known as the 'Clarendon Code'. As a result, some dissenting sects
which had formed in Wales during the Cromwellian period were
persecuted, including the Quakers in Montgomeryshire and some
Baptist sects in South Wales. Many members of these sects fled to
the New World to establish colonies there. Notable amongst these
was John Myles, who could possibly be called the originator of the
Baptist faith in Wales.

However, in 1689 the 'Glorious Revolution' came to pass with the accession of the Protestants William and Mary to the throne, ushering in an era of religious toleration both in England and Wales.

The increase in literacy saw new religious books being published in Welsh such as *Cannwyll y Cymry* (*The Welshmen's Candle*) by Bishop Pritchard and a Welsh translation of Bunyan's *Pilgrim's Progress* which, though John Bunyan himself was of the Baptist faith, was very influential on the Methodist revival of the late eighteenth century.

It was about this time that two organisations were established to increase educational opportunities. One was the Welsh Trust, which made available Welsh translations of the *Catechism*, the *Book of Psalms* and the *Book of Common Prayer*. The other was the Society for the Promotion of Christian Knowledge (SPCK) which had roughly the same aims. This society suffered initially from a shortage of teachers and the fact that teaching was through the medium of English in an overwhelmingly monoglot Welsh community.

Gruffydd Jones was a Welsh clergyman working for the SPCK. He was very dissatisfied with this situation and, with the help of a Carmarthenshire heiress and philanthropist Madam Bevan, set up circulating schools to teach elementary reading and writing skills in Welsh. The ensuing increase in literacy also had a great effect on the ensuing Methodist Revival of the late eighteenth century.

Three great figures were associated with the Methodist Revival in Wales: Hywel Harris (1714-1773), Daniel Rowland (1713-1790) and William Williams, Pantycelyn (1717-1791). Apparently, Harris and Rowland both had a religious conversion at different times in 1735 but they were not to meet until 1737 when both decided to combine their evangelistic mission. This date effectively marks the beginning of the Methodist Revival in Wales.

The catalyst of the conversion of these three great men was the work and preaching of Gruffydd Jones of Llanddowror, a small village a few miles south-west of Carmarthen. Hywel Harris was converted in Talgarth in Powys when he heard Jones preaching. He was so moved that he immediately started holding religious meetings at his home and very soon he was preaching all over Wales, often giving five sermons in one day. He was a man of passion and conviction who often caused controversy; this eventually led to a split with the other leaders of Welsh Methodism in the early 1750s. He returned to his home in Trefecca, a village near Talgarth, and established a religious community which later trained aspiring Methodist preachers.

Methodism started as a movement within the Anglican Church of England with revival as its main theme. Daniel Rowland, unlike his friend Hywel Harris, was actually made minister in the Anglican Church at Llangeitho, Cardiganshire in 1734, but he did not commit himself completely to Christ until he heard Gruffydd Jones preaching in 1735. Harris became a noted preacher and thousands came to Llangeitho from all over Wales to hear him preach. He was so successful that the Anglican authorities, alarmed at his fervour, sacked him from his position as curate. However, he had by now established a strong following, which built him a chapel not far from the church. Here he continued as one of the most influential preachers ever produced in Wales.

William Williams' reputation as a hymn writer and poet is legendary. He wrote nearly a thousand hymns during his time, many of which are well known in chapels and churches of all denominations in England and Wales and also among the followers of rugby football. His proliferation of hymns and other music earned him the nickname of 'Y Per Ganiedydd' (the sweet singer). Williams' conversion came after he heard a sermon by Hywel Harris. He too joined the Anglican Church and was ordained deacon in 1740. Later, he concentrated more on the Methodist movement and became a leading light in preaching Methodism all over Wales, at the same time selling his hymn books and supporting himself by selling goods such as tea.

Towards the end of the eighteenth century, new leaders emerged in the cause of religion in all denominations. Thomas Charles (1755-1814) made his home town of Bala a centre for Methodism in North Wales. Surely we have all heard the story of the young girl, Mari Jones, walking several miles to Bala to buy a copy of the Bible in Welsh. This act inspired Charles to establish the British and Foreign Bible Society at the beginning of the nineteenth century. He was also instrumental in taking Welsh Methodism out of the shadow of the Anglican Church in 1811 to align them with other Welsh nonconformist groups.

The Methodist Revival of the 1750s inspired other nonconformist groups to renew their activities, leading to another group of eloquent preachers such as Christmas Evans (1766-1838) of the Welsh Baptists. He was born into poverty in Llandyssul in Ceredigion and was of distinctive appearance: he had lost an eye due to a fight in his youth. However, his conversion resulted in his ordination as a Baptist minister. Like Thomas Charles, much of his mission work was carried out in North Wales. His years of travelling during his mission also earned him a nickname after that other famous Baptist minister, 'the Bunyan of Wales'.

This missionary zeal amongst the nonconformists led to a period of prolific chapel building in Wales which lasted throughout the nineteenth century. Every village had a chapel of some denomination and it was estimated that on average a chapel was being built every eight days. Since this was also a period of large scale industrialisation with increasing numbers flocking to services, these buildings were usually very large, many with galleries. The second Methodist chapel in Goginan, the Dyffryn, was erected in 1865 and is an example of this trend. It was designed so that, should the congregation increase as was anticipated at the time, there was room to erect a gallery.

This period also saw much civil unrest in Wales because

government reports portrayed the Welsh as ignorant and lacking moral standards. Such reports blamed the predominance of the Welsh language as a medium of communication, especially in the field of education. The patriotic backlash boosted nonconformity and its values. These unfavourable reports were deemed synonymous with the authority of the Anglican Church, and a census on religion in 1851 showed that Anglican worshippers were in a minority in Wales.

The large-scale development of the extractive industries like coal mining saw a rapid growth of densely-peopled communities which also encouraged the rapid growth of chapels. They became centres of culture and the tradition of choral singing dates from this period. Chapels held classes in tonic sol-fa, and since sheet music was often written in this notation, many people could join choirs. The choral tradition in Goginan was very strong throughout the nineteenth century and well into the twentieth.

Chapels encouraged the choirs partly as an attempt to keep people away from the lure of the demon drink. In an industrialised village like Goginan, intoxicating liquor presented a problem. For example, about 300 adults attended services at Dyffryn Chapel in the early 1860s but only 100 were members. Drink presented a stumbling block to full chapel membership in those days, as facilities for drinking were available 24 hours a day, seven days a week, until the Sunday Closing Act of 1881 which was considered as a nonconformist repressive measure.

We have already seen how certain elements of the national picture were reflected in the Melindŵr valley. Let us now briefly trace the specific development of the various nonconformist religions in the Goginan area.

The first traces of Methodism came to the district via a miner called William Jones from Anglesey. Around 1756 he started holding services at his home in Aberffrwd (mouth of the stream), a small village in Cwm Rheidol. The village already had a very strong religious tradition with regular meetings being held there and in Llwyniorwerth, a farm about two miles from Goginan. In 1763 Hywel Harris visited this farm as part of his mission. The religious fervour spread up the Melindŵr valley to Dollwen and further up to Nantyrarian at the head of the valley. Long before the nineteenth-century revival of the lead mines, Methodism was strong in the area thanks to the efforts of many faceless stalwarts who gave the movement a strong foundation. However, to hear sermons in a chapel, one had to travel either to Penllwyn, the next village down the valley, to Aberffrwd over the hill in Cwm Rheidol, or east for five miles to Ponterwyd. Sunday schools and prayer meetings, however, were regularly held in various houses or farms in the valley such as at Cefncoed, Penbompren, Penbryn, Troed-y-rhiw, Goginan Fawr, Goginan Fach and Blaendyffryn.

During the 1830s the population grew rapidly as the silver-lead mine increased production, so individual houses and farms became too small to contain the congregations. It was decided to find a site in Goginan where a Methodist chapel could be built. By 1843 the first one had been completed, along with a chapel house to cater for two families. The opening ceremony occurred in April 1843 with services in Welsh and in English. Why have a service in English? In the 1840s many mining families had arrived in Goginan from Cornwall and Devon, bringing the expertise and experience they had gleaned in the tin mines. Most of them were Wesleyan Methodists but since there was no suitable place for them to worship, many supported the Calvinistic cause at the new Methodist chapel.

What of the other nonconformist groups? Wesleyanism had never been the predominant religion of Wales, though John Wesley (1739-1791) made nearly fifty journeys to the country and preached at Tregaron and Cardigan in 1768. Wesley met Hywel Harris in Bristol in 1739 and was invited to come and preach in the Principality. However, Wesley decided that Wales could only

The inhabitants of the village of Goginan celebrating the Silver Jubilee of King George the Fifth. The photograph was taken in the field outside Dyffryn Methodist chapel.

An early photograph of the Methodist and Baptist chapels in Goginan. Adjacent to Jezreel chapel house (bottom left) is the small vestry which was once a small school and in 1829 became the first Jezreel chapel. Behind the house is the Pavilion. On the right is the Dyffryn, with the vestry and chapel house.

206

be reached through the medium of Welsh and left the mission to Harris and his followers.

So it was 1800 before Welsh Wesleyan Methodism took a hold in Wales through the work of Dr Thomas Coke, whose first mission circuit covered the whole country. For a short period, development was quite rapid with the publication of the first hymn book in 1802/3 and a Wesleyan Welsh periodical in 1809. However, this successful time was followed by a period of financial dire straits. In 1815 there were separate Welsh and English circuits in South Wales and a dearth of Welsh preachers, so that even to this day Wesleyan Methodism is not strong there.

In the late eighteenth century, nonconformism was strong in Aberystwyth. In 1784 the Tabernacle, a huge Calvinistic Methodist chapel (now sadly turned into a club) had been built and the Baptists had a chapel erected and opened in 1797. In 1802, the pioneers of Wesleyan Methodism, John Bryan and Owen Davies, journeyed from North Wales to Aberystwyth, preaching in various locations as they went. Here they met William Parry and a Mr Jones and held preaching services in the courtyard of the Talbot Hotel in the town. Even the town crier was involved to announce the services, which drew huge crowds.

Towards the middle of the century the religious revival swept through all denominations. In 1858 Tre'rddol (dwelling on the meadow), a small village about eleven miles north of Aberystwyth, became a great Wesleyan Revival centre; the chapel, built in 1809 and enlarged in 1845 held services during the corn harvest at five o'clock in the morning which had a capacity congregation. Now this chapel is a museum to the history of Wesleyan Methodism amongst other things.

By 1811 Wesleyan Methodism was quite well developed in Ystumtuen, a village in the hills a couple of miles south-west of Ponterwyd, with the society meeting in local cottages. By 1822 a small chapel had been built, to be replaced by a larger building in

1840. Its relative isolation meant a dearth of ministers visiting. Even here, however, the religious revival was felt and in 1859 the chapel was further enlarged.

The fervour led to two other chapels being erected, one at Aberffrwd and the other (more significantly as far as Goginan was concerned), Horeb Chapel in Cwmbrwyno. Again, it is possible that the influx of Cornish miners to Cwmbrwyno lead mine was influential in the chapel's early development, though services were conducted in Welsh for much of its existence.

In Goginan itself, the influx of tin miners had a significant impact on Wesleyan Methodism. This influx was due mainly to the fact that Lord Lisburne had leased many of his lead mines to a Cornish company which brought in workers from the south-west of England. Most of these families were of the Wesleyan Methodist faith, so a society developed here in conjunction with that of another lead mining village, Pontrhydygroes, and preachers were interchanged between the two villages. By 1842-43 this society was strong enough in Goginan to merit a meeting house. In 1861 land was leased for an English Wesleyan chapel in Goginan at Troedrhiwcastell (now a farm) at an annual rent of £1.10s a year. The erection of the chapel cost £300.

John Taylor and Son, an engineering family from the Midlands, were very influential in the development of both the Goginan and Pontrhydygroes (Lisburne) mine and were very sympathetic to the Wesleyan cause as they appreciated the part which the two chapels played in the lives of the mining families. However, with a transient population which depended very much on the fortunes of the mine, attendances fluctuated. As the mines' fortunes declined towards the end of the nineteenth century, so did the chapel in Goginan and it was closed in 1887. Some miners moved to Aberystwyth to continue their religious interests there. Others remained in Goginan where they learnt the Welsh language (very similar in many ways to Cornish) and became integrated into the activities of the other local chapels.

The third nonconformist faith prevalent in the village was that of the Baptists. The growth of this faith increased in Wales after the passing of the Act of Toleration in 1689 but it took another hundred years for there to be a rapid expansion, largely due to the eloquence of preachers such as Christmas Evans. Even so, numerically, the Baptist faith in the Aberystwyth area was relatively weak compared with the large numbers who flocked to the Calvinistic Methodist chapels. For example, the strongest Baptist chapel in Cardiganshire in 1800, Bethany in Cardigan, under an eloquent minister called John Herring, saw on average 563 people attending morning services, 353 attending Sunday School and 781 people attending the evening services, compared with 1,022 people on average attending every service at Tabernacle Methodist chapel in Aberystwyth. In the early 1800s, any additional chapels around Aberystwyth were small and scattered in distribution, though the chapel at Penrhyncoch, about four miles to the east, was an exception.

As the lead mines expanded, so did the growth of the Baptist faith in the lead mining villages such as Talybont, Cwmsymlog and Goginan. The first sermons for the Baptists in Goginan were heard in a small schoolroom owned by Thomas Jones in 1820 with one preacher, Jesse Jones, visiting from Aberystwyth and the other, John Davies, coming from Penrhyncoch. They were followed by other preachers who were part of the Baptist mission and despite some opposition, their visits were a great success. In March 1821, six people were baptised. Among these was a Mrs Jones from Troed-y-rhiw, a farm where preachers of other nonconformist faiths regularly stayed; intriguingly the family were regular Anglican churchgoers. Also baptised were her son, HW Jones, who later became a Baptist minister, the housewife at Goginan Fach farm, a maid at Nantyrarian farm and Thomas Jones, a lead miner.

There is an interesting story as to how HW Jones became a Baptist. The Methodists in Goginan had scheduled a rather cantankerous old man called William Goodman to preach, but since he was not very popular with the congregation and his religious views did not sit comfortably with the Methodist faith, a replacement had been found. So Goodman went to Troed-y-rhiw to stay the night, where he got into a furious argument with HW Jones on the merits of baptism. Apparently, Goodman won every argument and the two parted on rather bad terms. However, as time went on, Jones became increasingly disturbed by Goodman's argument and was eventually converted and baptised.

When Thomas Jones eventually left the area, the little schoolroom was converted into a permanent house of God with services every Sunday and a prayer meeting during the week there, as well as at various houses in the district. A Sunday School was also established.

In 1829, a strong wind blew off the roof of the small chapel, a source of great sorrow to the community. The building was nearly abandoned, but with the help and encouragement of the chapel at Aberystwyth and many friends in the neighbourhood they persevered until it was repaired. While repairs were ongoing, services continued at various farms like Troedrhiwcastell, Troed-y-rhiw, Nantyrarian and even at the Mill on the eastern extremity of the valley. Here, John Jenkins, a member of the established Anglican Church, opened his house to the Baptists.

The chapel reopened, but its success was short lived, for there followed a lean period when many left the church and others moved away. WH Jones himself, a stalwart of the small congregation, left to attend Bradford College leaving only two members of the congregation able to pray in public. By 1834 this was reduced to one and, in desperation, Mrs Jones of Troed-y-rhiw pleaded with her other son to come and read at the services, even though he was not a member. Services therefore consisted of two readings and two prayers. This rather unsatisfactory situation persisted until a Reverend Simon James took over the ministry at Penrhyncoch. By his hard work and encouraging sermons, he managed to revive the spirits of the little church in Goginan. Many returned to the chapel and many were baptised.

During the 1830s and 1840s the lead mine developed and so too, in keeping with the other chapels in the village, did the congregation at the Baptist church. Eventually, the size of the congregation exceeded the capacity of the little chapel and plans were made for a larger building. A stone high up on its front wall indicated that this larger chapel was built in 1842. (Another stone marked 1829 is obviously a commemorative reference to the earlier chapel.)

Finances must have been at a premium during this period as the following notice was circulated to members of the congregation and others seven years later:

The Case of Jezreel Baptist Chapel at Goginan near Aberystwyth.

This commodious Meeting House has been built on a piece of ground granted us upon a lease by Pryse Pryse Esq. MP of Gogerddan; and it measures 38 feet by 32 feet. After all we have been able to raise among ourselves, there still remains a debt of £300.00 on the chapel, which presses very heavily upon us. In order to clear this sum, we are constrained to solicit the aid of the religious public, and we hope that this appeal will not be made in vain.

Signed

William Owens   John Mason
Lewis Thomas   John Thomas
Deacons
Sept. 1849

Another interesting little titbit I gleaned was:

Agreement between Jezreel and Cwmsymlog Chapels, and David Jenkins, Pastor:

Salary of £2.15s.0p a month between the two churches

Three months' notice both ways

Dated 23rd November 1850

Attendance figures in all three chapels reflected the great spiritual fervour that swept the whole of Wales in the 1840s and early 1850s. Jezreel chapel's membership increased from 39 in 1846 to 160 in 1859 when 36 people were baptised and several people were re-admitted to church membership. The figures fluctuated during the 1860s, probably reflecting the economic fortunes of the mine, and by 1871 there were 117 members.

Similar fluctuations were seen in attendances at the Dyffryn Methodist Chapel. The Revival of the mid-1850s saw a rapid increase in membership and in 1859 a new leasing agreement was agreed with Gogerddan Estate that owned Blaendyffryn farmland and the chapel land, to extend the area to cater for a bigger cemetery and provide a site for a larger chapel. By the end of 1863 the new chapel was completed using local timber, stones from a quarry on Blaendyffryn land and corner stones from a quarry at Cwmbrwyno. Much of the labour was carried out voluntarily by members and £527 was collected towards the expense.

Following the opening of the new chapel, attendance figures soared and for a time every pew was taken – as were the benches provided for families who could not afford pew rental. However, the expansion was short lived. The building of Wesleyan chapels at Cwmbrwyno and Troedrhiwcastell as well the erection of a new Methodist chapel in 1866 in Cwmerfin to the north resulted in a drop in attendances at the Dyffryn. Then from the 1870s onward

Jezreel chapel in the 1950s.

the lead mine's profits fell, leading to a further decline in numbers.

Despite the fluctuations, the Sunday School was a feature that flourished almost continuously in the chapels throughout the latter part of the nineteenth century and for most of the twentieth.

Attendance at Jezreel Sunday School hovered around 100 members each Sunday during the 1860s and 1870s. However, by 1885 the average attendance had dropped to 33.

Similarly, the Sunday School at the Dyffryn helped to maintain the membership of the chapel more than any other organisation. As the lead mine flourished in the mid-1850s, Sunday schools became great venues for serious spiritual debate. Discussions raised during these sessions would be continued in the workplace during the ensuing week. Deep underground in the levels of the mine, brisk debates would occur on the merits of the various denominations; these in turn would encourage miners to do more research by reading widely and joining the book clubs which were run at the Druid Inn. This thirst for knowledge continued throughout the twentieth century and many illustrious scholars joined various professions from these schools, notably W Ambrose Bebb and Gordon Matthias from the Dyffryn. Ambrose Bebb distinguished himself in the field of education in the University of Wales, Bangor, while Gordon Matthias reached the top of his profession as a consultant in Harley Street, London. Many became teachers and lecturers, while others became very successful ministers of religion, notably the late Reverend Byron Howells and the Reverend Evan Mason Davies.

In 1871, St Matthew's Anglican Church was erected and opened on the eastern outskirts of the village as a sister church to Llan Bangor (Bangor church) in Capel Bangor. Unfortunately, despite many efforts, I have been unsuccessful in obtaining any information on the history of the church. One can only surmise that enough people of the Anglican faith came to live in Goginan to justify the building of the church. Even though a minority of the village population were Anglican churchgoers, St Matthew's continued to provide services every Sunday for over a century. In the latter years the little community held its services every Sunday afternoon, mainly thanks to the efforts of Mrs Iris Richards (nee Boon).

On sunny Sunday afternoons in my childhood, my grandfather used to take me for walks through the woods near the Royal Oak. I still remember the warm feeling of good-will I used to have – don't ask me why – when, at about half-past two the sound of St Matthew's bell used to echo faintly across the valley. Then, in common with the other places of worship in the village, numbers dwindled. to such an extent that it became no longer viable to continue. Now the building is crumbling with most of its windows smashed by vandals.

Undoubtedly, the religious revival of 1904 led by Evan Roberts must have had an influence on chapel attendances for a short period as this revolution, unlike earlier ones, was much publicised in the newspapers and political leaders like David Lloyd George were much affected by its fervour. However, by the middle of 1905 the fervour had largely died down and all places of worship in the village reverted to the gradual decline in attendances which continued throughout the twentieth century. What caused this sad trend? In the nineteenth century we saw that economic forces were largely responsible for the fluctuations in attendances. To a certain extent it was the changes in economic factors that also influenced material and social factors in the twentieth century. The two world wars, especially the second, led to a great social change in human behaviour. As people became emancipated in their perceptions of the world at large, so their ties to the immediate locality and their places of religion were loosened. This was furthered by developments in transport, which gave access to alternative attractions on a Sunday.

I think one of the underlying feelings some of us youngsters had during the late thirties and forties was one of entrapment on Sundays. The theme seemed to be 'Thou shall not...' In many ways this rather repressive feeling did not manifest itself when we were children and the ritual of attending chapel three times every Sunday was a way of life. But as the hormones became more dominant, there was a desire to get away to the wide world beyond. Thus in our youth it became very tempting to skip the evening service in summer and pedal our way down to the excitement of the promenade at Aberystwyth. Many young people moved away either to find employment farther afield or to get married. In consequence the average age of chapel goers rose, with the middle aged and elderly increasingly keeping the establishments alive.

The growth of materialism was another factor which overshadowed the image of God for increasing numbers of people. Whatever the reasons, all the places of worship in the village now present a very sad picture.

Jezreel sadly ran out of people as the stalwart worshippers one by one passed away or grew too old and infirm to attend services. The severe gales of October 1987 blew off part of the roof – an echo of the first chapel in the 1820s. Then there were people to repair the damage; this time there was no one. The building gradually deteriorated despite spurious promises to restore it for other purposes. Most of the pews were removed; fortunately the beautiful pulpit was moved to the chapel at Penrhyncoch and the Mason and Gamlin American organ which my mother played for so many years found a home in what was then the vestry of the Dyffryn across the lane. I went to the cemetery recently to visit my mother's grave and was thankful to see that at least the grounds and graves were being attended to, thanks mainly to the efforts of the Reverend Evan Mason Davies. But, on glancing through the broken windows, I was shocked to see the chapel occupied by a herd of cattle amongst all the rubbish that had accumulated.

Unfortunately, a similar fate has befallen the Dyffryn Methodist Chapel recently, where once again looking through the broken windows I noted that the building had been stripped of its furniture and even the floor had been removed. Thank God, the flame of worship has not been completely extinguished, as about fifteen worshippers under the leadership of Gareth Jones, his wife Mair and John Roberts of Penbryn farm continue to hold services. Here again there seems to be the completion of a cycle, as what used to be the original chapel in 1843 became the vestry of the chapel built in 1865, but has now reverted to its original function.

What I find even more distressing is that these three buildings, once the spiritual and social centres of Goginan, are being allowed to disintegrate slowly in an undignified fashion due largely to legal wrangling by bureaucratic authorities as to what, legally, should be done with them. For nearly two centuries these were the focal centres of the village and surely deserve a more dignified fate.

So how does one remember Dyffryn, Jezreel, St Matthew's and the two Wesleyan chapels, Troedrhiwcastell and Horeb in Cwmbrwyno? What made the people of the valley attend these buildings regularly every Sunday for generations? Was it purely religious fervour fired up by the evangelistic missionaries who periodically brought religion to the fore, or was there a personal, deeper need within people brought on by the harshness of the way they lived to find some form of salvation?

Personally, I believe it was a combination of all these factors. I am sure the exploitation of the miners in the nineteenth century at the hands of the owners made them feel that their very being was at the mercy of others, so much so that it was vital to grasp at any moral framework or discipline which would help them endure the type of life they were forced to live. So chapel and church offered them a way out of their miserable life towards eternal salvation.

But then, who guided and controlled them at these places of worship? It was the very people who controlled them during their hours of labour: the owners and captains, who by dint of their position and wealth in society, automatically assumed spiritual control by being elected elders of the places of worship. The fear was the threat of fire and brimstone to anyone who transgressed, a threat which the illiterate pieces of fodder would take very seriously. Even so, the promise of eventual freedom and salvation, despite being clothed in such ominous terms would, as in the case of slaves of an earlier time, offer some hope. Then came the revivals, which, by their very fervour would transport people out from their humdrum lives onto a higher plane of ecstasy. There is no doubt that many people were enlightened and transformed during this period and life took on a new meaning.

I was intrigued to hear my friend Evan Mason Davies referring to 'churchianity' as opposed to Christianity. The more I ponder on this word, the more I perceive its significance. I often wonder how much the physical ritual of attending the building every Sunday became more important than any spiritual benefit one would glean by such an exercise. The very process of dressing in our 'Sunday clothes' and the Pharisee doctrine of 'not doing things' on Sunday became so much more important than the true meaning of our faith.

Whatever it was, it was a way of life which I for one am so glad I went through, in that it gave me set parameters of human behaviour. Whenever I transgress these, my conscience lets me know. I thanked Goginan School for my basic education; I can certainly be thankful to Jezreel Baptist Chapel for a basic spiritual framework to my subsequent life.

CHAPTER THIRTEEN

Goginan at War

THE DAY WAR STARTED was a great disappointment to me. It was Sunday, 3 September 1939, a beautiful sunny day. Obviously something dramatic was happening as we didn't go to chapel that morning. But my excitement knew no bounds when I fiddled with the knobs of our Cossor wireless and heard Mr Chamberlain, the Prime Minister, tell me that we were at war with Germany. I was the first one in the village, probably in the county, to glean that momentous knowledge! I rushed over to my uncle John's house bursting with self-importance to enlighten him on the situation, only to be told to shut up and not to bother him because he was listening to the news that we were at war with Germany. It was a very deflating experience, I can tell you.

In the ensuing months very little seemed to be happening down our way as far as the war was concerned. In fact our relatively remote position meant that the real horrors of war did not reach us. Though a huge boulder had been thrown into the world pool, we seemed to be affected only by the smaller ripples. It was rather like being in the relatively calm eye of a storm while the thunderous clouds circled round on the horizon.

The ripples took many forms. One of the first caused excitement and some annoyance: having to find black materials to cover the windows after dark. Our old windows were not quite square, so attempts to make wooden frames to hold the blackout material proved very frustrating. Any small chink of light would result in a shout of "Put that light out!" or something stronger from officials appointed for such a task. Eventually, my mother had to succumb to using drawing pins stuck into the frames to keep the stuff in place.

Tom Evans, Claylands and Eben Richards, Hafodau were our first Air Raid Patrols or Wardens. Every evening as it got dark, one or the other would patrol the lanes of the village wearing a navy-blue boiler suit and a gas mask on their backs, and a black tin hat with a big white 'W' on the front to distinguish them as somebody important. How I envied the khaki satchels which held their military-type gas masks, compared with our rotten cardboard boxes with string to put them round our necks!

Tom was a tall, slender man with fair hair. He lived in a house on the main road with his wife and two children and also his wife's brother William David Bradshaw, who was a deaf-mute

Ioan Bebb's aircraft when it landed on Disgwylfa in the 1930s. In the photograph are my grandmother, Annie Evans, the Druid Inn, on the left; in the centre is Mrs Benjamin, Tanyrochr with her granddaughter Morfudd standing in front of her; while on the right is Mrs Margaret Evans (Maggie Bradshaw), Claylands with her daughter Valmai in front.

but quite a mischievous character. Tragedy hit the family when their son Randall, a rear air gunner in the Royal Air Force, was killed when his aircraft was shot down over Germany; he was one of two service personnel from the village to die. The other was a notable and very successful businessman who had close connections with Goginan where his relative, Llewelyn Bebb, owned the largest farm in the locality. His name was Ioan Bebb. Before World War II, I have vivid recollections of his visits to Goginan in his aeroplane, in which he gave aerobatic displays to entertain the inhabitants of the valley. The moment the sound of his aircraft was heard, every chore was forgotten and all rushed into the open air to marvel at his skills as he looped the loop and flew very low over the valley – everyone except my mother, who was forbidden to leave the living room where I would be hiding under the table! During the war, Ioan used his skills as an aviator in the service of his country as a test pilot and it was during one of these test flights that he was tragically killed.

The few cars in the village also took on the livery of war by having masks with horizontal slits fitted on to their headlamps to reduce the light emitted and having white flashes painted on the mudguards to make them more visible at night. The local buses had similar treatment and their inside lights were turned to a cold blue and were hooded.

Another early event was the distribution of gas masks to all and sundry, which I think brought home with a shudder the reality of what might happen even in Goginan. We were all summoned to the village school where, under the supervision of local bobby PC Jones, we were lined up and fitted with a gas mask – a rather unpleasant ordeal. I still remember the claustrophobic feeling and the musty, rubbery smell as the contraption closed in on my head and the feeling of isolation as one looked out at the world through the cellophane-like eye piece, ever conscious of one's heavy breathing. I remember the strict instruction of how to put it on: 'Put your chin in first before pulling the straps over your head'. My box was marked 'S' for small; smaller children had masks with a Mickey Mouse face on them to make them a little less hideous. Babies were put into gas-proof containers – it must have been a very frightening experience for them. Thank goodness there was never any call to use them, though they had to be updated periodically with a bright, metallic green charcoal nozzle.

Then came identity cards. I am not sure when these were first introduced but I think we all had them, though possibly children's names were added to their mother's card to start with. They were a light blue colour and called National Registration Identity Card. Inside was our name, address and a number. My mother's number was ZHDC 71:1 and I think mine was ZHDC 71:2. It being wartime, these cards were accepted by nearly all as an essential security measure, though I never recollect any of us being asked to produce them.

Food provision in those early days was not a great problem, though rationing began in earnest early in 1940. Being in the country, many of the essentials were produced on local farms; I remember some farmers used to sell all their butter and survive on the small supply of margarine issued on the ration books! I believe one or two milk suppliers were brought to book for diluting their milk supplies. However as the war progressed, food supplies became more of a problem. Luckily for me, my needs were very simple as I turned up my nose at most food. Apart from the aforementioned American cereal called 'Force', I enjoyed eating any form of potato, especially boiled potatoes made into a mush with milk. To eke out supplies a concoction called 'tea soup' – milk and tea with sugar, a little butter and pieces of bread – went down very well.

During those days, John Davies the shopkeeper, Richard Mason the butcher and Jack Saycell the milkman increased in stature as our source of sustenance relied very heavily on these august gentlemen. I think meat provision proved to be the greatest problem. Very often my mother would look askance at the little lump of grizzle of varying colours (sometimes with a slight tinge of green) purporting to have had its origins in some creature or other. But she managed to produce a Sunday dinner largely dominated by vegetables from our garden.

As time went by there was a great reliance on tinned food imported from North America. I don't think people would have survived without the tins and packets of dried egg they could purchase from Mr Davies at the shop. The waxed, light brown cardboard boxes had pictures of the American Eagle and the Stars and Stripes in blue I believe, and held the equivalent of a dozen eggs; I think we were allowed one box per family per week. For mothers, vanilla essence became a Godsend. Desserts became very difficult to make unless the ingredients involved only local produce, though the occasional tin of pears, peaches or even pineapples could be found if one was lucky. It was a wonder what delicacies could be concocted using vanilla flavouring. Parsnips could magically appear on the tea table as a delectable banana-flavoured sweet! When my father returned from London in 1942 he became a whizz-kid at creating meals out of almost nothing. I always remember how he produced a sumptuous evening meal using as its base a tin of Campbell's vegetable soup, completing the table decor with a single rose in a jar. He also became very useful with his shotgun, regularly producing rabbits for a pie or trout from the Melindŵr stream for an evening meal.

Most households had an adequate supply of potatoes as local farmers would allocate one or two rows in their field to each family in return for assistance with the harvesting. Potato planting days were exciting. Each family would start out in the morning, complete with Wellington boots, buckets and the ever important tea flask and lunch, and trek down to the field where they would find their allotted rows already manured. Then, under the fatherly eye of the farmer, came happy hours spent between planting the seed potatoes about eighteen inches apart and, more importantly, gossiping with the planters of the next rows – being a village there was usually plenty to gossip about. Lunch time was a big occasion when everyone sat on upturned buckets covered with sacks and shared whatever was available. The afternoon session would end after the last potato was planted. Then came the almost sacred period when the farmer with his horses and plough would cover the seed and one could almost feel the silent prayers going up for fair weather and a good crop in the autumn.

Summer would be 'pay up' time when the more able of the village ladies (most men were away in the forces) would assemble complete with pitchforks to toss the hay for quicker drying. The stronger folk would then hoist it on to the carts for transport to the farm's hay sheds. We children would play a spoiling game by surreptitiously clambering onto the top of the cart and sliding down, bringing much of the hay with us. Even so we were given the thrill of riding on top of the hay back to the farm. Autumn would bring a repeat of spring's proceedings when the potatoes were harvested and the sacks would subsequently be delivered to the homes by the farmer. The coalition government introduced 'the potato week' in spring and autumn, when schools closed so that children could help with the potato harvest.

Despite the worry and deprivation these were also good times, in that people talked and helped each other, giving the village community a vibrant quality. Whenever those on active service returned home on leave, they would be given 'welcome home' concerts in the vestry of the Methodist church. Much to their embarrassment, they were made to sit on the small stage while the villagers entertained them with song and verse. The highlights of these evenings were the tea that was provided and the presentation of some article of clothing – scarves, socks, balaclavas or gloves – which the ladies of the village would knit in the colours of the various services: khaki for the army, navy blue for the navy and air force blue. The chapels also arranged weekly or fortnightly cultural societies of readings and story-telling organised by the various ministers, which would help pass the dark nights of winter.

Despite our peripheral position well away from the main theatre of war, the government did its best to keep up morale through the Ministry of Information. This body would arrive, especially in the twilight of summer evenings, complete with screen and movie camera and would show very heartening films in the school playground about the conduct of the war. These were particularly exciting evenings for residents of a village without electricity for whom going to the cinema was a rare occurrence.

We also felt we had some part to play in helping the war effort by collecting sundry items which were deemed of use. Every Saturday my friend Danny and myself were designated to collect waste paper from households in the village. It was rather a dismal chore as a lot of shoe leather was wasted in gathering a very puny amount. However, on a certain Saturday our trek took us to Troed y Rhiw, a very old farm. In answer to our request, farmer Dilwyn Griffiths directed our footsteps towards the old barn where he told us that there was a stack of old books, papers and magazines which he would be glad to get rid of. We climbed the ladder to the loft and... wow! We were greeted by stacks of books and magazines extending across the entire floor to a depth of about two feet. We were in a paper heaven. No more trudging the paths and lanes; all we had to do was to sit on our bottoms and rip away. We were sure this would solve most of the country's paper shortage. For several weekends we sat there merrily ripping away and filling our sacks, but at the cost of subsequent feelings of guilt and regret at the loss of what were probably valuable old tomes worth thousands of pounds today.

We were occasionally asked to bring bundles of old clothes for collection at the school, in return for which we were given little toys such as aeroplanes made of balsa wood which could be made to fly using rubber bands.

Then there was the Home Guard. Since most of our able-bodied young men were called up to serve in the forces, the threat of invasion in the summer of 1940 necessitated that middle aged and older able-bodied men were required to enlist as Local Defence Volunteers. I well remember the first recruitment meeting of these elderly personnel. They were required to bring with them any weapon or tool that could be of use in thwarting an enemy advance. They were all issued with the only piece of uniform available at that stage, a khaki armband with the letters 'LDV' printed on it. It was a motley crew; most of them were in working clothes, cloth cap or trilby hat and overalls, carrying an interesting variety of 'weapons'. One or two had double-barrelled shotguns but most were armed with walking sticks, umbrellas or pick axe handles; some of the agricultural fraternity came armed with hoes while the more aggressive types brought pitchforks, some still caked with manure!

When Adolf Hitler heard that Britain was preparing to repel the German invasion by forming a Home Guard, it was said he flew into a rage and vowed that this 'murder squad', as he called it, would be wiped out. He might not have been so alarmed had he been able to catch sight of the Goginan LDV at that time. However, there was no doubt that these people would have given their lives in the line of duty, even at that stage.

Slowly and steadily the group became more recognisable as a fighting force, with the arm bands replaced by proper khaki uniforms, weapons and ammunition. When my father returned from London in 1942 he joined the local branch of the Home Guard. Every weekend after parade he would come home, place his gun behind the back room door and hang his webbing pouches containing live bullets, creams against mustard gas and other interesting items on a hook nearby. At the age of ten I would inspect all this paraphernalia closely. What the present Health and Safety legislation would make of that, I dare not guess.

Sunday afternoon was the time for major military operations in Goginan. These would take several forms, such as parade duties of marching, or sloping and ordering arms. There were also manoeuvres in the local woods or in the disused silver-lead mines that dotted the locality. On certain Sundays things got really serious when they were taken to a firing range with all the local top brass present. On the 'home' parades on the main road in the village there would be a regular uniform and weapons inspection when all brasses had to be shiny and boots well cleaned. Most of the troop took this task quite seriously, though not all!

I remember a fellow called 'John bach' – little John – though being only five foot nothing there was no comparison with his namesake in Robin Hood. Regulations meant nothing to him, though it was possible he did not understand them as I don't think he was very high in the intellectual stakes. He was a farm labourer and his boots usually bore all the markings of the farmyard. He always wore his cap at right angles to the regulation position and his marching resembled trekking over a ploughed field. However, he somehow survived without taking his responsibilities too seriously.

The man in charge of this group was a World War I sergeant

called Gordon Armitage, a well-built man of medium height with a completely bald head and a face that commanded some respect. His only drawback was that he had a pronounced stutter. One Sunday afternoon, Sergeant Armitage was putting his platoon through their paces by marching and countermarching them up and down the village's main road, which consists of a straight stretch about two hundred yards bounded at both ends by a right-angled bend. As the troop was approaching one of these bends, the sergeant decided to change his usual command of 'About turn'to 'Halt' to give the lads a break. When the troop was about ten yards from the bend he started to give his command with a stuttering "H – H – H – H". He quickly changed it to "S-S-Stop, you buggers!"

One afternoon we were very alarmed when my father arrived home with his face covered in blood. Apparently, they had been on hand grenade practice in one of the disused lead mines One of the troop (retained largely because he was a farmer – a reserved occupation – and could get some useful petrol for transporting people around) was being given instruction in using the hand grenade. He got through the first two bits of instruction: "Pin out! Take aim!" but then he completely lost it! "What do I do now?" he calmly asked. Everybody else was petrified – as one would be if someone was holding a live grenade. "Throw the bloody thing!" the sergeant in charge shouted as everybody took a dive to the floor. So John very nonchalantly lobbed the grenade underarm and that it landed about four feet away in soft sand. Hence my father's blood-spattered face.

It was a lovely Sunday afternoon when the manoeuvres task was to approach a certain area of the local woodland where there were some 'enemy' soldiers hiding, without being detected. To help them locate the position a blanket or sheet had been fixed on to the branches of a nearby tree. Two members of the troop

– I shall call them Bill and Dai – got to the position quickly. After a cursory look around and seeing nobody, they decided to have a rest and a smoke. They sat down under a tree resting their backs against the trunk, enjoying the cool shade.

"Dai," said Bill, "is it raining?"

"Don't be stupid," replied Dai, "Look, the bloody sun is shining."

Dai looked at his wet cigarette, squinted up through the leaves at the blue sky and perceived the 'enemy' up on a branch above him having a pee, with the added quip of: "Yoo hoo, you're dead!"

Ah, the fortunes of war!

Also about this time, the parade ground was disrupted by the addition of sand-banked barriers near the bends on each end of the road to prevent any enemy vehicles travelling at speed through the village.

Whatever we think of the Home Guard and despite how they are shown in *Dad's Army* on television, they were quite an impressive force. Had they been needed, they would have been an effective deterrent in a time of invasion. They were eventually disbanded in 1944.

Another enterprise, which I believe was organised by a Baptist minister, the Reverend David ap Morgan, in the early days of the war, was the First Aid group which held weekly meetings at the village school. I managed to obtain a photograph of this august body and it is pleasing that villagers from all walks of life learned how to save lives. It is also encouraging to note in the photograph a shield, which I presume meant that the group had distinguished itself with its efficiency. Most of the people involved were well-known inhabitants of the village, and since the group was formed early on in the war, many of the young men in the photograph had yet to be called up to serve in the forces.

Since I was acquainted with most of them, I thought it would be a good idea to include their names

Back row from left: *my cousin Leslie Prosser Davies before he joined the Royal Air Force; my aunt Lill (I didn't know she had such talent); Tommy 'Bach' Lewis; Maggie Williams (Lizzie Williams the teacher's sister); Dei John Thomas, Queen Street (before he joined the army); Gladys Morgan (D ap Morgan's niece); Fanw Leonard Davies (now MacLean), who worked in the top shop.*

Front row: *unknown to me; Eben Pryse, Llwyndel; Alun Howells, Eagle House who used to work for the Automobile Association; Llewelyn B Bebb, Blaendyffryn; D ap Morgan; PC Jones, the village bobby.*

I strongly believe that we had a German spy in the village. Around 1940, when I was nine, a strange lady came to take up the parlour of my grandparents' house, the Royal Oak. She kept herself to herself and I only knew that she was still around because empty tins of pineapples appeared in the rubbish dump on the other side of the stream. She wasn't Welsh or even English so I thought she must be a German spy. To add to my suspicions, on certain dark nights when the German bombers came over, little lights would flash in the trees behind the Royal Oak. But no one took the matter up and eventually she disappeared. She might have been caught and shot but nobody informed me of her fate.

In 1940 a group of evacuees, accompanied by two teachers from Anfield, Liverpool. arrived at the school for distribution amongst village families. Their average age was around eight or nine. They looked lost and frightened, each one with his or her blue and orange tab and a label with their names and addresses. Each had a small case or a brown paper bundle tied up with string containing all their belongings. It must have been a frightening experience to be gawped at by village kids and looked over by prospective adult strangers who spoke an alien language. They were all allocated singly, or in pairs if they were of the same family. The only one left over was Billy Tunstall, not because he looked different but because he was twelve years old. His two brothers and sister had already been allocated but no one seemed happy to accept an older child. Eventually my grandmother and aunt Mary agreed to take him in at the Druid Inn.

Most of the children gradually adapted to this alien environment; many had never seen green fields or animals before. They were soon assimilated into village life and entered into the corporate spirit. Many of them had lovely singing voices and came to my mother to rehearse for the 'welcome home' concerts. One little boy, I think his name was Colin Woolley, could hardly speak on account of his terrible stutter but once he started singing with his golden voice, the stutter disappeard completely.

Most of the evacuees eventually returned to their homes but Billy, who had seven siblings, decided to stay on and settled permanently in the area. He was apprenticed by my uncle Harry Ashley-Jones as a hairdresser, got married and established a hairdressing business with his wife in Aberystwyth. He served on the town council and became quite a prominent member of the establishment. He spoke Welsh fluently and was considered quite a character in the town, with the gift of the gab and a liking for beer! Just before he died, we were reminiscing about the early days when he first arrived as a boy in Goginan, and he told me a very amusing anecdote. Next door to the Druid Inn at that time was the Methodist Manse occupied, I think, by the Reverend Iorwerth Edwards. He and his wife had taken in Kenneth Joyce, a young lad with snow white hair. It was tea time and Billy was enjoying some food which he rarely got at home. There was a sudden commotion outside and they all rushed out to see what was going on. There was little Kenneth up in the apple tree pelting the minister below with apples.

"Come down, Kenneth, my boy!" called the Reverend in his best ministerial voice.

"F★★★ off!" was the reply from the tree.

It took quite a time to persuade Kenneth to relinquish his position. Eventually he re-entered the house but never settled down in the strange environment and had to be taken back to Liverpool.

Many years later, Billy visited his home district in Liverpool and went to his local to try and relocate some of his boyhood acquaintances. During his conversation with the barman, he mentioned the name of Kenneth Joyce and was very surprised when the barman pointed to a man with very fair hair sitting nearby reading a newspaper. Billy introduced himself and they had a pleasant conversation reminiscing about those early war days. Then the conversation drifted to their current life and occupations, which apparently went something like this:

"What are you doing now, Kenneth?"

"Oh, I'm working in Manchester at the moment. I'm just home for a few days' rest."

"Work going well?"

"Oh I can't complain, up and down, you know. I'm working nights."

"What do you do?"

"I'm a burglar!"

Even Billy had no answer to that one.

No bombs were dropped anywhere in the vicinity of the village, though we would hear enemy planes which we claimed to recognise by the irregular throb of their engines, pass over on their way to Belfast and Northern Ireland at night. One stir of excitement occurred when a German plane, probably being chased, dropped a stick of three bombs close to the village of Dol-y-bont, near Borth. Everyone who could, travelled to the site to marvel at the three craters.

I should have witnessed what was probably the only dog fight that occurred over the Goginan area. It was a lovely summer's early evening, probably in 1941, when it occurred. However, I was not at all interested, because someone had managed to get Danny and me a packet of five Woodbine cigarettes and some matches. We wended our way up past the field where the sheep mart was regularly held on certain Wednesdays and did not stop until we were about two miles into the hills, safely away from any prying eyes. There we lit the precious weeds which resulted in a ferocious wave of coughing and watery eyes. It would have been so much better to have watched the dog fight.

As the war progressed things seemed to ease off, even though rationing was still very much in evidence. When I was admitted to Ardwyn Grammar School in Aberystwyth, my mother had to use some very scarce and valuable clothing coupons to get me the full uniform that the school insisted on, despite the shortages of war. Hard though it was, on reflection I think that this was a very good policy as it gave the school a status to which all had to aspire.

In 1942 the Americans joined the war in Europe and we had to get used to the Yanks with their smooth uniforms and plentiful dollars walking our streets, though we did not see too many of them in Goginan. Nevertheless we had to learn a new language dominated by 'Any gum, chum?' Whenever convoys of American army lorries came through the village, we were out in force cadging anything we could from the troops. I remember these convoys increasing in number sometime towards 1944 and on one occasion as D-Day approached, it took a convoy all day and well into the night to pass through. It stopped for lunch, and those troops who were lucky to park in the village were entertained to a Welsh lunch by the mums and dads whose children were serving elsewhere in the armed forces – and we children got our fill of candy and gum. At about the same time, hundreds of American bombers came over from the west, at times filling the sky. It was a very exciting time, filling everyone with anticipation that something big was about to happen.

The end of the war was greeted with great jubilation which culminated in a party and a huge bonfire on top of the *Castell* – the old iron age hill fort overlooking the village. This was probably the first time a party had been held there since the fort dwellers themselves had cultural meetings in their enclosures. I am sure a few ancient ghosts were disturbed that evening; they wouldn't have been too pleased with the songs emanating from inebriated mouths, which would have made them sigh as they remembered the dulcet tones of their harps and pipes!

CHAPTER FOURTEEN

Post-War Culture in Goginan

IMMEDIATELY AFTER WORLD WAR II ended, there seemed to be a sort of social and cultural revival which permeated life. This is not to say that social life was stagnant during the war. I have mentioned the 'welcome home' concerts, the cultural meetings, the eisteddfod in Jezreel Pavilion and the village choir, all of which continued throughout wartime. However, with the return of the younger folk there seemed to be a sort of renaissance in community life and people wanted to join in various activities.

Football had been a favourite pastime for many generations; even during the war there was the occasional soccer match between Goginan and arch-rivals Ponterwyd, often during the Christmas holiday season. I remember one of these encounters taking place when I was a young boy. A neutral venue in Cwmbrwyno was decided upon. Unfortunately, there was a dearth of level land there and the chosen field had a gradient of about one-in-ten. During the first half one side kicked down-slope while their opponents had to climb a hill to get anywhere near the goal. Much of the time was spent in retrieving the ball from the bottom of the slope – a distance of about one hundred yards. I think Goginan won the toss and chose to play down-slope for the first half; by halftime they were winning about ten–nil. By the second half the poor Ponterwyd players were so exhausted that, though they managed to score about half a dozen goals, they did not have enough energy left to make up the deficit. It was rather a rough match and it ended in a bad-tempered fashion with Dai Pen-wal being pummelled by a Ponterwyd player who was kneeling on his chest. It's funny how little incidents like that stick in one's mind.

Football of some sort has been played in the locality for many centuries, and I am grateful to Mr Gwyn Jenkins (now of Talybont) for allowing me to peruse his book, *The History of the Aberystwyth and District Football League, 1934 to 1984* in order to glean some information on the part Goginan played in the league.

According to Mr Jenkins, an organised form of the sport dates from the 1870s. However, it was in 1934 that a real fervour for the game was engendered when the Aberystwyth and District Football League was formed. It ceased for the duration of World War II but was reformed in 1946-47 with a renewed post-war enthusiasm. However, this was not a very successful season as the executives were faced with many administrative and practical problems, not helped by the atrocious weather conditions early in 1947 when all matches had to be cancelled due to prolonged snowfalls. It was also difficult for teams to organise equipment and pitches in the dire post-war economic conditions.

The 1947-48 season saw a real renaissance with eighteen teams entering the league, making it necessary to have two divisions. The first division was made up of established teams, mainly from Aberystwyth, while the nine new village teams formed the second.

It was about this time that a committee was formed in Goginan to see if the village could muster enough young (or not so young) players to form a viable team. I can't remember who the chairman of the inaugural committee was, but my great uncle John Hughes was the natural choice to become secretary and I had the privilege of working closely with him.

First on the agenda was the matter of finance. To set the ball rolling, my mother and I organised a variety concert in Dyffryn Chapel vestry to raise funds. I thought the posters, which I designed with my fair hands, were revolutionary in that they were drawn in colour on a background depicting a huge football. By today's standards they were 'crap', but they succeeded in bringing a large and enthusiastic crowd, helping to set Goginan United on a fairly firm financial footing.

The next deliberation was the choice of equipment. My father had taken me to London for a holiday and I was lucky enough to the see Arsenal play at Highbury. In my fanciful dreams, I could envisage Goginan United decked out in their red shirts with white sleeves, royal-blue stockings and white shorts. However, I found our relatively meagre finances would not stretch to such an elaborate kit, so it was decided to have red and white quarters on the shirts and that the players should provide their own shorts and stockings.

Then came the need for an adequate pitch; we were initially fortunate in acquiring a field by the River Melindŵr from Dilwyn Griffiths of Troed-y-rhiw farm. The first goal posts were furnished by my grandfather and he undertook to put up the nets before each home match.

The initial team was composed almost entirely of locals and had a number of talented young men. In goal was Tommy Bray; he was a bus driver but managed to work his schedules so that he would be free every Saturday afternoon. He was only about five foot six or seven tall, but once he had divested himself of his dentures he became quite an acrobat in goal. He was a bit of an enigma in that he used to miss the simplest shots but would make up for it by saving the most difficult ones by hurling himself bodily across the goal.

The team was fortunate in having Glyn Williams as centre-forward; his quick-silver feet would bamboozle most defenders and his tally of goals was impressive. As was that of my cousin Leslie Davies; though he lacked stature, his skill and speed with the ball made him a formidable opponent. My other cousin, William John, Leslie's older brother, was reliable both in defence and attack and controlled the centre of the field. In central defence were my friend Danny Evans and Cyril Evans (no relation), both of whom were stalwart defenders. I always became very nervous when Cyril went into the attack as he would often go for the ball with his head about three feet from the ground and head it as strongly as if he were kicking it. Then there was Islwyn Owen who used his height advantage to the full. I cannot recall the other players in the original team, though I would appear on occasion to fill in, especially if the opposing team was considered weak.

I was deemed to be a decent left winger at grammar school, playing for my class team 4E with Peter Parry who appeared for at least five local teams in the league, and Gordon Edwards who was a stalwart for Talybont and Taliesin. I was guaranteed to score two or three goals each match. I was given trials for the school first team and used to enjoy myself worrying such noted players as the late Billy Lewis who played for Aberystwyth Rovers. However, when it came to playing for Goginan, I usually was more of a liability. For some reason, especially if my father was on the sideline, my poor feet ceased to function and I would slope off, head down in shame, much to his disgust. But you can't win them all.

Later on, Danny and I were pressed to play for arch-rivals Ponterwyd who, despite having a great stalwart in Geraint Howells (later Lord Geraint), were regarded as relatively weak. Geraint, who was over six foot tall and muscular with it, played at centre-half and could kick the ball from one end of the pitch to another quite easily without proper boots. Mr Jenkins' book reminded me of the Christmas Day match between Goginan and Ponterwyd in 1952, when Ponterwyd found themselves short of

Goginan United in 1951

Back: *Mr Nelson, Viv Morris, Cyril Evans, Tommy Bray, Islwyn Owen, Danny Evans, Bill Howells, Mr Edwards.*
Front: *Iorwerth Price, Tubby Edwards, Jock Duncan, Glyn Williams, Fred Jones, Leslie Davies, Alwyn Thomas.*

a few key players due to the holidays. Geraint got in his car and travelled all the way to Caernarfonshire on Christmas morning to bring two Aberystwyth University students who were regular star players in the team to play in this vital match. He then drove them all the way back that evening – I can't remember if this was a triumphant return or not.

A couple of years later, Goginan was forced to import some able players either from Penllwyn, a village down the valley, or from Aberystwyth. The 1950-51 photograph includes some of these stalwarts who managed to keep the team in a respectable position in the league, though they did not win any major trophies during this golden age of local soccer. Viv Morris travelled from Aberystwyth for several seasons to play in defence while those two skilled forwards Tubby Edwards and Jock Duncan, also

Goginan, 1970–71

Back: *Gwyn Roberts, Dai Jones, Meirion Davies, Mike Ingram, Ambrose Roberts, Dai Parry, Handel Rees, Colin Baxter, Idloes Roberts, Haydn Fleming*. **Front**: *Wil Davies, John Jones, Gerwyn Jones, Ifor Pugh, Geraint Jones, Arwyn Roberts, D H Evans. Mascot: Mathew Parry.*

Goginan, League Cup Winners, 1982–83

Back: *Brian Ashton, Paul Edwards, Raymond Davies, Raymond Evans, Arwyn Roberts, Alwyn Jones.* **Front**: *Tony Price, Martin Williams, Paul Morgan, Idloes Roberts, Tom Morgan, Alun Williams.*

from Aberystwyth, added strength to the attack. Fred Jones and I believe Alwyn Thomas came from Penllwyn.

Bill Howells was given the responsibility of training the team and preparing the pitch, ably assisted by Iorwerth Pryse, a postman who worked in Capel Bangor. The remaining administrative members of the time were David Edwards from Llanbadarn and Mr Nelson who, though a comparative stranger to the village, gave able support to the administration. In his work, Bill was ably assisted by his dear wife Sally, who regularly entertained the teams to an after-match tea at Jezreel vestry.

After a few seasons, the difficulties of maintaining a viable team saw the village dropping out of the league. In 1970, however, a new enthusiasm for the game led to its revival, with a new strip in the rather unusual colours of mauve and yellow. The new team boasted some very skilful players and in season 1974-5, created one of the biggest upsets of the decade. At the time, Penrhyncoch was the team to be reckoned with in the league and cup. Goginan found themselves in a semi-final tie of the league cup with the favourites and after two bruising matches where they managed to withstand the Penrhyncoch attack, Goginan managed to score in the last few seconds of extra time and win a place in the final. After such a contest, the final against Tregaron was an anticlimax, but a single goal by Idloes Roberts, Penbryn, saw Goginan lift the cup.

Goginan was successful once again during the 1982-83 season when the skills of seasoned players like brothers Idloes and Arwyn Roberts saw the team once again lifting the cup, this time at the expense of Bryncrug. Having been involved in the embryonic stages of the team, it is very heartening to read of their later successes.

To return to the immediate post-war period, another event which proved very popular for a time was the annual sports meeting. This involved not only the usual athletics competitions but also horse trotting races and even dog racing. The initial meeting was held in one of Blaendyffryn's fields up the Melindŵr Valley in Cwm Graig (rock valley). Then the venue was changed to a slightly more convenient site on Troed-y-rhiw 's field, the same one that was later used by the soccer team.

The 'mile' course followed the same track as the trotting horses, so distances were rather approximate. There were fast bicycle and slow bicycle races along the same track; the latter required great skill as the wheels had to be kept moving and balance was vital. The dog races intrigued me, as the track was a straight run of about two hundred yards. Just beyond the finishing post stood the post office's Morris Eight with the back wheels jacked up. One had been removed and string was wound around the hub, then unwound and drawn out to the dogs' starting point. On the end of the string was a rag which would serve as the 'rabbit'. I assume that John Moses or Dick y Post would have put some rabbit scent on the rag to entice the dogs. Whatever it was it worked well, as once the engine of the car was started and put into gear, the revolving hub would drag the 'rabbit' quickly across the field with the dogs in hot pursuit. I remember my friend Gareth Jones, Gwarllan had a little dog called Prince which was guaranteed to win races in his class. Unfortunately these events, interesting and popular as they were, gradually waned and faded from the calendar, as did the agricultural and flower shows which were held in hired marquees for a time.

In July 1954 a *Cambrian News* reporter under the pseudonym of Crwydryn (Wanderer) wrote an short article on Goginan and the Melindŵr Valley and called it 'The Valley of Song'. Music has dominated the valley for well over a century and during the heyday of the lead mine a great variety of music went on under the leadership of several notable personalities. I have already mentioned the brass band which played a leading part in any special village occasion. I once read a report from 1880 in the *Cambrian News* about an eisteddfod which was held in a specially constructed marquee – in the school playground, I think. I know proceedings started early in the morning with a procession through the village of the chairman, the secretary, the adjudicators and a host of other dignitaries led by the Goginan brass band. There were two sessions and judging by the nature of the competitions, there was little difference between that eisteddfod and the ones we used to enjoy in the 1930s and '40s. But back then there were a number of addresses by dignitaries whose general theme was the importance of the Welsh language in the local culture. Competitors came from Aberystwyth and many of the surrounding villages. Aberffrwd in Cwm Rheidol figured prominently amongst the winners in the musical sections. Bow Street also produced many individual and choral winners, with JT Rees as the conductor of the choirs. Altogether it sounded like a very sophisticated day.

Though the 'welcome home' concerts ceased after the end of the war, there were others, notably the annual Boxing Night concert organised by St Matthew's Church. The church itself had no hall, so the concert was always held in Dyffryn Methodist's vestry. Since this was the only occasion organised by the church, it was regarded as very special and had to be good. Being the day after Christmas, it was guaranteed to have a capacity audience. Two long tables were arranged at the back of the vestry and the audience was entertained to a tea before proceedings commenced. This was a fundamental part of the occasion and the whole affair was rather rudely referred to as a '*cwrdd* buns' (a buns meeting) though the fare was of a much more sophisticated nature. The whole affair was under the control of Mrs Davies the shop so it was bound to work like clockwork.

The concert itself followed the usual pattern: local kids did their turn and my uncle John provided half an hour of 'entertainment' with his fiddle. He would take ten minutes to play Genievieve or some similar violin piece accompanied by my mother on the pianoforte, while the other twenty minutes would be used getting his stand ready, finding a suitable location for him to lean due to his disability, and tuning the instrument to the piano. Still, it was all taken as part of the entertainment and it was usually worth the wait as he could coax some very pure sounds from the violin.

Sometimes, since my cousin Fanw worked for Mrs Davies, Dick Leonard, Fanw's father, could be coerced into performing. However, he would not appear until half the concert was over and there were palpable sighs of relief when he arrived. He had a magnificent baritone voice but in his retirement was very reluctant to learn any new pieces of music, so the audience would be regaled with Welsh folk songs or his old favourite 'Mae'r airship wedi dod' (the airship has come). Whatever his offering, he was guaranteed tumultuous applause, as was Dick y Box, a very notable character in the village. He once had aspirations of entering the ministry and had the personality and panache to sway audiences, and his comic and other recitations were tremendous. Another buzz of excitement would run through the audience if Mr and Mrs John from Cwmbrwyno appeared. Mr John had a very good baritone voice and his wife was a very good contralto; once she had divested herself of her fur coat the audience would be thrilled by songs and duets.

However, the highlight of the evening was the culminating sketch produced and directed by Mrs Davies herself. Weeks before the concert, we would all make our way to her front room for rehearsals and planning. One sketch included my friends Danny and Cyril, my aunt Lill and myself. Rehearsals went well even though the play was in English. It involved taking photographs on stage and I had managed to make a passable replica of a camera on a tripod using one of Mr Davies' biscuit tins, a black painted cotton reel to represent the lens, three broomsticks painted black for the legs and a piece of black sheeting for the hood.

The play, which should have lasted about forty minutes, was going great guns with everyone remembering their lines until about ten minutes before the end. My aunt, who had a considerable role, had two very similar cues: one about five minutes in and one near the end. Unfortunately, Lill mistook the second of the cues for the first one and so about thirty minutes of the play had to be repeated. When she came to the dreaded cue the second time, she froze so that there was a pregnant silence of about a minute. During this time the Tilley lamp which had been introduced that year, started playing up. These lamps had to be pumped at regular intervals to maintain a constant light, and after doing half an hour's overtime it was in urgent need of pumping. The light blossomed and waned between very bright and very dim as the poor lamp struggled in its death throes. Not only that, Lill's eyes went up to the flagging filament and seemed mesmerised. The outcome was a premature lowering of the curtain to rather bewildered applause and the demise of Lill's career as an actress. Still, they were good days which added so much to the cultural life of the village.

After the opera Y Trwbadŵr had visited many local villages, I suddenly realised the wealth of young talent there was in Goginan and set about, with the aid of my mother, to create a variety group of singers and actors. At the initial meeting in our house, it was decided that we would call ourselves 'The Goginan Youngsters' – these were the days when fancy names were not yet in vogue. Being stringent times any uniform would have to be very simple, so a red tie, white shirt and grey flannels made up the boys' apparel while the girls wore white blouses, red bow ties and grey skirts. The only exceptions to this get-up would be my mother as accompanist who could wear any dress she chose, and John Moses Evans with his jokes, who offered to be a compere for any concerts.

The group concentrated on variety with solos, duets, trios, recitations and sketches separating groups of choral songs.

The Goginan Youngsters

Back*: Gareth Jones, Glyn Williams, Rona Davies, Danny Evans, Winnie Jones, Goronwy Owen, Irfon Meredith.* **Middle***: Nanno Wright, Tegwen Howells, John Moses Evans, Gwynne Evans, Olwen Evans, Daphne Jenkins, Gwyneira Howells.* **Front***: Leslie Davies, Byron Howells.*

Though the voices were untrained they created quite beautiful sounds. The repertiore varied from Welsh folk songs and a few sacred anthems to popular ballads of the day. We hear a lot of fuss made of the vocal contributions by young people on radio, CDs and television today, but I very rarely hear anything that came near to the standard and quality of our soloists during those concerts. Firstly there was Tegwen Howells (now Tegwen Jones of Talybont). She gave a wonderful performance as a very young sprite in *The Troubadour* and it was very fortunate to have her join the group. She had such purity of tone and wonderful interpretation – a quality so rare in contemporary singing. She was joined in the soprano section by my childhood friend Nanno

Wright (now Rees) and one of our 'imports' – Winnie Jones from Ponterwyd. What a lovely sound they created. My cousin Rona had returned from the WAAFs and possessed a uniquely beautiful contralto voice; she was joined in the alto section by Tegwen's sister Gwyneira and Mrs Davies the shop's granddaughter Daphne Jenkins. The tenor section included my friend Glyn Williams, ably assisted by Gareth Jones, Gwarllan and our other 'import', Irfon Meredith from Ystumtuen. The bass section was led by my other cousin Leslie, Rona's brother, and included Goronwy Owen and myself.

As a choral group, we competed successfully in many cultural meetings. Once, we decided to enter a competition at Llanwrtyd Wells. A special prize was to be awarded for the singing of the hymn 'Abide with Me' in memory of some notable personage from the town. The adjudication which we received was the shortest that I think I have ever heard: "Lovely, lovely, lovely!" I shall never forget that, or the feeling of pride I felt in being associated with the group.

We also heard some wonderful recitations. Byron Howells, Gwyneira and Tegwen's brother, was about ten years old at the time, but such was his tremendous talent as an elocutionist that his inclusion in the group was a must. It was obvious even then that he would move on to an illustrious career. Then came the comedy section which usually included my childhood friend Danny Evans who, though lacking the refinements of vocal accomplishments (he was a bloody awful singer), more than made up for it in his acting talents. Then came Glyn 'jack of all trades' and myself. We had a large suitcase filled with odds and ends of clothing – hats, coats, skirts, blouses – and a variety of props. We made an agreement that, while one or two sketches would be standard, we would add spontaneity by hunting down jokes which would lend themselves to being enacted on stage. During the journey by hired bus, the three of us would get our heads together at the back and decide on suitable jokes. Then each would decide which character to play in the general theme. Sometimes a fourth or fifth character had to be co-opted. Though it sounds rough and ready, it is amazing what freedom one had without the confines of a proper script and such skits were very well received.

One time at the Woodlands (now a tea room) in Devil's Bridge, Glyn and I had decided to sing the old duet 'Oh no John!' where he would take the part of the lady. There were no changing rooms so we had to go outside into the woods to change. Unfortunately, Glyn had forgotten the 'fillers' for his bra and we had to use handfuls of wet leaves! It was a very wet night, so both of us presented a bedraggled picture even before we started. Whenever Glyn moved around on the stage he left a trail of wet leaves, and by the time the duet ended he was completely flat chested!

I am so glad that I undertook that venture and even though I have been engaged in theatrical productions all my life, those days will never be forgotten.

1952 was a notable year in the annals of the village choir. The National Eisteddfod of Wales paid a visit to Aberystwyth and, along with most of the local choirs, Goginan was invited to join the mass choir which was to perform at the pavilion on the Saturday evening. It was also found that Goginan was the oldest established choir in the area and the BBC decided to make a filmed feature of it during the run-up to the performance. Much was the excitement as the vans and the cameras arrived in the village. Though the choir's actual singing was not filmed – the camera crew decided to stay outside the vestry and record from outside – there was much interest, real and synthetic, in the members' lives and their struggles to get to rehearsals. The important thing, as with all such features, was to get a story.

The choir in action

The dress code was not stringent, as can be observed from the varied 'get-ups'.

Back row: Glyn Williams, Top House; Gareth Jones, Gwarllan; Dei Hugh Evans, post office; Cyril Evans, Blaendyffryn; Islwyn Owen, Jezreel Chapel House; gentleman from Capel Bangor; Goronwy Owen, Jezreel chapel house; Dilwyn Griffiths, Troed-y-rhiw farm; Mr Williams, Maesbangor; Bill Davies, Rhiw felen; Jim Jones, Alltygwreiddyn; Leslie Prosser Davies, Queen Street.

Third row: Megan Davies, Queen Street; John Moses Evans, post office; David Griffiths, Troed-y-rhiw farm; Ceiriog Gwynne Evans, Lynn Cottage; William Evans (Bill y Go'), Royal Oak. **Second row**: Lill Evans, Royal Oak; Mair Jones, y Shop; Margaret Jones, Y Wern; Beryl Jones, Llwyngwyn; Mrs Pryse, Troedrhiwcastell farm; Bethan Bebb, Blaendyffryn farm; Joan Dench, Tŷ Sgwâr; Betty Ashley-Jones, Druid Inn; Maggie Williams, Bangor House; Tegwen Howells, Dollwen; Katie Parry.

Front row: Rona Davies, Queen Street; Mrs Meredith, Capel Bangor; Edith Olwen Williams, Top House; Marged Ann Morgan, Bank farm; Maggie Jones, Hyfrydle; Kate Jones, Gwarllan; Irene James, BlaenMelindŵr; Miss Williams, Maesbangor; Sally Davies, Queen Street.

Accompanist: Olwen Evans, Lynn Cottage; Musical Director: Llewelyn B Bebb.

Gareth Jones lived in Gwarllan, a small holding situated near the church, but for the purposes of the story, he and Cyril Evans who worked at Blaendyffryn farm, also a mile from the village, were made to take their bicycles about four miles up the road so that they could be filmed whizzing round the corners above Cwmbrwyno on their way to rehearsal. Cyril had to go to the middle of a wheat field with the conductor of the choir, Llewelyn Bebb, who farmed Blaendyffryn, standing near the gate. The script in Welsh went something like this:

LB: Hello, Cyril, are you coming to rehearsal tonight?

CE: Yes I am.

Not exciting and gripping stuff but it added to the story.

Obviously with such an epic production there were 'glitches', as when filming had to be abandoned for the night due to fading light to be continued the next day. Unfortunately when filming did resume, it was discovered that one or two of the ladies had appeared in a completely different outfit! I think the tragic part was that the choir itself never saw the finished product, though it did appear on televisions in the London area.

As with most cultural activities there comes a time to move on, whether due to people getting too old to continue, the increasing advent of television and similar attractions or because there was an exodus of people from the district. Whatever the cause, there was a gradual waning of such traditional culture in the village. However, the 'good old days' still live in the memory and many of us who remain feel fortunate to have participated.

CHAPTER FIFTEEN

Dei Bwtsh
and Bill y Go'

M Y TWO GRANDFATHERS WERE real characters. They had very different personalities but both made quite an impact on village life in the early twentieth century.

David Evans (Dei Bwtsh) was born in Bethesda, a small slate mining village in North Wales on 11 November 1867. His father was a butcher, hence the nickname David acquired – even though the nearest he came to the profession was possessing pigs, some of which were slaughtered each autumn to keep the family in meat for the winter. His early history is rather vague to me, but he must have moved to the Aberystwyth area in his early twenties because he met and married Annie Griffiths in 1891. Annie was born in Llanrhystud, a village about ten miles south of Aberystwyth, on 20 July 1871. She was the illegitimate daughter of a chambermaid, Mary Griffiths, who was made pregnant by the lord of the manor where she worked. After a short stay in South Wales where their first son John Lloyd was born in December 1892, they moved back to Goginan where they took tenancy of the Miners' Arms in the centre of the village, but soon moved to take over the Druid Inn. They then had seven more children, my father Evan being the fourth.

To say that Dei was a character is an understatement. I have only vague memories of him as he died in 1936 at the age of sixty-nine. I remember he was a slim man of rather short stature with wisps of white hair framing his bald head, a short, white clipped moustache and very penetrating blue eyes. My only vivid memory concerning him is entering his front bedroom in the Druid when I was four, to take him a tin of Colman's mustard. He died soon afterwards; I fervently hope that it was not the mustard or my visit that precipitated his passing. He left a series of adventures and anecdotes that could be the basis of an amusing book.

Dei was an enigmatic character; he could be kind and gentle, excitable and vitriolic, brave and terrified. He was known to venture on his own into dangerous situations but also to cower in terror at what others might seem rather trivial.

My father related the following anecdote about Dei's bravery. Every spring when the temperatures rose and the air was fresh and clear, all the mats and carpets were taken out of the Druid and hung outside on the hedge across the main road. On one such occasion, Dei decided to inspect the carpets after a few hours in the fresh air – only to find that every mat and carpet had vanished. After a few moments of pregnant silence the wisps of hair above his ears started twitching, his hackles rose and his usually mild language took on a much rosier hue. "It's those bloody gypsies, I bet you," he shouted to no-one in particular. "Get me my bike, I'm going straight down to their bloody leader and I'm not leaving until I get them all back!"

Every year during winter, over a hundred gypsy caravans camped on the banks of the River Rheidol near the railway bridge at Pendre, about two miles east of Aberystwyth. My father and a few other friends, knowing that it would be impossible to dissuade Dei, offered to accompany him. Apparently, entering a gypsy encampment alone, especially to accuse someone of a misdemeanour, was very dangerous. However, Dei was adamant: "I don't need anybody; no bloody gipsy is going to get the better of me, I can tell you. I'm going to get those carpets back if it's the last thing I do." Off he went down the road, much to the consternation of the little crowd that had gathered. Four hours later, a beaming Dei re-appeared pushing his bicycle proudly, followed by a caravan containing his mats and carpets.

Then there was the other side to his character. In summer when the weather was muggy, Dei kept a wary eye on the sky for the appearance of any dark cloud which threatened thunder. At the first clap of thunder in the distance, Dei dropped everything and scuttled into the cupboard under the stairs. Woe betide anyone who dared to open the door of that cubby hole to enquire as to his condition; they would be met with a torrent of verbal abuse. Dei would remain in his hole until the storm had cleared completely.

Dei kept a good garden; there was never a weed to be seen and he nurtured his vegetables with such love and care that the quality of his produce was admired throughout the village.

For some reason, Dei developed a love-hate relationship with the village policeman, PC Matthias, who lived next door to the Druid Inn. His wife Mary was very familiar with Dei's wife Annie and they were in each other's kitchens several times a week. One morning, Matthias appeared at the back door of the inn as Dei was tapping one of the beer barrels that had arrived by horse and cart from the brewery in Aberystwyth.

"Good morning, Dei," the policeman said. "Stocking up for tonight, are you?"

"Well, yes, Matthias, there was a lot of drinking last night by the miners who came over from Cwm Rheidol. I don't know how some of them got home, considering the state they were in when they left here."

"This drinking to excess – very foolish, Dei. Oh, by the way, Mary asked me to come in to ask if we could take a couple of onions from the garden. She's making cawl and we've run out of onions."

"Of course you can. Help yourself, you know where they are."

"Thank you Dei, you'll get some back once my onions grow big enough."

So it was: neighbour helped neighbour. But this was to come to an end on the second Saturday in August, when the annual Agricultual Show was held in Capel Bangor. Most of the village made the annual pilgrimage and quite a few entered their flowers and vegetables in the various competitions. After a while, Dei heard the following announcement: "… And the winner of the competition for the best onions – and what a quality entry it is – PC Matthias from Goginan!" The wisps of hair above Dei's ears twitched more than they had ever done before and a volcanic eruption seemed in the offing. It was more than he could stomach to see the prize going to someone else, especially since he recognised the onions as being the very ones Matthias had taken for Mary's cawl the week before.

"…and the winner of the competition for the best onions is… PC Matthias from Goginan."

One stormy night when no one was in the Druid apart from a shepherd who had decided to stay the night instead of braving the elements to reach his hut on the foothills of Pumlumon, Dei decided to close the doors early. However, at about nine o'clock there was a sharp knock on the front door. Reluctantly, Dei went to the door and there, seated on a white pony, was a man dressed from head to toe in weatherproof clothing. He wore a sou'wester, pulled well down over his eyes.

"Good evening, guv'nor," the stranger said. "I'm so sorry to bother you on a night like this, but I wonder if you would be kind enough to serve me with a pint of your ale. I'm soaked to the skin so I won't get down from my pony. I'm on my way up to Ponterwyd but I thought a pint would go down very well."

"Certainly," Dei replied, "I'll get you one right away."

Dei brought the stranger his pint, which he drank avidly.

"Thank you very much. I wonder if I could have another – I didn't realise I was so thirsty."

Dei got him another, and a third.

"I think I'll have one more for the road," said the stranger, "and then I'll settle with you."

Dei brought out a fourth pint, only to discover the stranger had vanished. The tufts of Dei's hair bristled once again and another volcanic eruption developed in his chest which he let forth, giving the poor shepherd in the bar a full and vitriolic account of the treachery of some people.

The next evening Matthias, having finished his rounds, came in for a drink with his old pal Dei. Since the bar was closed, Dei took him into the back kitchen where they sat facing each other in front of the fire. Dei gave a full account of the previous night's misadventure, to which the policeman made sympathetic grunts and growls. But Dei suddenly noticed that Matthias' black uniform trousers were covered on the inside of the thighs with white horse hairs. Matthias had noted that the shepherd's white pony had been put in the stable for the night. Nothing was simpler than to don the shepherd's waterproofs, saddle the pony and bring it round to the front door. I was never told how Dei reacted to this deception.

Another time, Dei's sow was constipated. For three days it had lain on its side in the shed next door to the Druid and had passed nothing. People came and went, each one offering sympathetic advice as to a cure.

"Give her a drop of sherry, Dei. I hear it worked wonders when John Morgan's pig had the same problem."

"Try forcing some stout down its throat, Dei. I heard it cured the problem with Tom Pugh's cow."

So it went on, until nearly all the available drinks had passed down the poor sow's gullet to no avail.

Eight-year-old John Moses then passed by. "What's the matter with the sow, Mr Evans?" he asked, innocently.

"She's constipated, John bach."

"What's that, Mr Evans?"

"Damn you, she can't shit! What does Herbert teach you in that bloody school?"

John Moses beat a hasty retreat.

Who should then approach, a little worse for wear, but PC Matthias. He was just finishing his beat and his last port of call had been the Maesbangor Arms in Penllwyn, two miles down the road.

"What's the problem with the sow, Dei?" he asked.

"I'm not quite sure, Matthias. I think she's very constipated. I've tried everything but nothing seems to move her."

Matthias looked intently through bleary eyes at the sow and stroked his chin. By now, quite a crowd of bystanders had congregated.

"Right, I'll soon cure her. Stand back, lads. Dei, bend down there to see if anything is happening at the back."

Dei bent down, peering intently at the sow's posterior, when Matthias took a huge leap and landed squarely on the sow's stomach. Not even the sow could withstand that, and the contents of her stomach exploded from the rear with such force that poor Dei had no time to move out of range. The sow was cured but at the price of a new set of clothes for Dei!

Another anecdote concerns William David Bradshaw. His family had come from Ireland to work in Goginan's lead and silver mines in the mid nineteenth century and, unlike many other mining families who had come from Cornwall, Devon and Ireland, settled permanently in Goginan and were assimilated into the life of the village. Though William Defi, as he was called, could not speak and was deaf, he had a great sense of humour and was not averse to playing a trick or two on his neighbours. His sense of humour seemed to leave him, however, when the dreaded time came to cut my hair 'basin fashion' when I was young. For a time my uncle John undertook the task but he

"…Dei, bend down there to see if anything will happen at the back."

was so meticulous in his style that the ordeal usually took well over an hour, by which time he would have lost his patience and I was like a demented wriggling worm on a fishing line. So he thankfully passed the burden over to his pal William Defi. The problem was that William Defi did not believe that scissors should be sharpened and the agonies I endured in the garden shed during that tugging and snatching ordeal, accompanied by the occasional frustrated clip on the ear and a disgusted 'Daputh!' – William Defi's only vocal expression of disgust – gave me a phobia about barbers.

Though William Defi did not drink very much when I knew him, there was a time in his younger days when he frequented the Druid Inn quite often, sitting on his usual stool close to where Dei used to draw pints for his customers. In those days, lighting from the two paraffin lamps was dim and William Defi took advantage of this by surreptitiously slipping a toy spider attached to black thread into a pint of beer while Dei, probably chatting to the customer, drew a second pint. Much was the consternation when on lifting the glass, the customer discovered the offending insect. With a few oaths and mumbles of apology, Dei would empty the beer into the slop bucket under the counter (possibly to be strained later and returned to the barrel) and proceed to fill a clean glass. At the same time, William Defi would whip the little spider out of the glass and into his pocket. Apparently, this little escapade would be repeated two or three times in an evening and I don't think Dei ever discovered the source of the spider infestation in his pub.

I wouldn't say that Dei was an alcoholic but in the mornings he was unable to sit down for any long period of time and would serve himself a small nip of whisky whenever he was in the vicinity of the bar. Since he was in this vicinity rather frequently, he would be very slightly the worse for wear by lunch time on many a day.

Dei had a phobia for neatness. There was never a weed in the garden and he even gave the main road outside the public house a sweep every day. All was well until the farmer at a small holding called Blaenrhosydd took to bringing his dairy cows down to graze in the field next to the school. For some strange reason, the cows would always make a stop outside the Druid and relieve themselves of the contents of their stomachs nearly every day. This was too much for Dei, who appeared a few mornings later carrying a bunch of corks which he strongly urged the farmer to push into the beasts' nether regions before they passed the pub on subsequent days.

However, Dei was a staunch churchgoer and was Vicar's Warden for many years at St Matthew's. The whole family would have to dress in their Sunday clothes and troop off to the church for morning service at ten o'clock. They had to sit in the front pew just under the pulpit. This was not due to ultra piousness but because the Reverend Morgan was subject to sudden epileptic fits and it was the warden's duty to keep a wary eye on him during the sermon lest he should succumb to a fit and topple out of the pulpit.

On one occasion, my father had been sent down to the post office on an errand before going off to church. As was quite usual on a Sunday morning at the post office, with four young children to dress and care for, Mary Elizabeth was in a bit of a dither. So when my father arrived all spruced up in a new velvet suit, Mary Elizabeth handed him one of the very young children to hold while she attended to one of the others. Unfortunately, the child had not completed its ablutions and was happy to relieve itself all over the front of my father's velvet suit. With many apologies, Mary Elizabeth produced a damp cloth and wiped the offending deposit off the suit. Since all were in a hurry, the cleaning process was a bit cursory and my father had to run to the church smelling in no way like a bunch of lilies. He crept in and sat at the far end of the pew enduring the stares and smirks of his siblings. Horror of horrors, his father motioned him to take his usual position under the pulpit next to him. Slowly, Dei's nose started twitching and gave my father a slow enquiring stare. My father never told me the outcome of that encounter.

Dei slaughtered the pigs he kept – scalding the skin with boiling water before cutting up the body parts in preparation for salting. Normally a butcher would be hired for the actual killing and the cutting; in Dan Jones' time the charges were around one shilling for the slaughter and an extra sixpence for the cutting up. Once the carcass was cut up and salted, the parts were hung up on the rafters from whence slices could be cut as required. Dei had a special back room in the Druid where the salting took place; in my childhood it was called *y lle halltu cig* (the place for salting meat). Even today there are still one or two hooks remaining on the rafters as a reminder of this very important process in the life of the family.

Soon after slaughtering a pig, Dei would travel to the sales in Aberystwyth to buy a piglet. There was one occasion when, after buying a piglet and putting it in a sack which he slung over his back, Dei decided to walk up to the top of the town. Near the old clock, the fishmonger always had a stock of Dei's favourite fish, locally caught whiting. (Dei used to ask one of the drivers of the brakes – the horse-drawn passenger carts which travelled regularly to Aberystwyth from Goginan – to bring him some home, but since one of these good people had brought him a packet of ceiling whiting instead, he travelled down personally to get them). Apparently, as he approached the top of Great Darkgate Street the piglet managed to escape through a hole that had developed in the sack. Dei rushed through the crowd shouting, "Stop that bloody pig!" as the piglet dodged its way between the legs of astonished people. The piglet took the easiest course down the street and, as coincidence would have it, ran through the only open door – that of the police station. The police, on seeing that the cause of the hullabaloo was that strange character from the Druid, quickly put the piglet in a cell. I would have loved to overhear the altercation between an agitated Dei and the police sergeant, but I believe that Dei was charged with being incapable of controlling an animal and had to pay a small sum as bail to get the piglet released. I assume he got the money back later.

Dei attended my aunty Dora's very posh wedding. Her husband Billy Gwynne, one of the nicest gentlemen I ever met, was an officer in World War I and was married in uniform. (He was a very young officer and received many taunts. When he was leading his troops in France, the whole platoon rendered a chorus of 'A little child shall lead them on the way'.) Dei had to wear top hat and tails for the wedding and, to the accompaniment of some flowery language, my father had to assist him in dressing for the occasion. A stiff wing collar, attached to the shirt by a front and back stud, became a source of great discomfort throughout the ceremony, even more than his grey top hat which, from the photograph I once saw, seemed to be held up by his ears.

Early the following morning my father was summoned into Dei's bedroom and was surprised to see him sitting up in bed, steaming, and still wearing his shirt and wing collar from the day before. My father had used a new-fangled front stud where the top slid into the base and separated into two pieces with a slight twist, as opposed to the ordinary stud where the hinged top button could be turned to slide through the slit in the collar. Dei had never encountered one of the new studs and after a long period of pulling and twisting, resigned himself to sitting up in bed all night still dressed. I don't think my father was flavour of the month for a considerable time after that incident.

The saying goes that behind every great man there is always a good woman. Well I don't think Dei could be called a great man – a significant man, certainly – but behind him was a great though long suffering woman who controlled and steadied him through his rather turbulent life. Annie was slim and upright; not what I would call beautiful in the glamorous sense but most attractive with dark brown eyes and flowing black hair which, even in her last years in her nineties, was still dark and reached right down almost to her waist. She had an upright, regal posture with her hair plaited and rolled into a tight bun at the back of her head. What I remember most about her was her calm nature; I never once heard her raise her voice or speak ill of anyone. Unfortunately, her eyesight started failing in her thirties and by her early forties she was blind. But this tragedy seemed to give her a new inner peace and if anything she became even more tolerant in misfortune.

Two of Annie's sayings always remain with me. When strangers were introduced to her, she would ask quietly what he or she did. This has always stayed with me and I think it has helped me to look at people in the light of their contribution to life rather than their appearance or utterances. The other saying, she used in reply to any selfish complaints and whinges I hurled at her: "Never mind, bach, things will soon be better."

As a child, I used to visit her in her 'black hole' (she used to spend much time in her later years in the back kitchen which had only one small window opening onto a covered area at the side of the house). On entering, I would be greeted by: "Who's there?" Then I would grope my way in the darkness towards the only source of light emanating from the glowing embers in the fireplace. She would always grab my elbow and say, "Oh, it's you. Come and sit beside me, bach." As my eyes got used to the utter gloom, several shapes would gradually materialise and I would often discover that we were not alone. In a non-conformist village such as Goginan, it was strictly frowned upon for women to drink. So if the desire for the demon drink overcame the conscience and guilt of certain ladies in the village, they would slip in to the Druid by the back door and ensconce themselves in my grandmother's 'black hole'. It always amused me to hear the sighs of relief as the pints of Guinness or other prohibited imbibements emerged from under the coats before the gossip recommenced.

Annie survived Dei for over thirty years and died in my aunt Betty's home in Capel Bangor at the age of ninety-four, still as upright and uncomplaining as ever.

Bill y Go' (William the blacksmith) was a completely different personality. There was little enigma surrounding him. In many ways, one could call him a practical man who was predictable in his behaviour and carried himself through life with pride. William Evans was born on 6 December 1871, the third of five children. His father, Thomas Evans, was born in 1846 in Nebo, Cross Inn; his mother, Anne Evans, was born in Trefeurig, north of the Melindŵr Valley, in 1843. William married Margaret Jane Hughes in 1892. She was the daughter of John and Sarah Jane Hughes and sister of my great-uncle John. On both sides of the family the connection with the silver-lead mines was strong. Sarah was the daughter of Captain John Boundy who had worked in the tin mines around St Austell in Cornwall before moving to a superintending capacity at Cwmsymlog mine, where his son WH Boundy met with a fatal accident in 1877 at the age of thirty-five.

William and Margaret settled initially in Trefeurig and had three daughters – the youngest being my mother, Olwen. For many years, William worked as a blacksmith in several of the local lead mines. He would either walk several miles each day to and from some of the remote mines or stay the working week at the mine's barracks – walking home on Saturday afternoon and returning very early on a Monday morning.

I think it was during one of the periods when the fortunes of

William Evans (Bill y Go') with his eldest daughter, Lill, outside the Royal Oak.

the local lead mines were precarious and work became uncertain that Bill decided to seek work in London. I don't know why, but it seems he walked all the way to London from his home in Trefeurig. Whether he went alone or accompanied some sheep drovers (cattle droving had ceased in 1870), I can't say. However, he had little luck in finding work so he walked to South Wales before returning home and resuming work in the mines.

In 1910 the family moved over the hill to take up residence at the Royal Oak in Old Goginan, and for a time Bill combined his work as blacksmith at the lead mines during the day with being a pub landlord in the evenings. In its early days the Royal Oak was frequented by Goginan miners, but since that mine had ceased to be worked the clientele came mainly from other mines in and around the district. As the lead mines closed, the number of customers dwindled and the Royal Oak eventually closed. Even so, the fabric of the interior remained unchanged and when I was a small boy, I could easily envisage what it was like at the pub when my mother was young.

It was an interesting house, full of nooks and crannies to explore when the weather was cold or wet. What was the living room in the 1930s used to be the drinking room. I don't think they called it the bar, as that title was reserved for the room behind where the beer casks and bottles were stored. Connecting the two rooms was a small hatch five feet above the floor through which the beer glasses were delivered. Each side of the fireplace were two settles, one of which still remained – the other had been removed to make room for my grandfather's easy chair.

There used to be three round tables in the drinking room which my grandfather, being a skilled carpenter as well as a blacksmith, had made. The circular wooden tops were surrounded by a slightly raised steel rim and the tops themselves tilted ever so slightly towards the centre where there was a minute hole. One of these tables survived and I was always puzzled by this hole. My grandfather eventually explained its significance. Apparently, poor miners or their wives used to visit the pub during the day with a pint and a half sized bottle. My grandmother filled these to the brim with beer but only charged for a pint. Thus, my grandfather found that he was losing a halfpenny, quite a significant sum in those days, on each bottle. Since the miners were rather a rough, rowdy lot and spilt a lot of beer during altercations, my grandfather put a jug on the shelf under each table into which the spilt beer would find its way through the minute hole in the centre. This was then strained and put back into the barrel; thus reducing the financial loss incurred due to my grandmother's generosity. So it seems that both my grandfathers had a rather dubious streak as far as spilt beer was concerned!

There were certain objects in that front room which remain vividly in my mind, such as the imposing china replica of Wallace, the great mediaeval martyr for Scottish independence, dressed in his kilt with a huge dog at his feet. I never could understand why a Scotsman should dominate the mantlepiece of a Welsh public house but the name Wallace, or de Waleis, means a Welshman, so there was some connection. On top of the three-cornered cupboard was a beautiful china swan which also fascinated me, though I was never allowed to handle it. Then there was the grate with its brass handles which my mother in her youth laboriously cleaned and polished. The oven was no longer used, having been replaced with a paraffin one situated in the old bar room. (I don't know how many times I burned myself during my early childhood by placing my inquisitive little mitts on the top of that bloody thing!)

The room had been decorated with a bright flowery wallpaper for good reason, as I discovered. Before this had been applied, the old wallpaper was scraped away – a task which took several people more than a day. The next procedure was to fill up the holes in the stone wall. This was done by soaking lumps of scrunched-up newspaper in a sort of paste made up of flour and water and stuffing them in the holes between the stones, then trying to smooth the surface as much as possible. Then the garish paper was applied, with the flowers serving to hide most of the dents which had not been sufficiently smoothed down.

Across the passage was the parlour with its wide open fireplace. There was no oven here, so this was a place to rest and relax; in fact it was seldom used except at Christmas time when a fire was lit in the grate. The room had rather a musty smell which was soon forgotten as the novelty of sitting somewhere new took over. I also remember a wide, winding staircase up to the first floor where there were three bedrooms and a box room full of dust, boxes of wonderful trinkets and a stack of musical instruments.

The back of the house was interesting as my grandfather had put a corrugated roof between the back wall and the steep rock face; one side was used as a very primitive washroom where the face and hands were given a cursory splash every morning in a pan containing cold water. I don't think that this was a favourite

"Come outside and say that!"
A probable scene from the Royal Oak in its heyday.

pastime for Bill as his attack on the cold water could be heard all over the house; rather reminiscent of a bird splashing its feathers in a stream. The other side was much more exciting, especially in wet weather, as a torrent of water would emanate from the rock. This flowed into the permanent little pool where many frogs lived and where my grandmother kept perishable foods, milk and lemonade cool in summer.

Then there was Bill's 'grotto' – his shed. He led an active retirement and was always fashioning something or other in either wood or metal. His experience in the lead mines stood him in good stead as he had built himself a huge bellows, rather like those used in the mines to heat and fashion iron bars into various shapes. Bill would surprise and delight me with a whole host of toys: tanks, destroyers, sailing yachts, kites and waterwheels to be worked in the stream, to name but a few. He once built me a tipping lorry with real windows and hinged doors. I often wonder what became of it because it was built so sturdily that it would never have disintegrated of its own accord.

Bill had the only water closet in the village – well, it was a loo that was built over a stream which flushed the waste products away into a marsh about a hundred yards downstream. Going to the loo when the little stream was in spate was a truly exciting experience.

During the summer, certain days were devoted to cutting the grass on the greens which lay on the other side of the lane running past the house. This was meticulously done by Bill and his eldest daughter Lillian using a couple of sheep shears. The following week, the same task was undertaken on a much larger scale in the cemetery of the Baptist chapel. Bill would wield the scythe while his wife and Lillian would be on their knees with their shears, trimming round each grave and braving encounters with snakes which found shelter among the gravestones.

It was also Bill's task to dig graves. This was a laborious job done solely with a pick and shovel. After clearing about two feet or less of the topsoil, one encountered solid rock. To a certain extent the task was made slightly easier in that the shale was well jointed, but to dig down about six feet was a gargantuan task. To add to the problems, the water table was reached after two or three feet. Since the ground was wet, many people asked Bill to build a brick vault to keep the coffin from rotting too quickly. Bill lined the base either with cement or slabs of rock. On many occasions, funeral directors would give the wrong dimensions for the vault, allowing no room for the coffin's brass handles. During committals, the coffin would be solemnly lowered into the grave, only to come to a sudden halt with a crunch at the top of the vault. Bill would have to lower himself into the grave and remove the handles after the mourners had departed, before starting on the task of filling the grave again. On very rare occasions in rough weather, especially if it was very cold and wet, the prospect of remaining soaked to the skin would get the better of him. He would then take a running leap into the grave and land on the coffin, which would lower itself neatly into the vault *sans* decorations. I always.wondered why one drawer in his shed contained so many brass handles!

Setting such misadventures aside, Bill's contribution to the maintenance of Jezreel Chapel and the pavilion in the next field over the years was tremendous. Since the high winds of 1987 blew most of the roof away, the chapel has fast deteriorated into a ruin. If Bill had been alive, I have no doubt that he would have been there immediately with his ladders, replacing the missing tiles. The beautiful pulpit has been taken to another chapel in Penrhyncoch and most of the pews have long since vanished. But the scraps which remain bear testament to the beautiful work he did of painting and graining all the woodwork nearly sixty years ago.

Bill's love and understanding of all types of wood led to his creating all sorts of furniture for the house – objects which were built to last. Each spring when the sap was rising, he also used to teach me how to make whistles from pieces of willow. We would select a branch of suitable thickness from the willow tree overhanging the stream in front of the house and cut off a section about six inches long. Then we would score the bark right around the circumference of the section with our penknives, about three inches from the end of the piece. The next process would be to wet the bark (I never found out why) and very gently tap the wetted section with the handles of our knives. After a few minutes of patient tapping, the bark would release itself and could be gently slid off the wood. Then holes and notches would be cut in the wood and the bark, which would miraculously be transformed into a creditable whistle. I tried to repeat this process a few years ago to prove to my wife that I really was a country lad but alas, not a peep!

Bill also practised water divining with a forked piece of hazel, holding the two ends with the backs of his hands facing inwards to create tension on the wood. It was quite eerie to see the point of the fork suddenly turning to face the ground despite my grandfather's efforts to keep the point upwards. It wasn't a gimmick either, as he was occasionally called on to find springs in the ground for the creation of wells. I'm afraid that ability passed me by, despite several frustrating attempts on my part.

One of his great hobbies was fashioning walking sticks from hazel. When the desire roused him, one would see him going out very early in the morning armed with a billhook. He would return a couple of hours later carrying the stem and root of a hazel sapling, which he transformed into a beautiful walking stick. When it was carefully varnished, he would give it to some deserving person. At eisteddfod time, he usually won the competition for the most elegant walking stick.

Music was his great passion and his bass voice provided the

Bill y Go' teaching two young spectators the art of fashioning a walking stick from a hazel sapling outside the Royal Oak.

backbone of choir, opera and chapel for many years. I have already mentioned his contribution as a sort of master of ceremonies at the annual Good Friday eisteddfod, and it was interesting to see him sprucing himself up for the event in front of the mirror. In his younger days, he would stiffen his moustache tips and 'quiff' with a dab of Brilliantine. I remember a dear old neighbour of his, Marged Ann Bradshaw, once calling in at the Royal Oak when Bill was in the process of preparing his hair. She watched him with a mixture of amazement and hilarity.

"I see you're out to make a mark today, Bill," she said. "I'd go with him to keep an eye on him, Marged, if I were you. I'm sure with that quiff, the women will be swooning all over him."

"Do you think so, Marged Ann?" Bill replied, looking at her gravely over his spectacles. "I'll tell you what; why don't you go home and practise doing the same to Tommy's hair. I'm sure he needs a bit of romance in his life."

Unfortunately, poor Tommy, Marged Ann's husband, was as bald as a coot with just one or two straggly hairs on his head.

As with Dei Bwtsh, Bill y Go' was blessed with a good wife who kept him in line in her own quiet way. My grandmother was a tiny lady, less than five feet in height – a characteristic which she passed on to all her daughters. Yet she had a tremendous strength of character. On many a night at the Royal Oak, so my mother told me, the miners became very unruly. Once the acceptable limit of noise was reached, my grandmother would grab the biggest and often noisiest miner by the lapels and push him back on to his seat. Then the finger would come up under his nose with the charge: "Sit there and shut up!" Amazingly, regardless of their size, they would obey her and remain as meek as lambs until it was time for the bar to close.

During my childhood, I would spend nearly every Saturday at the Royal Oak which was like a second home to me. I would spend my mornings playing amongst the trees surrounding the house or across the little stream where my grandmother had her washing line. This was like a small amphitheatre which had a flat raised area flanked by two large oak trees. This was a favourite spot as in my flights of fancy, it became a magnificent stage where I could act out the great dramas in my mind.

From a very early age, I had been hooked on the operettas which the grammar school in Aberystwyth put on annually at the King's Hall (where I later had the privilege to act in the grammar school's operas). I have acted and directed musicals in many theatres in and around London since that time, and I can honestly say that I have seldom experienced the warmth and atmosphere which emanated from that theatre. I felt so sad when it was decided to destroy it.

My little 'theatre' by the washing line saw the re-enactment of the school's operettas, with performances running each Saturday for weeks. Then it would be time for dinner prepared by my grandmother and my aunt Lill: cawl in a basin followed by meat and vegetables. For some reason, I would eat vegetables there but, much to my mother's frustration, would turn my nose up at them at home.

If the weather was fine, we would spend part of the afternoon having a picnic on 'Banc bach' – a small grassy area next to the ruined building which housed a big waterwheel when the mine was in use. Apparently, this is where I learnt to walk; it was also the site where cryptic messages could be sent to my mother by my grandmother and aunt on the other side of the valley. They would hang cloths of various colours on the gorse bushes. A blue one meant 'come over after tea'; pink, 'I shall be over tomorrow morning' – and so on.

At about four in the afternoon the *Car Melyn* (yellow car) would arrive. This was a horse-drawn van which travelled each Wednesday and Saturday from Powell's Bread Shop in Aberystwyth to deliver bread and a variety of other goods such as cakes to the rural areas. I can still savour that lovely aroma emanating from that van. Richard Jones the bread man would give me a ride back to the village.

In 1950 my grandmother succumbed to a bad bout of shingles on the face and neck and died at the age of seventy-six. Her funeral was the last occasion when a bier was used to carry the coffin to the cemetery in traditional Welsh style. Her grandsons had the honour of carrying the bier for the first part of the journey. Then at regular intervals, teams of four men would take over and move back to the end of the line until their turn came again. This was all synchronized by the funeral director. I had never experienced this kind of procession before and it still stays vividly in my mind.

As was the custom, the lady mourners would be inside the chapel before the cortege arrived. I could never understand the passion some Welsh ladies had for funerals. I would often perceive my aunt and her sister-in-law all dressed in Sunday black, complete with sniff rag, on the way to a funeral – anybody's funeral, whether they knew them well or not – and the sniff rags would be used liberally during the proceedings. There's sentimentality for you!

Bill y Go' survived his wife for seventeen years, living for a time on his own in the Royal Oak. I remember one incident which amused me very much during this time. When electricity arrived in Goginan in the mid-1950s, most villagers welcomed it as a positive move into the modern world. Not so my grandfather, who insisted that a paraffin lamp had served him well throughout the years and saw no reason to change to these new fangled devices. However, he very grudgingly conceded to have the living room wired up for one single bulb, steadfastly refusing any addition. He used to switch it on for just enough time to light the paraffin lamp. He eventually moved to live with his other daughter, Sarah Ann, and died in 1967 at the age of ninety-six. He was buried by the family in the plot which he himself had built in Jezreel cemetery, and the village mourned the loss of another pillar of society.

CHAPTER SIXTEEN

Marie and Betty

SOMETIMES WE ALL HAVE idle thoughts as to how long we shall be treading this earth. I often make a mental roll-call of my family to see who has reached the promised age of three score years and ten, who carried on a bit longer and how much longer. It seems that most of my male relatives have popped their clogs when they were in their seventies or eighties but most of my female forerunners have gone on to their eighties at least. Recently, my aunts Marie and Betty beat them all by becoming the first centenarians in our family. Now, does this mean that I will emulate them? Except for the fact that I am a boy and probably have the wrong genes, I see no reason why not!

Anyway, Marie celebrated her one hundred and second birthday on 3 April 2006. However, she died peacefully on 3 January 2007. Betty, on the other hand, is still going strong. What made them live so long? Other than genes, I can't think of any common factor that could account for their longevity. The two sisters were as different as the proverbial chalk and cheese. Marie had a very jovial nature and seemed to wear her heart on her sleeve. Nothing seemed to worry her, and truth to tell, I don't think she delved very deeply into the serious side of life. As the daughter of a publican and being a landlady, she was not averse to strong drink, especially whisky. Betty took a much more serious attitude to life; she was and still is a worrier. Strangely, despite her upbringing in the Druid Inn, she was to all intents and purposes a teetotaller, only imbibing a little for medicinal purposes or to be 'sociable'.

Marie was born on 3 April 1904 at the Druid Inn, the sixth of eight children. She spent most of her early life in Goginan, working in and around the pub. Like many other young people of the time, she and her younger brother Dan left the village to work in the dairy industry in Peckham, London, where they lived for a considerable period. Eventually she met and fell in love with a London City policeman, Arthur Moore, and soon afterwards they were wed.

Arthur, in keeping with his colleagues in the city, was huge – not in width but in height. He was about six foot eight inches tall and had enormous feet, about size fourteen. Eventually, sometime after the end of World War II when he retired from the force, they both came back to live for a short time at the Druid, before becoming landlords of the Commercial Hotel in Tre'rddol (now the Wild Fowler). Arthur would look after the public bar where the locals gathered, while Marie established herself in what she called her 'special room', where she entertained the upper and professional classes. Apparently she was a fine hostess and soon attracted a regular clientele, especially from Aberystwyth. Her discretion was absolute, and many notable personages from the town found her room a secure refuge whenever they were engaged in dalliances with the opposite sex. I shall say no more! Though he was a cockney, Arthur was surprisingly popular with the local population and was readily accepted as the landlord. His enormous height and feet probably had something to do with it – and the fact that he was an ex-bobby.

I went to the Commercial once when I was young with my father and Jack, his second cousin. Jack once lived at the Maesbangor Arms in Capel Bangor and had come for a holiday from South Wales. He was a small, slight man with dark brown eyes and a cloth cap which he wore at a very rakish angle, pulled well down over his left eye. He was quite posh in that he drove a little car. During his stay, he gave my father and me a lift to the

Mary behind her beloved bar at the Wild Fowler when celebrating her one hundredth birthday. Below, with her husband Arthur after their retirement from the Commercial Hotel, Tre'r Ddôl.

Commercial. We were greeted effusively by Arthur and were immediately asked what we wanted to drink. My father drank very little and I think ordered half a pint of what he called a 'shandy gaff' (I think it was an ordinary shandy); I had a lemonade, being under age, while my 'uncle' Jack decided on a double whisky and soda (drink-driving was not yet seen as much of a problem). There followed a period of friendly chat in which Jack spoke at length of the joys and advantages of living in Tylorstown. Then, out of the blue, Arthur looked at Jack and said, "That will be one pound seventy two, please."

"What do you mean, one pound seventy two? You bloody well invited us to have a drink!" Jack replied, bristling and rising to his full five foot, four inches. " I'm not paying a halfpenny for your drink."

Arthur very calmly reached forward and picked up Jack's cloth cap that was lying on the table. He walked over to the front door and threw the cap into the middle of the road, where a passing bus promptly ran over it.

"Do you see that cap in the road?" Arthur said, quietly gazing down his rather purple hooked nose at the still bristling Jack.

"Of course I do. You threw the bloody thing out!"

"Well," said Arthur, "now you can follow it!"

So ended what could have been a pleasant afternoon visit.

Eventually, after some thirty years or so, Arthur and Marie retired from the victualling trade and moved to a small terrraced house about ten yards from the Commercial. Thus ended a lengthy tradition both for them and the pub itself, which was extensively renovated and its name changed to the Wild Fowler.

Within a few years, Arthur passed away and Marie moved to a flat in Portland Street, Aberystwyth, where she lived on her own until she was ninety-six years old. During this time she kept remarkably healthy; her secret was a bottle of whisky a week and one Guinness a day. I remember one occasion when she and her sister Betty, who had a flat in North Parade, decided they should go on holiday for a change of air. Eventually a destination was agreed upon – the Belle Vue Hotel on the promenade in Aberystwyth! Apparently they both felt the need to keep an eye on their respective flats in the town.

Living alone in the flat became a little depressing for Marie, so eventually she was given a room at the Deva Old People's Home on the promenade. During this time, I used to telephone her regularly to enquire after her well-being. One such conversation went something like this:

Me: How are you?

Marie: I haven't been very well.

Me: What's been the matter?

Marie: I've had trouble with the waterworks.

Me: Have you been to the doctor?

Marie: Of course I have.

Me: What did he say?

Marie: 'What the hell's the matter with you again?'

(The doctor knew her well and had a good sense of humour.)

Me: What did you say?

Marie: 'Well, doctor, you know I've left my little flat and am now living with all those lovely men in the Deva. I'm having a whale of a time there and I think I'm pregnant! Stupid fool, it's his job to find out what's wrong with me.'

Indeed, Marie had a very good time at the Deva and would always be washing dishes in the kitchen or helping the girls do the beds. Every week she would visit the sweet shop to buy Jelly Babies for the other residents, whom she called 'the old folk'. One would always hear her singing as she walked down the corridors to visit the bed-ridden in their rooms.

She was fortunate in having many visitors who brought her bottles of whisky, her favourite tipple – so many that Betty had to ration the supplies. I received a telephone call from the Deva one day telling me that Marie, who was now one hundred years old, had fallen and hurt herself rather badly. I dropped everything and rushed down to Aberystwyth, picking up two speeding tickets during the day. I arrived just after lunch and rushed to her bedside. There she was, bundled up in bed, her face black and blue with bruises. I softly enquired as to how she was feeling. She opened one eye and said: "Oh, it's you. Come back tomorrow, bach, I'm going to sleep now." One hundred and fifty miles and a speeding ticket for three seconds of conversation! I could have murdered her. I didn't feel much better as I returned home fuming and got another speeding ticket. Even worse, I eventually found out the reason for her bruising. Betty had secretly hidden a full bottle of whisky behind the wardrobe in Marie's room. Marie had found it and proceeded to drink most of it in one session. So the verdict was drunk and disorderly in charge of a whisky bottle!

About three years ago, Cecele and I decided to take the sisters for a nostalgic trip around the countryside. For some reason they chose a ride to Tregaron, then on to Lampeter and back to Aberystwyth via Aberaeron. While Betty was interested in the shops, Marie was impatient to get to Aberaeron and visit the Feathers Hotel. There, they inevitably ordered fish and chips for lunch, the sisters' idea of a *cordon bleu* meal. Betty decided to treat us all to a pre-lunch drink: a mineral water for Cecele, a half of lager for me, a Coca Cola for Betty and… an American Dry Ginger for Marie! I thought I had mis-heard her, but there it was, a ginger ale, which Marie sipped very sedately. Then Betty, escorted by Cecele, left for the ladies' toilet. The moment they disappeared, I felt a tug on my sleeve and a hoarse whisper in my ear: "Take this slop away and give me a double whisky. Betty won't know as both drinks are the same colour!" For ninety-nine, I thought that was pretty sharp thinking.

For Marie's hundredth birthday a party was arranged at the Deva, which was attended by the Mayor of Aberystwyth. The previous day, we had a lunch-time party at her old pub the Wild Fowler, so that her old village friends could meet her once again. We organised it with a second cousin of ours, Yvonne John, who had looked after the two sisters for many years. The party lasted from noon until half past one, during which time Marie saw the outside of eight whiskies. We thought the last one 'for the road' should be diluted with a little water. But once she had tasted it, she almost threw it back at me in disgust!

The next morning was her official birthday with telegrams arriving from the Queen, Rhodri Morgan, Peter Hain, the Minister for Wales and a few other dignitaries. At nine o'clock in the morning, I telephoned the home in fear and trepidation lest the demon drink had got the better of her. To my surprise I gathered she was up, bright as a lark and helping to wash the breakfast utensils. She was a remarkable lady.

Eventually, old age caught up with her and, when the Deva was closed, she was transferred to Tregerddan Old People's Home in Bow Street and finally to Cwmcynfelin, a couple of miles north-east of Aberystwyth. One often hears horrible stories about the treatment of the elderly, but these homes provided excellent care. The kindness shown to my aunt by the wonderful staff was exemplary and made me wish that I would also be able to end my days there. She was so happy in the home and very popular with the staff, as she had been with all who came into contact with her.

After she died, it surprised me to find out that she had suffered congenital heart disease since she was eighty. She had travelled a very long road since her early days in Goginan and it was so nice to think that she left this world with no enemies or anyone who thought ill of her. On a facetious note, my thoughts turned to her choice of interment: cremation. With all the spirits she had imbibed to her very last days, would the flames ever be extinguished?

Whether Betty was the chalk or the cheese, I don't know, but she is certainly a very different personality from her sister. Life for her seems to have had a more serious, contemplative quality. She was born on 11 January 1906 at the Druid Inn, the seventh of eight children. Being the youngest daughter, she was destined to stay at home and assist her parents with the domestic chores around the house. Thus her early life was spent almost entirely in the environs of the village. She enjoyed her time at the local school and various jaunts among the surrounding hills and woodlands, picking blueberries when they were in season for her mother, who made as many as six pies at a time to feed the large family.

Many of her earliest memories centred on life within the Druid and her liaisons with its clients. About two years ago when she was ninety-nine, she surprised my wife and me by bursting into song; it was an Irish ballad which, I later learned, she had picked up from some Irish 'navvies'. In the early twentieth century, they had worked on the track of the *Tren Fach* (little train) which plied from Aberystwyth to Devil's Bridge. This train was first used to transport goods and local workers to and from Aberystwyth. Each evening these Irish workers made their way to the Druid, so that Betty had ample opportunity to listen to their banter and songs. I can't quite remember the number of verses which she sang in English, but we were amazed at how word-perfect she was after a span of around ninety years.

In later life, Betty spent some time working as a secretary in Aberystwyth. She was musical and possessed a fine soprano voice. She sang in concerts and was the soprano lead when the local choir gave performances of *Y Trwbadŵr* in the early 1930s. Quite remarkably, she performed the same role just after World War II.

Betty and Mary enjoying a leisurely holiday in Caersws.

She also had a remarkable talent for playing the piano by ear, so that she could accompany herself with many of her songs.

Being a very attractive young lady, she had no end of suitors in her early life, but the gentleman who finally captivated her heart was a hairdresser from Aberystwyth, Harry Ashley-Jones. Besides owning a salon in Pier Street, he also had establishments in Carmarthen which were run by his sons and daughters from a previous marriage. It was Harry who apprenticed Billy Tunstall, the evacuee from Liverpool who billeted with my grandmother at the Druid. Billy stayed in Aberystwyth as a hairdresser for the rest of his life, an opportunity for which he was eternally grateful.

Though Harry was quite a bit older than Betty, they enjoyed years of love and marriage. We used to tease Betty that she really had married him for his double-barrelled name! In reality, however, they were a well-matched couple. They married in 1946 and spent their honeymoon in Salzburg, Austria. Cecele and I visited the city a few months ago and it was surprising how much Betty remembered about its beautiful buildings and her visits to Berchesgarten, one of Adolf Hitler's retreats during the war. However, what struck her most was the abject poverty and lack of food suffered by the Austrians immediately after the war.

After a short time living at the Druid, Harry bought a large property called *Maes Heulog* (sunny meadow) in Capel Bangor. It was a solidly built, five-bedroomed detached house, which was soon filled with fine quality furniture including Betty's favourite piece, a baby grand piano. She also acquired a little white poodle which remained with the family for many years. The pair visited several auctions and sales in large manor houses in their grey Vauxhall car, and gradually added many fine antiques to the house. Betty gained a very creditable knowledge of the value of furniture, pictures, crockery and fine art – especially if they were antiques – and developed a very shrewd eye for a bargain.

Harry had a passion for fishing and had leased a lake called *Pwll Glas* (blue lake) up in the hills near Ystumtuen. On the banks of the lake was a small bungalow and, oh, the thrill of being taken up there for the afternoon in the Vauxhall. He had a large telescope in the sitting room which stood on a tripod and was trained to look out over the lake. As a small child, I had a passion for telescopes but the nearest I got to possessing one was a six inch little toy with a magnification of plus two. But I used to gaze at two objects in my mother's Graves of Sheffield catalogue: the bicycle with the 'North Road' raised handlebars which I eventually got, and a page devoted to various telescopes which I never got. So it was ecstasy to be able to gaze at this magnificent instrument and even to look through the eyepiece. I couldn't see a darn thing as it was adjusted to ancient eyes, but it was a thrill nevertheless. Then there was the tea with real cucumber sandwiches – it's amazing how things taste great when everything else is so fine.

For a time, Harry also leased another lake closer to Ystumtuen, called 'Pond yr Orfa'. He would invite his shopkeeper friends in town to go up for a spot of fishing. He also engaged an old chap called Richard James, who had a little cottage overlooking the lake, to keep an eye on things. I believe Richard was a distant relative of mine. He had been a Baptist minister for a period but it was rumoured that he had become a little 'loco'. I'm not quite sure whether this was true or not, as he seemed to know what he was doing and poked quiet fun at people. When I was a child, he used to come to afternoon communion services at Jezreel Baptist, arriving about ten minutes before the service was due to finish. Everyone would look at each other in trepidation; since he was a retired minister, he was guaranteed to stand up just before the last hymn and pray very loudly for up to twenty minutes.

Anyway, Richard would do his job for Harry a little too conscientiously, for the moment one of Harry's friends arrived at the pond, he would immediately accost them as to what authority they had to fish. If authority from Harry was not forthcoming in writing, Richard would stand or sit about three yards away from the 'interloper' and throw stones into the water until the fisherman gave up in disgust.

Eventually, Richard was admitted to a mental institution in Carmarthen for his last days. Hughie Griffiths the coalman, who was a close neighbour of Richard's in Ystumtuen, visited him quite often during this period. As Hughie was about to leave after one such visit, Richard asked him to wait a moment as he had prepared a little parcel to remind Hughie of their friendship. He brought out the parcel which was wrapped in brown paper and tied with string, from some hidden location, and charged Hughie not to open it until he had arrived home. This Hughie duly did, although he was intrigued that it weighed a lot for such a small parcel. Could it be a book – a Bible perhaps? On arriving home, Hughie could wait no longer and hurriedly opened the parcel to find a brick wrapped in one of the institute's monogrammed towels. I really think that for all his quirks, Richard had a wicked sense of humour.

Harry died in his early eighties and left a much younger widow with surprising little money and no pension. Apparently, since he was the owner of the business, he had not paid any national insurance for such an eventuality. So Betty, after a blissful marriage, was left to build her life up once again. She sold the large house in Capel Bangor and bought a smaller property in Aberystwyth. Buying and selling antique furniture soon garnered her a little capital and she was able to move into a larger property. By this time, Marie had moved into a flat in Aberystwyth so that each could support the other. It was rather strange really, because their perceptions of life were very different. However, woe betide anyone who tried to come between them.

Betty moved into the Abbeyfield Home in Great Darkgate Street and continued what had now become a hobby for her: buying and selling items found at auctions. Even today, her perspicacity and business mind is as clear as ever. Just over a year ago, she visited a local auction room and bought a small bedside table which she fancied. It was very light, and as she was leaving the premises with the table under her arm, an elderly gentleman came trotting towards her, perspiring and very red in the face. His face fell as his gaze rested on the little table. My aunt became very concerned and asked him what was the matter. He explained that he had visited the auction rooms earlier in the morning when the articles for sale could be viewed, and had set his heart on acquiring the table. He pleaded with her to sell it to him but my aunt, with many apologies, told him that she needed it to place near her bed. Very dejectedly the gentleman turned away; then with a sudden change of heart my aunt called him back and told him that as he looked so upset, she would sell it to him for what she had paid for it – seventy-five pounds. The gentleman immediately regained his composure, thanked Betty profusely for her kindness and departed carrying the table with a new spring in his step. On enquiring as how much she had actually paid for the table, she mentioned the sum of twenty-five pounds! As to the propriety of undertaking such a course of action, she evoked the principles of supply and demand. I felt a great pang of envy and wished that I had inherited her eye for business.

During the outing to Tregaron and Lampeter I mentioned earlier, Cecele accompanied Betty into a draper's shop in Lampeter across the road from the university entrance. Apparently, this establishment was of high repute, and Betty was a regular client when Harry was alive. Betty had an aura about her that immediately attracted the attention of at least two of the female staff. Even at her ancient age, she would gravitate to the high quality items (I always guide her to the cheaper clothes!). Cecele was very amused to eavesdrop on the conversation which went something like this:

Betty: That's a very nice dress, do you think you have it in my size?

Assistant: I'm sure we have madam. What are you, size eight or ten?

Betty: I'm not sure, bach. Anyway, how much is it?

Assistant (looking at label): That's a hundred and twenty pounds, Madam.

Betty: How much? I bought a cottage for less than that a few years ago!

After trying to buy another dress which was much cheaper and finding that it was the uniform worn by the staff themselves, they departed with Betty muttering about the price of things.

The same thing happened when I took the sisters to tea; I think we had four teas and some Welsh cakes at a total cost about eight pounds. When Betty heard how much it was, a question that was inevitably asked, she immediately demanded that I should take it all back! At her advanced age, I think it is very difficult to come to terms with the concept of rising inflation and the cost of living.

A few years ago, Betty managed to endure the relatively long journey from Aberystwyth to Trowbridge for a week's holiday with us, and what a model guest she was. She was enthusiastic about everything she saw and everywhere she went. She seemed to have boundless energy and her favourite activity was to visit the shops, especially the antique and charity shops. Ever the pragmatist, she decided that at her age it was more practical to buy clothing for herself and Marie in charity shops for a reduced price, rather than paying considerable sums for outfits which might have little use. As my father-in-law used to say when he was eighty: "I never buy my bananas green any more!" What amused Cecele, who was nearly half a century younger, was Betty's constant enquiry as to whether she was getting tired and if she would like to rest and have a cup of tea.

Yes, Betty is a remarkable lady and obviously a survivor. She walks up and down the stairs several times a day in the home, even though there is a lift for the convenience of the elderly. She gets pangs of nostalgia at times and feels the loneliness of one who is left behind, now that her whole family and contemporaries have departed. Even so, she lives in great comfort at the Abbeyfield home, enjoying the comfort, the excellent food and the care which Mrs Hilda Leeman and her staff provide.

I look forward to celebrating her next birthday with her in January. We celebrated her hundredth at the Belle Vue Hotel, with many of her friends and acquaintances braving the cold weather. Who knows, we might be able to celebrate a few more with her in the years to come.

CHAPTER SEVENTEEN

Cameos

EVERY VILLAGE SEEMS TO have its characters and Goginan is no exception, as I have shown in this book. Another character was Richard Williams, or Dick y Box as everyone knew him. Dick had an unfulfilled ambition, that of becoming a Methodist minister. I don't think that there is any doubt that, had he received the proper training, Dick would have been an inspiring addition to the clergy. However, I think that he was too much of a dreamer to achieve his goal.

I think Dick lived at Box Cottage for his whole life, hence his nickname. He was the youngest of four children. I believe John Williams was the oldest; he was married to Edith Olwen and had one son, Glyn, who inherited many of Dick's talents. Then came brother David (Dei Box), whose antics used to keep me in stitches when I was very young. He used to chase me around the trees near the Royal Oak until I would collapse with laughter. These episodes would often occur when I had a full belly, but being violently sick was a small price to pay for the hilarious enjoyment. Their sister, Kate Mary, was my mother's great friend when she was young; unfortunately she became victim of tuberculosis and passed away at a comparatively young age.

Eventually, Dick was left to live at Box Cottage on his own and followed his own dreams. When electricity came to the village, Dick shunned the idea of modernising; I don't think it arrived in the house until he passed away.

In some ways there was a little of Walter Mitty in Dick; he

dreamt of life as a successful minister and would emulate the famous ministers of his time. During the thirties and forties, it was the practice of all the places of worship to hold *Cyrddau Mawr* (big meetings) once a year, when at least two ministers of note would be invited to preach. There would usually be one evening session with a sermon, to be followed the next day by meetings in the afternoon and evening, with two sermons at each session. Quite a few of us youngsters would jib at the prospect of this feast of 'sermonising', but Dick would be in his element.

On one occasion, Jezreel Baptist Chapel engaged the services of Jubilee Young, one of the foremost Baptist ministers of the time, and his equally talented nephew, Young Haydn. They could rouse great fervour with their eloquent and inspiring sermons. Dick attended every service, sitting in a pew by the door to one side of the pulpit, as if he were in the wings listening to a wonderful performance and wishing he could step on to centre stage and perform in the same way.

For weeks after this great event, Dick slept and dreamt sermons, and would regale any house he visited with an almost verbatim reconstruction of one of them, complete with *hwyl*, Bible thumps and expansive arm movements. He was so good at it; he had all the attributes – he was a consummate actor with a commanding voice for exhortation, a soothing tone for the more poignant bits and a beautiful lyrical tenor voice to tug at the heartstrings when required.

However, Dick's dreams seemed to preclude any thoughts of doing practical work; he was quite happy to be on the dole for much of his life. This gave him more freedom to develop his 'performances'. Much of his reading was devoted to the published sermons of his heroes, and he could quote large passages from texts to impress his listeners.

He had a fund of recitations, both serious and humorous which, when he could be coaxed to perform, would keep his listeners at local concerts enthralled, with loud shouts for an encore which Dick, revelling in the adulation with a slight smile on his face, would politely decline. 'Keep them wanting more' was his motto. Eventually his conscience, or the authorities, caught up with him and in later life he was obliged to take a job as the village postman.

Funnily enough, Dick revelled in his new job. As long as he commenced work on time, there was little other restriction on his movements during the day. Rural people do not seem to have the sense of urgency which one finds in urban areas, so that the time letters or parcels arrived was of little consequence. Dick therefore could take his time and enjoyed passing the time of day over a cup or two of tea in quite a few houses during his round.

One very sunny August day, Dick had to walk to one of the extremities of his round, namely Brodawel (the quiet vale), a house at the bottom of the Melindŵr valley, and then up the valley side to a small holding, Ty'n y Pwll. After Troed-y-rhiw farm, Dick felt he was far enough from civilisation to be able to divest himself of his trousers since it was so hot. After all, he was sporting a new pair of striped underpants and it might lighten the day for Mrs Boon and Iris at Brodawel. So, rather than having to carry his trousers with him, he decided to hang them on a tree to be retrieved on the return journey. I can only guess what reception Dick received at Brodawel. However, on the path down to Ty'n y Pwll he was received by a gaggle of geese. Whether the sight of Dick's bare legs or his striped underpants attracted them, I don't know, but they took a fancy to him and Dick had to flee in a hurry with the offending birds snapping at his nether regions. I don't think Ty'n y Pwll received any mail that day and I can only assume that he remembered to retrieve his trousers on the way back.

Dick passed away a few years ago and the village mourned the loss of another great character.

The chase.

Dick on his round, delivering mail to the inhabitants of the Dollwen, Goginan.

Peter Davies was an enigma. He was born to Eluned Davies in the mid-1940s at Hyfrydle (beautiful place) in Goginan, but since she was away for a considerable time on government work, Peter was largely brought up by his grandmother, Margaret (Maggie) Jones. I remember him as a quiet, pleasant, blonde, curly haired little boy who often visited us when we lived next door. He went regularly with his grandmother to Jezreel Baptist Chapel and, though there was a considerable age gap between us, he often followed me around. I was at the 'love of the sea and anything that floated' stage and I commandeered anything that could be made to resemble the action of rowing. I had acquired the chassis of a handcart with large wheels and found out that by sitting on the chassis on a small plank of wood, I could 'row' myself by pulling the wheels backwards, rather like a wheelchair in reverse. I let Peter use my 'rowing boat' too.

He proved to be very bright and automatically entered Ardwyn Grammar School in Aberystwyth where he excelled in both academia and sport. He was a champion sprinter in the school's athletics house competitions and was chosen to represent Cardiganshire in the relay competition. During his early childhood there were signs that he was very gifted in elocution, and it was at the eisteddfod in Goginan that he won his first prize for reciting the Welsh hymn 'Dyma gariad fel y moroedd' (Here is love like the oceans) in a competition for children under six years of age. During his latter years at Ardwyn, his thoughts turned to Christian matters and, with his eloquence, despite a slight speech impediment, he felt his future lay in the ministry. To this end he visited many places of worship as a lay preacher.

During his later years at Ardwyn, his great promise in the literary world led the then editor of the *Cambrian News*, Douglas Wright, to offer him free tuition as a reporter. His talent soon led him to the post of radio and television columnist for the national newspaper, *Y Faner* (*The Banner*). About the same time,

Peter as a child on my 'rowing boat' outside Rose Cottage, once the home of Absolom Francis, the mining superintendent in the nineteenth century.

he became one of the presenters of *Sgubor Lawen* (*Happy Barn*), a weekly Welsh variety television show on Harlech Television (HTV).

On leaving Ardwyn School he was accepted for teacher training in Trinity College, Carmarthen, where, under the able tuition of Nora Isaac, he could have developed into one of Wales' great actors. Under teachers such as W Beynon Davies at Ardwyn, Peter had immersed himself in Welsh culture and the Arts, and he was only seventeen when he won the first of the thirty bardic chairs, including the chairs at the Urdd (Welsh League of Youth) National Eisteddfod in 1966 and 1967. There is little doubt that he could have gone on to win the Crown or even the Chair at the National Eisteddfod of Wales had he persevered. He was an excellent elocutionist and could hold his own with the very best in the country. Since he could not drive, I gave him lifts to many competitions where he would invariably win the main elocution competition.

Despite Peter's many achievements in the world of literature and broadcasting, there seemed to be something in his makeup that prevented him from reaching his true potential. His outlook on life completely changed as the 1960s wore on, and he became a great exponent of keeping public houses open on Sundays. He went on something of a mission, spreading the word, and like Dick y Box, his orations were given a greater poignancy by emulating well-known preachers. Peter was an enigma. He could discuss any topic on an equal footing with the most illustrious of scholars, yet be totally comfortable and happy amongst his mates in the Druid Inn or in the Coopers Arms in Aberystwyth.

He was the first to confess that he could have made much more of his academic studies. On leaving Trinity College, he spent a period teaching in schools in North Wales living like a hermit in a small cottage near Bethesda. Eventually, he received a lecturing post in Monmouth College where he remained for twenty-five years.

During this time he met his future wife and was married at Jezreel Baptist by the Reverend Roger Jones. My mother had the privilege of playing the organ for the service. Peter was very fond of my mother and when he visited the village, he would spend a lot of time at our house. Unfortunately, his marriage

Peter Davies, Goginan

was not a success. He began to be plagued by gastric problems which forced him to retire early from lecturing, and he returned to Goginan to live for a time with his mother. The demon drink gradually increased its hold on him. Still, flashes of the old Peter often came to the fore and there was some demand for his considerable talents. About a year before his untimely death, he appeared as Saint Padarn in a Welsh television programme, to some acclaim.

In his latter days he lived with his partner, Heather, at the old School House in Goginan, where he received all the love and care that could be given to him. His health deteriorated rapidly and he was admitted to Bronglais Hospital where he remained in a coma for five days. Despite great efforts by the hospital staff and the support of many friends who regularly visited him – including three ministers of religion, an Irishman, Willie Mahon, who played the pipes at his bedside, and Glynis and 'Rocket' who took turns for two nights reading his favourite poet, Waldo Williams – Peter quietly slipped away with Heather at his side.

One of Peter's dear friends over many years was Lyn Ebenezer. In his tribute, he spoke of Peter as a man who had been born a century too late; he envisaged him as being totally at home in the midst of the old nomadic saints, but he added that, unlike Saint David, Peter would never be satisfied with drinking only water!

At the time of his death, it had been a few years since I had met him but I always had a soft spot for Peter. Like many of his friends and acquaintances throughout Wales, I felt that we had lost a great potential talent, and can only surmise what could have been had he managed to reach the peak of his many abilities.

I remember hearing the phrase *breuder bywyd* (the fragility of life) when I was young. I can't remember whether it was the title of a poem or the name of a song, but it often returns to my mind when people are, for whatever reason, struck down in an untimely fashion. Like Peter, it can be used to refer to another of the brightest stars ever produced in Goginan.

Frederick Byron Howells was born in Goginan in 1940, the fifth of six children to Bill and Sally Howells. Their first-born was Dewi, who had an illustrious career as a captain in the navy. Second was Meurig; he worked locally before getting married and moving to Bow Street, where he took an active interest in local affairs, especially that of the local soccer team. He died recently after a fairly long illness. Gwyneira and Tegwen, the third and fourth children, were musically talented. They both moved away after getting married. Gwyneira now lives in Penrhyncoch, while Tegwen and her husband Goronwy reside in Talybont. Geraint, the youngest of the family, tragically died at a very young age.

Byron enthralled us with his performances as an elocutionist at the age of nine or ten. Even then, it was almost a certainty that he would become a leading light in the world of the arts and literature. At Ardwyn Grammar School he showed his outstanding talent as an actor and his qualities as a leader. He was greatly influenced by W Beynon Davies, who guided his studies in Welsh and Scripture. Years later, it was with great rejoicing that Beynon, himself a regular worshipper and lay reader, received the news that Byron had decided to become a minister of religion.

During his youth, Byron enjoyed many adventures with WJ Edwards and Tegwyn Jones of Bow Street. In 1961, Byron and WJ joined a group of young people from Ammanford in Carmarthenshire on a visit to Berlin. Since their journey was overland, they were obliged to show their passports and visas at the border between East and West Germany. Unfortunately, the East German authorities deemed that there were irregularities in their documents and they were thrown into a cell at five o'clock in the morning, where they languished for a period with only one orange between them. Byron's humour sustained them until they were released. They were then advised by a more helpful woman, in rather broken English, that the border did not extend into the heavens and that it was possible for them to fly into West Berlin. This is what they eventually managed to do, taking off from Hanover.

On leaving school, Byron spent a period working under the guidance of R Alun Edwards at the county library. Then he went to the University of Wales, Bangor where he became one of the stars of the university's social programme, especially the

inter-college cultural competitions like the eisteddfod. It was during this time that he met and fell in love with Eirian from Conway, and soon afterwards they were married. Following his arts degree in Bangor, he returned to the Theological College in Aberystwyth where he obtained the title of Bachelor of Divinity. Then, on 7 September 1967, at the age of twenty-seven, Byron was ordained as minister of the Calvinistic

Byron with one of his boys.

Methodist Chapel at Trawsfynydd and its sister churches. Byron and his wife entered wholeheartedly into their new life, partaking in the activities of several associations and societies in the area, notably the Young Farmers' Club.

After a few years of faithful service in Trawsfynydd, the family moved to Bryngwran in Anglesey. However, heart disease began troubling him, and he was forced to leave his calling in Anglesey to live once more in Bangor.

Byron was a 'man of letters', writing plays and scripts for a variety of occasions. A testament to his considerable abilities was his victory in the National Eisteddfod of Wales on at least nine occasions in the 1980s. His children's novel, *Pysgodyn yn y llwch* (*A Fish in the Dust*) was published in 1982 to great acclaim and won a prize at the Swansea National Eisteddfod. He also won acclaim for an essay he wrote on the influence of his friend, Dan Jones, on his early life.

In 1989 he passed away at his home in Bangor, leaving his wife, Eirian, his children, Ifor, Elfed and Geraint, as well as many other relatives and a host of friends to mourn the loss of one of the most pleasant and talented people Goginan has produced.

I have already mentioned the enterprising Emlyn Jones who started many new businesses in Goginan. Emlyn became increasingly handicapped by the onset of the skin disease psoriasis which was to afflict him for most of his later life. He died in 1980 at the age of seventy; Dilys, his wife, continued to live in the village for a further nine years. Whatever satisfaction they gleaned from their enterprises, they certainly took pride in the success of their two children, Gwyn and Mair.

Gwyn Shop, or to give him his full name, Huw Gwynfryn Jones, was born in 1936, and very early in his life showed signs of brilliance – especially in science and technology. During my youth, I had many conversations with a young Gwyn, and was amazed and more often than not, flummoxed by the depth of his perceptions. On leaving Aberystwyth University, Gwyn was accepted to work at the Atomic Nuclear Station at Harwell, after which he became a lecturer in Nuclear Physics at Loughborough College. It was during his time at Loughbough that he devised the Torbeck Valve which revolutionised the water flow in toilet cisterns,a development of such significance that it was featured in the *Tomorrow's World* television programme. He subsequently opened his own factory in Welwyn Garden City to produce the valve, with great success. Many plumbing manufacturers adopted the valve, which is still used throughout the world.

Tragically, as in the case of other bright stars in the village, Gwyn died before his time – in 1987 at the age of fifty-one. He is survived by his wife, Norma, who has returned to live in the Aberystwyth area, and two daughters, Gaynor and Dilys. Norma came to the area as an evacuee in 1940, decided to remain in the area and is now a fluent Welsh speaker. Gwyn's memory is perpetuated by a prize which is annually awarded to promising students at Loughborough College.

In 1937, the Joneses were blessed with an addition to the family. Mair Shop, as her many friends still call her, was educated at Goginan School and Ardwyn Grammar School where her considerable musical abilities were nurtured, so that a brilliant career in this field seemed almost a foregone conclusion. However, her father's medical problem took a turn for the worse, and it was decided – in the traditional fashion – that Mair would have to forego her studies in order to help out at home. It was considered more important that the male offspring should be given every opportunity to progress.

So Mair, much to her chagrin, found herself taking over the village shop rather than pursuing her studies. Though her heart was not in the work, she battled on for over a year. Then her father's condition improved somewhat and Mair took the opportunity to apply for a place at the Cardiff College of Music and Drama. She was accepted for the following academic year, when misfortune struck again. Her father's condition suddenly deteriorated and he was forced to spend considerable periods of time in various hospitals, in a vain effort to combat the disease. So once again Mair was forced to abandon her dreams and return home.

Even so, she pursued her interests and developed into a fine singer, winning several prizes in the mid 1950s at local eisteddfodau. She also developed a keen interest in drama and became a member of the Cardiganshire Drama Company under the distinguished tutelage of Ithel Jones, Talybont. Her musical interests were further widened when her parents gave her a harp for her eighteenth birthday and, as an accomplished harpist, she received the honour of being accepted into the Bardic Circle – *Yr Orsedd* – at the National Eisteddfod of Wales in 1957, being given the title of *Telynores Rheidol* (Rheidol's Harpist).

Her considerable abilities as a harpist led to another very important stage in her life. In April 1962, Mair was invited to play the harp at a folk dancing course which had been organised by the Welsh League of Youth (*Urdd Gobaith Cymru*) at their headquarters at Pantyfedwen, Borth. It was here that she met the love of her life, Alwyn Selway, and a year later, in April 1963, they were married and settled in Colwyn Bay. In 1966, Alwyn was made headmaster of Llansannan Primary School in North Wales where he and Mair settled for the next thirty-eight years. They produced three very able children: Dylan who is now lives in Sweden, working as a surveyor; Buddug, who teaches in Mold; and Dyfrig, who works as a translator in London.

In 1976, Mair was invited to form a Welsh male voice choir. The Bro Aled Choir has since gone from strength to strength, giving scores of concerts both at home and abroad; their success culminating in winning the second prize at the 2007 Welsh

National Eisteddfod for Male Voice Choirs. In 2004 Alwyn and Mair moved to a new home in Mold where they continue to lead a very active life in the cultural activities of the area.

I think Mair's story again illustrates how when one door seems to close, another opens. Though she many not have achieved her initial ambition, other opportunities emerged to allow her to develop her talents, and it is so nice to think that another successful career had its roots in Goginan.

Mair Selway

CHAPTER EIGHTEEN

More Anecdotes and Other Bits of Interest

D URING THE PAST FEW months as I have tried to gather my thoughts on my early days in Goginan, I have been increasingly amazed at the vibrancy which seemed to emanate from the community. Many of my old friends and acquaintances from that time have been so helpful in adding to, or correcting, the memories I had of those days. Invariably the reminiscences centre on what people did or how they reacted with one another. Since little tit-bits are still reaching my ears, I am using this section as a sort of 'hoover' to sweep them all up.

In his book *The History of the Goginan Mines*, Simon Hughes recounts two very amusing stories. The first relates the story of two brothers who once lived in Goginan at a time when its economic fortunes were at a low ebb. One worked in a local lead mine, while the other was a butcher by trade, and was having a hard time to make ends meet. His life was further plagued by a large black dog which had taken a shine to him – or rather to his meat, parts of which he made off with whenever the opportunity arose. The butcher's profits were suffering due to the dog's purloining habits, so much so that one night the brothers hatched a plot for disposing of it. It was decided that the mining brother would bring a cartridge of explosive, a cap and some fuse home from work the following afternoon.

The next day, the butcher primed the cartridge and, when

the dog appeared, lit the fuse and threw it out of the door. The dog excitedly bounded after it and the butcher quickly closed the door with a sigh of relief in the sure knowledge that his precious meat was safe at last. There was a pregnant silence as he waited for the sound of the explosion that would seal the dog's fate. Having no clue as to the burning time of the fuse, he grew impatient and decided to ease the door open slightly to look for the dog's remains. There was no sign of the offending creature. It was then that the butcher became aware of an acrid burning smell and, turning round, was rather surprised to see the dog sitting behind him, tail wagging, with the cartridge at its feet eagerly awaiting a re-throw. The butcher flung open the door and rushed into the street just before the charge exploded, totally demolishing his establishment. What happened to the dog is not recorded but the butcher decided to cease trading.

Simon also records the story of an aged female ore dresser who worked in one of the lead mines around Goginan and lived in a remote cottage a few miles into the hills. It was a very wet and windy day, so she decided to adjourn to the Druid Inn along with some of her workmates before walking home, in the hope that conditions would improve before nightfall. However, conditions got worse and the landlord eventually asked them to leave, as he had to be up early the next morning. Nineteenth-century Goginan was not well lit after dark (nor was it during my youth) and the paths into the hills above the Melindŵr valley were treacherous in daylight, let alone for an old woman at night. Someone decided that she should be provided with some form of illumination, but in such atrocious conditions a lantern would be of little use. It was then remembered that one of the senior mine staff had a new fangled electric lamp – this was sent for and proved to be ideal for the journey. The old lady was then despatched home through the storm.

The following morning the old lady appeared as usual at her

place on the dressing floor, carrying the lamp which looked in a very poor state and had ceased to function. Its owner was not best pleased and asked for an explanation as to its current condition. Apparently, having arrived home and put on her nightclothes, the old lady found that the light refused to be extinguished despite every effort to blow it out. Even pinching the light had no effect. With a thatch roof, it would be dangerous to leave the light on, so she decided that the only safe course of action was to dowse it with water. Even then the light did not go out, so she had no option but to leave it in a bucket of water overnight. She was pleased to report that this eventually did the trick!

When the local lead mines closed, miners had to travel several miles to find work. Due to the long hours of work, walking such distances daily proved to be impracticable. So the mining authorities would build accommodation barracks where the miners could sleep during the working week. They would leave the village early on a Monday morning carrying provisions for the week, and return home on Saturday afternoons.

Every Monday morning, one miner – who I shall call Tom – would leave his dear wife in Goginan and walk the nine or ten miles across the moors to Dylife, a mining site a few miles north-west of Llanidloes. Tom had not had much formal education and as such was pretty illiterate. So to ease his comprehension a little, his young wife hit on the idea of cooking six pies of various kinds, one for each day's work. Thus, when all the pies were gone, it was time for Tom to return home for the weekend. The system worked very well for a long period, until, one particular week, some thieving wag decided to help himself to one of Tom's pies during the week. So by the fifth day, all the pies had been consumed. Tom packed up his meagre belongings and returned home, only to find his dear wife in a very uncompromising situation with another man from the village. What happened the following week was not made known.

Daniel y crydd (the cobbler) was another notable village character. Whether he had been a serviceman in an earlier war, or had had a severe accident is not clear, but Daniel had lost a leg which had been replaced by a wooden peg. Despite his handicap, Dan was quite an accomplished musician and played in the Goginan brass band. One summer's day, the band was invited to play at Aberdovey. A horse-drawn brake was hired to carry them to Ynyslas, where they embarked in rowing boats to cross the Dovey estuary. The concert went well and was without incident. However, the Goginan choir had earlier undertaken the same journey to sing 'Worthy is the Lamb' from Handel's Messiah at an eisteddfod in Aberdovey. The rendering of the anthem was going very well – until the stage collapsed!

The band's 'voyage' back over the estuary was a painfully slow one, probably due to a change in the tide. Tempers got a little frayed at the slow pace, as the prospect of a few pints at the Druid Inn began receding. Daniel became increasingly irate and to show his frustration, he stood up and stamped his foot. Unfortunately, it was the peg leg that he stamped, and the pointed end went right through the floor of the boat. Apparently, poor Daniel had to stand with his peg leg stuck in the hole for the rest of the crossing to prevent the boat from sinking.

Just after World War II a lady came to live in one of the remoter cottages overlooking the Rheidol valley. She had been working in domestic service for the gentry of London for years and so, despite the drastic change of environment, she still hankered for some of the high life – which Aberystwyth could offer to some extent. (To call life in Aberystwyth 'high' was a bit of a misnomer, but at least there was a choice of three cinemas in those days.) Thus, nearly every Saturday afternoon, she would catch the one-thirty bus from Goginan to attend a matinee screening. In summer, she would add to her pleasure by visiting Emlyn Jones at the lower shop to purchase a block of ice cream to enjoy while watching the film. One hot day, Emlyn, who had rather a sharp sense of humour, decided to let her have a large block of ice cream for a cheaper price. She arrived in Aberystwyth anticipating the feast, only to discover a huge pool of melted cream at the bottom of her bag.

On another occasion, it was a wet day and she decided to purchase a pair of Wellington boots. The bus arrived as she was in the act of putting them on, so she started running to catch it. Unfortunately, the boots were still tied together with string, and much was the hilarity amongst bystanders as they watched her chasing the bus with short steps which would have done credit to a geisha girl.

It's strange how gullible people can be at times. On one occasion the same lady arrived at the village shop after it had closed for the night. She apologised and explained that for the first time ever, her faithful clock had let her down and was inexplicably half an hour late. Emlyn looked at her seriously and advised her boil the clock for half an hour. The following week, she returned to enquire if Emlyn sold clocks; apparently hers had ceased to function completely after being boiled!

From time to time when I visited Goginan, I would come across the local paper *Y Tincer* (*The Tinker*) and would read of events such as weddings and meetings. Most of the time the names of the people involved would not be familiar to me. However, while looking through an old issue of the paper at my cousin's house recently, I came across an article by a Dewi Davies on the history of the Melindŵr valley. I found it so absorbing that I decided to get more information by visiting the Town Library in Aberystwyth. Miss Nia Richards very kindly furnished me with a host of past issues of the paper, from which

I include a few extracts below.

In the early nineteenth century, with such a small population, there was little opportunity for opening any form of shop in the valley. People relied on what they could grow in their gardens or on the one or two animals they kept if they had enough land. There were one or two farmers who saw an opportunity to make extra money by selling a little meat, which they transported in their carts.

However, with the rapid increase in mining activity in the middle of the century, the population quickly grew, giving an opportunity for shops to open. In the early 1850s there were two retail outlets in the village. There was Edward Morgan who described himself as a general dealer and had a shop called Victoria House, sited about half a mile to the west of Goginan on the main road; thus the shop must have been on the site of the Black Horse, which, when I was in Goginan school during World War II was a pig farm. Due to its name, we always surmised that it had been a pub but apparently the house had never been used for that purpose. At the time there was also another general dealer's shop near the Druid Inn owned by a Richard Williams.

A little later, it seems that the shop on the site of the Black Horse was passed on to a gentleman called John Sylvanus Williams who combined this activity with that of a cobbler. In Pleasant Row, near the top of the hill leading from the village to the Dollwen, an Evan Lewis described himself as a carrier and shopkeeper, while over the other side of the valley in the Geuallt, a thirty-four year old widow and mother of two girls, Sarah Pierce kept a shop. Also near the Druid Inn, Thomas Ody, a native of Wiltshire, opened a shop. Ody also was a lay preacher with the English Wesleyan chapel. Dan Jones also mentioned a 'fish woman' who travelled around the village.

Miners were usually paid monthly in the mid nineteenth

century, the salaries being distributed initially at the Druid Inn and later at the Mines' Office. During the earlier period, when the 'pay-out' was at the Druid, it was essential for the wives to accompany their husbands to ensure that the salaries did not go into the coffers of the public house. It was also noted that absenteeism at the village school increased very markedly on pay day.

To take advantage of this significant day, merchants came with their wares from considerable distances and established their stalls on the approach roads to the mine. I remember the older inhabitants of the village during my childhood referring to a stretch of road near the farm of Troed-rhiw-castell as 'Bwlch y Ffair' (the Gap of the fair).

Once the monthly salary was received, the sequence was firstly to pay the debt incurred during the last month for goods purchased, in order to be entitled to goods 'on the slate' for the coming month. Then any other debts, for instance to local shopkeepers, would be settled.

There were a few 'clubs' in Goginan in the mid nineteenth century whereby people could pay for goods by easy instalments. I have already mentioned the book clubs in and around the Druid Inn that had been formed.

On 3 January 1854, a Friendly Society was established which met in the house of a Morgan Morgan in Druid Village. The object of this club was to establish a treasury which would help members in sickness, old age and to pay funeral expenses. Members met on one Tuesday a month, when each would pay one shilling into a box. If a member fell into arrears with his payment for over four months, one shilling would be deducted from his benefit; this would rise to one shilling and sixpence if arrears continued for five months. However, anyone who lived over six miles away would be given six months to pay. If arrears were not paid within six months, the member would be expelled. All members had to be under forty-five and be of 'a peaceful disposition and sober in habits.' Members were elected by a majority vote, but election meetings had to have a quorum of eleven. Voters used black (no) or white (yes) sticks which were put in a hat to decide the fate of a candidate. Members would be eligible for benefits after a membership of two years when three shillings a week would be paid for the first two months, two shillings and sixpence for the third and fourth months, and two shillings for the fifth and sixth month.

A Clothing Club was also opened in the village by a William Davies, again with very strict rules. Members were expected to contribute half a crown every Saturday until their fund amounted to thirty shillings. Once that sum was reached, the member would be entitled to an article of clothing; however, the time he or she received the goods depended on when that person's name was drawn out of a hat. A levy of sixpence was charged if a member fell into arrears with the payment. Anyone leaving the district would be entitled to clothes to the value of the contribution paid in up to the date of departure. William Davies ran his business at Loveden Place in Druid Village, but the tailor shop and the club did not last long as Davies and his family suddenly left and were never seen again.

A John Richards kept a shop at Miner's House (I assume that this was right in the centre of the village on the main road) and described himself as 'grocer, draper, ironmonger and flour factor' and he issued a bilingual pamphlet to describe the goods he dealt in. He died at a comparatively young age but his widow, Sophie, whose three sons worked in the lead mine, carried on the business.

By 1870 it was noted that many other women kept shops in the village. Amy Jones, a forty-eight-year-old widow kept a shop in Druid Village as did the eighteen-year-old Mary Ellis in partnership with her sixteen-year-old brother, Edward. Some people showed considerable enterprise at a very young age.

Griffith H Jones arrived in Goginan as a single young man of twenty-two and described himself as a merchant. He lodged with an ancestor of mine, Captain Henry Boundy, and his family. Eventually he got married and it is significant that his son, Humphrey O Jones was one of the first to graduate at the university in Aberystwyth. Tragically, he was killed while climbing in the Swiss Alps during his honeymoon.

In addition to these retailers, there were many workers in the cloth trade in the valley: fullers and dyers and makers of home-spun cloth.

Just before my time a very popular venue was an establishment called 'Shop Leis'; I assume this referred to Elizabeth's Shop and, as far as I can guess this shop was sited somewhere near the Eagle House of my childhood.

So, by my reckoning there were at least eleven shops at different times in and around the village during the mid and late nineteenth century which seems to paint a picture of a very vibrant community during this time.

I think that there's a tendency at times to look with rose-tinted glasses at the past. The rough edges of reality seem to be smoothed out by a sort of mellowness which tends to hide the arguments and the harshness of life many years ago.

I was reading with interest some information about the village school when it was built in the mid nineteenth century and the problems emanating from the project. Since I live near Bath, I couldn't help comparing the difficulties associated with building the Thermae Baths recently, with those of erecting the school all those years ago. In Bath, it had been envisaged the project would be completed in time to celebrate the Millenium at a cost of around £13,000,000. In reality, it was finished in 2006 at a cost of around £50,000,000. Building contractors were changed more than once and severe penalties were imposed due to non-delivery of the project on time.

In Goginan, the School Board met in August 1871 to discuss the problem of catering for the increased numbers attending the school, at the time held in the chapel vestry. One plan which did not reach fruition was to use the Chapel House to cater for the younger children. Eventually, it was decided that a new school should be built on a headland slightly to the west of the village on land owned by a Thomas Bonsall, who was willing to sell it for £120 an acre or rent it at £8 a year. Five tenders were submitted by various contractors, with the one submitted by a Walter Thomas of Liverpool being initially accepted. Even so, it was decided to postpone any further moves for six months until the following spring. In the meantime the architect was asked to select suitable stones for the construction. He chose a blue stone which could be quarried at Penbryn, about a quarter of a mile away. The cheapest tender of £907 was accepted, that of a Thomas Griffiths from the village of Llanfihangel, a decision which the board would have cause to regret at a later date. This tender was accepted on condition that Staffordshire bluestone was used for the keystones of the building.

So far everything had gone smoothly, but problems soon began to arise. Firstly, Thomas Bonsall had died and his brother, John, who had inherited the land, refused to sell or rent the land to the Board. However, as the Board was in the process of finding an alternative site, John Bonsall relented and construction was allowed to continue at the same price.

Then came the second dispute, between the Board and the architect concerning his fee of £76. Lawsuits were threatened by both sides, but eventually the matter was resolved for a fee of £30.

A third problem arose between the Board and Thomas Griffiths, who said he had underestimated the cost of construction by £100. The outcome was that the Board had to look for an alternative builder, and a Thomas Jones of Dole, Capel Bangor, agreed to complete the work for a fee of £1,027. The Board agreed, on the condition that the building be completed by 13 May 1878, with a penalty of £3 for every week after this date.

The next stage was to obtain a financial loan from the government to cover the costs which had by now risen to £1,523. The loan was paid out in instalments of £200 or £300 at a time and the builder was paid piecemeal as sections of the work were completed.

Subsequently, the work continued undisturbed, except that the Board urged the architect to be more diligent as to standards and to ensure that the well was deep enough to supply a constant source of water for the school. (Obviously this condition was fulfilled as the water pump functioned efficiently at least up to the time when I was there).

So, unlike the Bath Thermae project, the school was opened on the appointed date and three pillars of the community, Doctor Evan Rowlands, the mines' doctor, the Reverend John Hughes, the incumbent minister of Jezreel Baptist chapel, and a Mr Edwards of Blaendyffryn farm were asked to make arrangements for the grand opening, including a tea party for the children and a public meeting in the evening.

Prior to the opening of the village school, the British School was probably held in the Dyffryn Methodist Chapel vestry, although there is also some information suggesting it was at the considerably smaller Jezreel Baptist chapel vestry. It must have been crowded, having around sixty pupils. The authorities could have sympathised with the headteacher's difficulties, but instead censured him for the low standards achieved in most subjects, the lack of adequate lesson notes, the shortage of ink bottles and the poor organisation of books. Their report of August 1866 saw the withdrawal of much of the grant to the school for the ensuing year. To add to the teacher's problems, attendance at school was not compulsory and absenteeism in good weather, when children could be put to work aged eight, did nothing to improve educational standards. There was also the problem that families, whether they had children at school or not, were often called on to fork out a penny or so a week towards its maintainance.

However, it was not all gloom and doom as there was a tea party for the children on 16 of August that year, given by the local housewives. Apparently, one hundred and thirty children gathered at three-thirty in the afternoon to process through the village, singing the multiplication tables as they marched, before returning to the school in time for tea. This could have been to show that some education was going on and parents were getting value for money, or just high spirits!

For many centuries before the village was established, there is evidence that farms had formed the basis of the economy since mediaeval times. They were under the control of the lords of the manor in the hundred of Llanbadarn.

I visited John Roberts recently at Penbryn farm and was fascinated to find that most of the rooms, with their stone floors, low-beamed ceilings and panelled walls, had not changed much from the time when Oliver Cromwell had possibly stayed there. John and his family came to Goginan over fifty years ago to take over the farm and though now over eighty years old, he continues to take an active part in the business. Over the years he has been a pillar of local society and, as a deacon of Dyffryn Methodist chapel, has taken a leading role in the maintenance of faith in the village.

I was intrigued by an early Ordnance Survey map of the Melindŵr valley to see that all the farms that are still in existence were mentioned, except Troed-y–rhiw. However, where it is now situated, the name Goginan Fawr was on the map. Since the name Goginan seems to have originated from the names of the two farms, Goginan Fawr and Goginan Fach, could it be possible that the earlier name of Troed-y-rhiw farm was Goginan Fawr?

The farm itself has been in existence for centuries and, like Penbryn, has featured strongly in the history of the valley. Recently, my friend Mrs Mair Selway kindly sent me a copy of a tape recording made in the 1970s or '80s at the Dyffryn vestry, of the reminiscences of Miss Lizzie Williams, my old teacher, Mrs May Williams, another local teacher, Miss Kate Rowlands, who became headmistress of Goginan school after David Herbert retired, and her sister Lydia Rowlands. Other residents made valuable contributions, notably my old friends George Richards and Gareth Jones. Sadly, apart from Gareth, who, leads the Methodist faith in the village alongside John Roberts, these worthy people have passed away. They have, however, left this unique heritage of glimpses into village life during the early twentieth century.

I was particularly intrigued to gather some historical titbits concerning Troed-y-rhiw. Firstly, the house itself is a remarkable example of the traditional long houses of the past, where the family lived in one part, while the animals were housed in the other. Also, within the house itself there is a secret stairway leading to a room where people of forbidden faiths, like the Papists, could be hidden to avoid persecution. From my point of view, after my forays during the Second World War to destroy valuable tomes to help the war effort, I was surprised to learn that this very building was an ancient tithe barn. These little gems slipped off the tongues of these people in such a matter-of-fact way, that I felt so guilty I didn't know!

Tithes date back to the time of Abraham and Jacob in the Old Testament and seem to have been an unquestioned contribution made by land owners throughout history. In most cases there was no objection from farmers that a tenth of their produce should be paid in tithes, as the proceeds went to the churches and abbeys who helped the poor and needy. However, with the dissolution of the monasteries in the sixteenth century, tithes found their way into the pockets of landed gentry. Also, whereas tithes traditionally upheld the salaries of the clergy, nonconformists felt it was unreasonable for them to support the established Anglican church, while caring for their own chapels. Many were sent to prison for non-payment and for obstructing the sale of farm animals. In 1846 the Tithes Commutation Act was passed, allowing the monetary payment of tithes. A very detailed survey was made of each agricultural holding to determine the exact acreage of each field and holding on a farm, and whether is was used for pasture or for ploughing and crops. Then the value of each field's produce was estimated and given a certain name.

For example, according to information gathered by Mr Davies, the acreage of Penbryn farm in 1840 was one hundred and six and was part of Glanrheidol estate. Cae March (the horse's field), a hayfield of three acres, had a tithe of three shillings and sixpence, whereas Cae Tan y Coed (field under the trees) with six acres, had a tithe of eighteen shillings and sixpence. It can only be assumed that the tithe was commensurate with the estimated yield of the crop. It is also interesting to note that forty-six acres were under the plough, a much higher percentage than is found in present-day farms.

Many of the names that were given to the fields at this time have prevailed. At Blaendyffryn farm there is a field called Y Talwrn (the meadow). I was very interested to learn from Mr Aled Bebb, a member of the family who worked the farm for many years, that this very field is mentioned by the fourteenth-century romantic poet Dafydd ap Gwilym. Apparently, he courted one of the farm maids and their tryst was located in this very field. So it is very fitting that during the village choir's performances of *Y Trwbadŵr* featuring the love life of the poet, Llewelyn Bebb MBE, the owner of Bleandyffryn at the time, took the poet's role.

Epilogue

OSCAR WILDE ONCE SAID, "The only way to get rid of temptation is to yield to it." Well, after many months of being tempted to bring into the open all the thoughts and memories of my days as a child and young man in Goginan, I have at last yielded and got it down on paper. How do I feel about it? I feel a sense of relief and quite a lot of satisfaction that all those wonderful characters who could have faded into oblivion have a chance of having their memory perpetuated in some small way.

When we moved to Trowbridge, I asked my neighbour what he thought of the town, to which he replied, "Well, it's not a bad little town." Goginan in my time was not a bad little village; no, it was a wonderful village full of wonderful people, people I was proud to know and who gave me such a great start in life.

Many things have changed with time. Some for the better: the spirit of culture remains very strong in the village, the inhabitants take pride in the appearance of the place and many people are attracted to come and live there, which augers well for the future. Then there are those changes which I personally rue: the closing of the shops and school, the demise of most of the places of worship and the covering of the ugly remains of the silver-lead mine – to name but a few.

However, whatever the material changes, the memories linger on. Whatever else, I hope that I have made a small contribution to the perpetuation of those memories and hope I can encourage people from other small rural communities to stir up reminiscences of their own localities and write them down before they are lost in the mists of time.